UNIVERSITY OF UTAH
ANTHROPOLOGICAL PAPERS

The University of Utah Anthropological Papers are a medium for reporting to interested scholars and to the people of Utah research in anthropology and allied sciences bearing upon the peoples and cultures of the Great Basin and the West. They include, first, specialized and technical record reports on Great Basin archeology, ethnology, linguistics, and physical anthropology, and second, more general articles on anthropological discoveries, problems and interpretations bearing upon the western regions, from the High Plains to the Pacific Coast, insofar as they are relevant to human and cultural relations in the Great Basin and surrounding areas.

For the duration of the archeological salvage project for the upper Colorado River Basin which the University has undertaken by contract agreement with the National Park Service, reports relating to that research program are being published as a series within a series, bearing numbers in the general sequence of the papers as well as their own identifying numbers.

The Glen Canyon subseries will represent a wider range of the sciences and humanities than the parent series itself. The project provides for studies of the natural history of the Glen Canyon area and its inhabitants so that the relations of the prehistoric cultures and their settings will be understood in depth. As contact with Western peoples and cultures has had a varying effect upon the native Americans and the land, some papers will be concerned with the Colorado in the more recent past. Most of the Glen Canyon publications, however, will be archeological reports.

SOUTHERN PAIUTE ETHNOGRAPHY

by

Isabel T. Kelly

Number 69   (Glen Canyon Series Number 21)   May 1964

ANTHROPOLOGICAL PAPERS

Department of Anthropology

University of Utah

UNIVERSITY OF UTAH ANTHROPOLOGICAL PAPERS

Begun by the late Jesse Jennings, and continued by James O'Connell and Duncan Metcalfe, the University of Utah Anthropological Papers are a comprehensive series of over one hundred archaeological and ethnographic monographs. They highlight significant sites and topics in the American West and are informed by a strong theoretical component.

First paperback printing 1964
ISBN: 978-1-60781-103-9 (paperback)

PREFACE

The strong Rip-van-Winkle flavor that pervades the present paper results from the fact that it was written in 1933 and 1934, on the basis of field data gathered in 1932. Completion was postponed because of my departure for Mexico where, except for a few breaks, I have remained during the succeeding years. As a consequence, for three decades the nearly finished manuscript reposed in the files of the Department of Anthropology of the University of California and only recently has been exhumed, for inclusion in the Glen Canyon Series of the University of Utah Anthropological Papers.

The text is substantially that of the version prepared 30 years ago, and the ethnography is unabashedly of the how-was-it-in-your-grandfather's-day approach. All detail remains in the telegraphic style, adopted at the time by the Department of Anthropology, at Berkeley. During the past few weeks, I have done considerable editing and, by way of introduction to various of the sections, I have prepared a number of sentences or paragraphs, as the case may be, mentioning a few general points, but leaving all detail in telegraphic style, to be set in indented form. The several unfinished chapters have been completed. No attempt has been made to bring either discussion or bibliography up to date, although to the latter have been added a couple of Steward's publications, the recent edition of Powell, and one or two other pertinent works.

In the course of 30 years in storage, the ribbon copy of the report has strayed. So also have some of the original Kaibab field notes made available by the late Dr. Edward Sapir (p. 4); his missing data are those that had been more or less thoroughly incorporated in my semi-finished report. Fortunately, those that pertained to themes treated in the unfinished chapters were intact.

Editing and revision are on the basis of the elderly carbon copy of my 1933-1934 manuscript. In many instances, the handwritten symbols used in writing Paiute words did not pass through to the carbon. Terms which come from my field notes have been checked against the latter, but some derived from Dr. Sapir's missing typescript could not be checked.

Needless to say, in perspective, an appalling number of gaps are evident on all scores, and I appreciate, belatedly, the enormous number of possibilities that were unexplored, as well as the fact that many points that remained confused might well have been clarified. Despite these lamentable defects and despite the archaic nature of the paper, it is some solace to think that the field endeavors herein reported probably salvaged a good deal of material that could not be obtained today from informants.

I should like to thank Dr. Robert F. Heizer for having arranged release of the material from the University of California and Mr. Albert B. Elsasser for having undertaken the chore of assembling, packing and shipping to Mexico the considerable bulk of notes, manuscript and correspondence. To Dr. Jesse D. Jennings I am indebted for the opportunity to rid my professional conscience of the present load--which, unfortunately, represents no more than a third of the 1932-1933 field data on Southern Paiute and Chemehuevi.

August, 1963

Isabel Kelly
Tepepan, D. F.
Mexico

TABLE OF CONTENTS

	Page
PREFACE	iii
LIST OF ILLUSTRATIONS	ix
ORTHOGRAPHIC NOTE, by Wick R. Miller	xi
INTRODUCTION	1
KAIBAB	5
Habitat and Population	5
Watering places and settlements	6
Seasonal cycle and economic clusters	22
Population: composition of settlement and household	24
Chieftainship	26
Neighbors	31
Subsistence	36
Agriculture	39
Wild plant products	41
Hunting	47
Salt	55
Shelter	55
Winter dwellings	56
Less substantial structures	58
Tipi	58
Sweathouses	59
Dress	59
Body clothing	60
Footgear	62
Hairdress and headgear	65
Adornment	66
Rabbitskin blankets	68
Crafts and Manufactures	69
Tanning	71
Weapons	72
Fire making equipment	76
Pottery	77
Basketry	78
Musical instruments	85
Communications and Trade	86
Routes	87
Commerce	89
Property and Inheritance	92

	Page
Life Crises	94
Birth	96
Adolescence and menstruation	98
Marriage	99
Death and mourning	101
Diversions	102
Dances	103
Games	112
Narration of folk tales	120
Kinship Terminology	121
Miscellaneous Social Data	131
Age terms	131
Names	131
Childhood	132
Division of labor	132
Greetings	133
Natural and Supernatural	133
The world	133
Nature lore	137
Omens	140
Souls, ghosts and spirits	140
KAIPAROWITS	142
Identification and Neighbors	142
Habitat and Distribution of Population	145
Economic clusters	149
Subsistence	151
Wild plant products	152
Hunting	155
Salt	158
Shelter	158
Dress	159
Crafts and Manufactures	160
Tanning	160
Weapons	161
Fire making equipment	161
Horn spoon	162
Basketry	162
Musical instruments	164

	Page
Communications and Trade	164
Routes	164
Commerce	165
Miscellany	166

SAN JUAN 167
   Territory and Neighbors 167
   Habitat and Settlement 168
   Subsistence 169
      Agriculture 170
      Wild plant products 170
      Hunting 171
      Salt 172
   Shelter 172
   Dress 172
   Crafts and Manufactures 173
   Trade 174
   Miscellany 174

PANGUITCH 175
   Identification and Neighbors 175
   Habitat and Distribution of Population 176
   Chieftainship 178
   Subsistence 179
      Wild plant products 179
      Hunting and fishing 181
   Shelter 183
      Winter dwelling 183
      Less substantial structures 184
      Sweathouse 184
   Dress 184
      Body clothing 184
      Footgear, headgear and ornament 184
      Blankets 185
   Crafts and Manufactures 185
      Tanning 185
      Weapons 186
      Fire making equipment 186
      Pottery 186
      Basketry 186

	Page
Communications and Trade	187
Routes	187
Commerce	188
Miscellaneous Social Data	188
BIBLIOGRAPHY	189
EXPLANATION OF PLATES	193

LIST OF ILLUSTRATIONS

Maps

Page

1. Area of the eastern bands of Southern Paiute . . . . facing p. 1
2. Sketch of Ankatɨ 15

Figures (in text)

1. Horn spoon and ladle 38
2. Bone knife for gathering mescal 44
3. Rabbit stick 51
4. Pattern of man's buckskin shirt 61
5. Yucca-fiber footgear 63
6. Moccasins 64
7. Face painting 67
8. Start of rabbitskin blanket 69
9. Handle of skin flesher 71
10. Bow and arrows 73
11. Water jar, coiled basketry 80
12. Twined-basketry techniques 82
13. Rattle used in "Cry" ceremony 85
14. Rasp and rasper used in bear dance 85
15. Menstrual scratching stick 96
16. Stick dice 114
17. Ring-and-pin game 115
18. Bull roarer 119

Plates

1. Landscape and vegetation 195
2. Kaibab seed collection and preparation 196
3. Basketry 197
4. Basketry, yucca footgear, clay dolls 198
5. Cradles 199
6. Juniper-bark dolls 200
7. Postures associated with bow and arrow, rabbit stick, rasp, rattle, and hand game 201

ORTHOGRAPHIC NOTE

At the request of the editor, I have provided a system for transliterating the phonetic record originally used by Kelly for the writing of Southern Paiute. The changes, which were carried out by Carol Stout, were made to achieve a more printable orthography.

The phonetic description given in Sapir's grammar (1930, 6-70) was used as a guide. The description is not phonemic, but because of Sapir's fine feel for phonetic system and because of the detailed phonetic description, it is possible to work out most of the phonemics of the language. There are, to be sure, unresolved points, in particular concerning glottal stop, glottalized consonants, initial /h/, and probably contrasts between /s-š/ and /c-č/.

The orthography found herein for the consonants is (cf. Sapir, 1930, 62 and 44 ff.):

Fundamental	Spirantized	Geminated	Nasalized
p	v	p	mp
t	r	t	nt
k	g	k	ŋk
kw	gw	kw	ŋkw
c, č	c, č	cc, čč	nc, nč
m	ŋw		
w	ŋw		

The same orthography is used for what Sapir called fundamental and geminated stops, and for fundamental and spirantized affricates. This practice leads to no ambiguity because the fundamental consonants occur only in initial position, and the other types (spirantized, geminated, nasalized) in medial (or intervocalic) position. Other consonants, which are the same in initial and medial position, are: s, š, n, ŋ, ?, h. The orthographies for the five fundamental vowels are: i, ɨ, a, o, u (cf. Sapir, 1930, 6). Long vowels are written double. A sequence of two identical vowels is rewritten with a medial glottal stop.

Some of the changes in symbols are minor and obvious; we list only those that are not:

Symbols used here	Sapir's symbols
k	q
c	ts
č	tc
g	Greek gamma
š	c
u	u, o
o	open "o"
i̵	umlauted "i"

Inasmuch as Kelly used Sapir's phonetic orthography, there were few problems in making the transliteration. The resulting orthography cannot be claimed to be phonemic, but it does have a phonemic basis.

In no sense have the Southern Paiute words been edited or "corrected." Phonetic and allophonic variations have been omitted, but all of the contrasts as well as ambiguities of the original are preserved. We find, for example, that voiceless vowels, which occur in certain predictable environments and can be phonemically identified with their voiced counterparts, have sometimes been omitted by Kelly. Thus, some of the words are recorded with a final consonant (all Southern Paiute words should end, phonemically, with a vowel), and some with nonpermissible medial consonant clusters that probably contained an intervening voiceless vowel. In most cases the missing vowel can be supplied by consulting Sapir's dictionary. A medial "w" usually corresponds to either /v/ or /ŋw/ of Sapir (medial /w/ is rare; see Sapir, [1930, 49]). If a contiguous vowel was nasalized the "w" was rewritten as /ŋw/. In all other cases we have retained the "w." The same was done with the rarely occurring "e," which corresponds phonemically to /a/, /i/ or /ai/.

In one case Kelly indicates a contrast--between initial /ʔ/ and /h/- that is lost in Sapir's material.

The Uto-Aztecan linguist will find much of value in this material. A good many of the Southern Paiute terms, particularly those listed in <u>Subsistence</u> (pp. 36-55), are not to be found in Sapir, and some that are given by him have more exact definitions or identifications here. These terms will be useful in comparative Uto-Aztecan linguistics.

Wick R. Miller

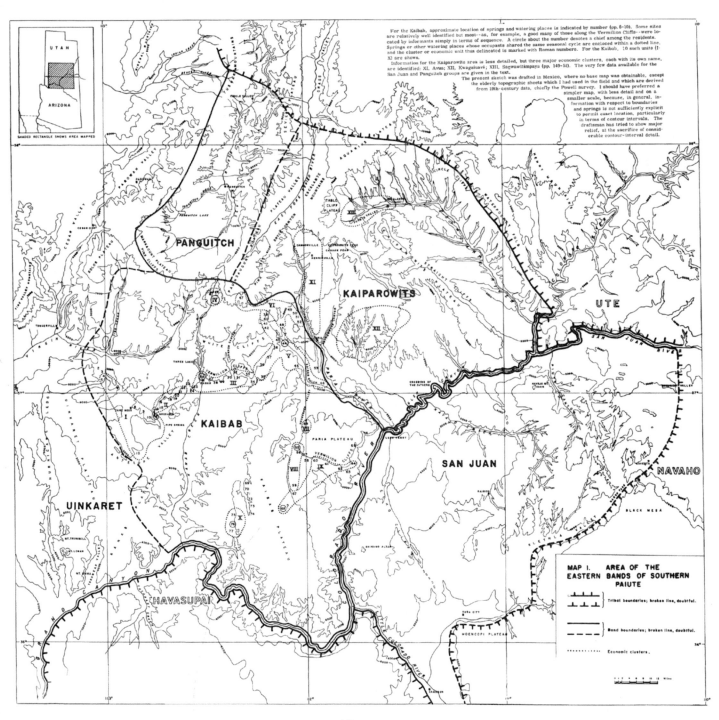

INTRODUCTION

The term Southern Paiute generally has been applied to the Ute-Chemehuevi groups living in southern Utah, adjacent Arizona, and southern Nevada. Through recent field work it is apparent that the Chemehuevi, to the west, merge ethnically with them, and in a previous paper (Kelly, 1934) the groups composing the combined Southern Paiute-Chemehuevi were enumerated and their respective territories defined.

The present study concerns the four eastern bands: Kaibab, Kaiparowits, San Juan, and Panguitch. Material on the Kaibab is relatively full, that on the other three, extremely sketchy. It seems advisable to publish on several groups at a time, rather than delay until the entire mass of data is in final form. (For the Shivwits, Moapa, Las Vegas, and Chemehuevi, particularly the two latter, information is quite full; for St. George and Paranigat, it is less detailed but adequate for a general outline. The Uinkaret are extinct and of them I have no account. Few informants could be located for the Cedar, Beaver, Panaca, and Gunlock groups, and the data are correspondingly scant.)

Once this happy situation is realized and the descriptive material from all the Southern Paiute is in order, it should be possible to view the panorama in perspective. Problems of culture change promise to be especially interesting. For example, agriculture, pottery, and the sweat house seem to have reached the Paiute at different times and by different routes. In a good many instances, it was possible to record the circumstances surrounding the introduction of new traits and, sometimes, even to establish the identity of the individual or individuals who were responsible for the innovation.

The second half of the past century was one of extraordinary cultural upheaval, particularly among the Kaibab, who had lived in comparative isolation. During these five decades, they were exposed to a veritable avalanche of new influences, which arrived from north, southeast and west. My four elderly informants had witnessed the introduction of the dog, of native agriculture, of pottery making, of the sweat house. They remembered the arrival of the first horses; although Escalante must have traversed Kaibab country much earlier, there seemed to be no recollection of his passage and, as far as effective introduction is concerned, the horse dates from the middle of the past century.

In post-horse days, the Navajo practically overran Kaibab territory, on trading and raiding trips. The Ute became frequent visitors--occasionally to steal children for the slave trade, but more often to barter and sometimes to hunt. They arrived with travois and tipi, both of which the Kaibab adopted from them, as well as the smoking of buckskin and probably the use of hair braids by the men. About the turn of the century, probably also from the Ute, came the bear dance; and from the Paiute to the west, the "Cry," which traces ultimately to the Colorado River mourning ceremony.

During the same timespan, informants witnessed the arrival of the Mormon settlers and the Powell parties, and the introduction of firearms. They saw their watering places taken over by the whites and the destruction of the plants that produced their old seed staple. They saw also the establishment of the Moccasin reservation and the herding together on it of the Kaibab survivors and a few individuals from neighboring groups.

This kaleidoscope of experiences and of exposure to culture change can only be described as dramatic. It must also have been traumatic.

Although their western congeners extend far into the Basin and Range, the four bands herein described are confined to the Plateau province. Here climate and vegetation vary directly with elevation. The tablelands above 7000 ft. receive considerable precipitation and support a fairly dense coniferous forest; between 5000 and 7000 ft. there are open stands of pinyon and juniper; and areas below 5000 ft. are desert upland, with sage and other shrubs. Because of winter snows, the high country was not considered suitable for semipermanent camps. Population was concentrated in the middle and lower levels, which are predominantly arid, with few perennial streams. Springs, which occur chiefly at the base of plateaus and cliffs, determined the location of the semipermanent settlements. The latter were conveniently adjacent to the valleylike flats, which supplied seeds and small game, and from them the higher country, essentially a hinterland, could be visited periodically for pinenuts, large game and other products.

This exceedingly brief, composite, and generalized pattern of land utilization seems to have held in a broad way for most of the Southern Paiute. It underwent, as is to be expected, modifications according to local conditions; the most important of these will appear in the discussion to follow. My interest has been primarily in subsistence and in relationship to habitat. In a low-pressure culture such as that of the Paiute, domestic economy rests on direct exploitation of the habitat. Information on other aspects of culture was tangential to the central theme of the study.

July and August of 1932 were spent at Moccasin, Arizona, with Kaibab and Kaiparowits informants; part of September, at Cedar City, Utah, with the Panguitch informant; and a few days in October, at Marble canyon and Tuba City, Arizona, with San Juan informants.

For the Kaibab, the principal source was Captain George (G), with supplementary data from Mose (M), Adam (A), and Sarah Frank (S), the latter the sister of A. Others provided miscellaneous information, especially Minnie Tom (MT), who was born in Cedar territory, of a Cedar father and a Kaibab mother, and who has lived many years among the Kaibab.

A number of Kaiparowits were mentioned by name but, at the time of my visit, few were available. One, Dick, had changed residence so often that it was difficult to identify his statements with locality; another, Tom, who gave data on the bear dance, had lived in Kaiparowits country but, by his own statement, was born and raised among the Ute. Joe Pickavits was so deaf that communication was uncertain. By default, the chief Kaiparowits source was Lucy (L), called also Rosie, middle-aged and a mediocre informant.

The scanty San Juan data come from Jodie (J) and Joe Francis (JF); the Panguitch material, from Rena (R), a lone survivor, now at Cedar City. With Kaibab, Kaiparowits and Panguitch informants, Katie Craig (KC) of Moccasin was interpreter; she is the daughter of Sarah Frank and "Chuarruumpeak," or Frank, of the Powell and Dellenbaugh accounts. Of the San Juan group, Jodie worked without interpreter; Joe Francis, through a Navajo-English interpreter.

The present data were gathered as a National Research Fellow in the Biological Sciences, for the year beginning July 1, 1932. Field funds were provided half by the University of California and half by the Laboratory of Anthropology and the American Museum of Natural History. The two latter institutions also provided funds for the purchase of ethnographic specimens and models, of which a number are figured here. Those in the American Museum are identified as AMNH; those delivered to the Laboratory of Anthropology are now in the possession of the Museum of New Mexico (MNM). Through the courtesy of the late Mr. Frederick Dellenbaugh, of the Peabody Museum (PM), and of the Bureau of American Ethnology, it was possible to consult the photographs taken by J. K. Hillers, of the Powell survey. Moreover, the Peabody Museum very kindly has permitted illustration of a number of specimens of the Powell and Palmer collections.

For a great deal of Kaibab material I am indebted to Dr. Edward Sapir, who generously made available his valuable manuscript notes on the ethnography of that group, as well as a number of photographs and sketches. His material is cited constantly in the Kaibab sections; when no page is indicated, reference is to his unpublished data. In addition, Mr. Frederick Dellenbaugh was kind enough to lend several pages of manuscript, unfortunately incomplete, on the Kaibab. For botanical determinations, I am indebted to Mr. John Thomas Howell, of the California Academy of Sciences. The helpful cooperation of Dr. A. E. Farrow, of the United States Indian Service, Cedar City, Utah, and of Mr. Othello Bowman, of Kanab, Utah, is acknowledged with thanks.

Native terms are given in an enormously simplified and, I am afraid, very inaccurate approximation of Sapir (1930, 539), whose system proved highly specialized for one with an untrained ear and no linguistic training. Translation of terms is that which was given by the interpreter, without attempt at closer analysis.

[Editor's note: See "Orthographic Note," p. xi, for discussion of phonemic transcription used throughout this volume.]

KAIBAB

Habitat and Population

The Kaibab occupied the area between the southern tip of the High Plateaus of Utah and the Grand Canyon. From the Pink Cliffs, which are the southern terminals of the Markagunt and Paunsaugunt plateaus, the country descends by a series of successively lower mesas until the broad upland of Kanab Plateau is reached. The first descent is marked by the White Cliffs, an abrupt white sandstone scarp of 1000 ft.; the second by the Vermilion Cliffs, a red sandstone bluff of approximately equal height; and the third by the Shinarump Cliffs, a low, irregular, and less impressive series of bluffs near the base of the Vermilion Cliffs. All of these great rock terraces are south-facing and have a general easterly-westerly course, but in the eastern part of the area they swing off to the northeast, where they are cut by the Paria River. At this point the Vermilion Cliffs turn southward, then northeastward to form the western and southern boundaries of the Paria Plateau; from the same point the great Kaibab Plateau extends southward, to terminate in the Grand Canyon. The marvelous scenic beauties of this country have been acclaimed since the days of Dutton, but even his classical reports cannot do justice to the majesty of the panorama of tiered and intensely colored scarp fronts.

On the Kaibab and High plateaus winter snows reach a depth of 8 to 10 ft., but at lower elevations the country is markedly arid. For the Colorado Plateau province as a whole, Bowman (1911, 287) states the precipitation below 7000 ft. to be less than 8 in. annually. Summer rains fill the local draws sporadically, but excepting the Colorado, there is only one perennial stream system, the Virgin. This heads in the north, between the Markagunt and Paunsaugunt plateaus, and flows south through Long Valley, where it turns west to receive its several northern affluents, Zion, North, and, outside Kaibab boundaries, LaVerkin and Ash creeks. Kanab Creek, the next largest stream, heads in the north, slightly east of the Virgin, and flows due south, dissecting the White, Vermilion, and Shinarump cliffs, and eventually reaching the Colorado through a tortuous canyon cut midway in Kanab Plateau. Unlike the Virgin, the Kanab is not perennial the full length of its course. Parallel to the upper course of the Kanab and 10 mi. to the east is Johnson Canyon, through which there is a small intermittent flow, which eventually joins the Kanab drainage. Many smaller canyons also dissect the cliff series.

To the north, the High Plateaus are covered by a fairly dense coniferous forest consisting of ponderosa pine, Engelmann spruce, Douglas fir, and alpine fir. The growth is sparser on the next lower bench; scattered pines occur at the foot of the White Cliffs (Pl. 1, d). Nevertheless, from the base of the latter to the Vermilion Cliffs, the vegetation is essentially juniper growth interspersed with scrub oak, sage and other shrubs. The same belt continues at the base of the Vermilion Cliffs and again on top of the Shinarump Cliffs, but the open stretch between these two bluffs is sage-covered. At present the whole desert country from the Shinarump Cliffs to the Kaibab Plateau supports a sparse growth of sage; there is pretty good evidence that, prior to the white occupation, this was grassland (Dutton, 1882, 104). With increasing elevation, pinyon, juniper, cliffrose and broad-leaved yucca appear on the Kaibab Plateau; at 7000 ft., ponderosa pine is the chief timber tree, interspersed with locust and groves of Gambel oak; at still higher levels, blue spruce dominates, in company with fir, balsam and groves of aspen. The summit of Paria Plateau, which is considerably lower than the Kaibab, is within the pinyon-juniper belt.

In the canyons, elder, squawbush, serviceberry and oak occur; about springs and along streams there are cane, tule, cattail, and other hydrophytes. Cacti are not characteristic of the region, but occur sparingly at moderate elevations. Mescal, or agave, is rare; according to informants, it is found chiefly in Kanab Canyon and below the rim of Grand Canyon.

Of all the Southern Paiute, the Kaibab occupied the richest game country. Deer abounded on the Kaibab Plateau. Antelope were less important but there were bands on Kanab Plateau and in the Houserock Valley-Marble Platform district. Mountain sheep were found in the rocky section by Zion Canyon and along Grand Canyon rim. Smaller game, too, was reasonably abundant.

Watering Places and Settlements

The higher plateaus are well watered but are unsuitable for permanent habitation because of the depth of winter snows. In contrast, the lower elevations are arid, and there campsites were governed strictly by the availability of water. Streams were of scant importance, and springs were the controlling factor in the location of settlements.

Springs occur chiefly in a long, almost continuous line, along the base of the Vermilion Cliffs, including the western and southern fronts of the Paria Plateau, and along the western slopes of the Kaibab Plateau (map 1). Here, intermittently during the year, most of the population was concentrated; camps were semipermanent in the sense that the occupants returned to them following hunting and foraging trips. The sites were strategically situated. Drinking water was at hand; the juniper-dotted slopes of the backing scarps provided fuel; the desert flats were nearby for rabbit hunting and seed collecting; and the higher plateaus could be visited periodically for deer, pinenuts and yucca fruit.

The important watering places along these two main loci seem to have been privately owned:

> A man owned a little land [sic] around a spring and lived there with his relatives and friends. If someone else came around, he could camp there too; a man liked to have company. He liked to move around and change springs too; he knew where he wanted to camp. But if he moved away, he would come back later to his own spring. When a man died they moved the camps but did not leave the spring.

Probably ownership of watering places was not as formal and individualistic as informants' statements suggest. It may have been a family affair, resulting from the fact that relatives tended to camp year after year at the same springs (pp. 24-6). Habitual occupation thus may have been expressed in terms of ownership. Yet in comparatively few instances did G or M hesitate in identifying the owner by name, and they stated their doubts clearly. It was reported that one spring (no. 76; see below) was "not owned by any one person," although several families camped there. A once-populous watering place (spring 65) was deserted following the death of the occupants; a certain man "found the spring and camped there; he thought he owned it." G doubted that the man living at 77 was really the owner but conceded that "at least he lived there."

Theoretically, watering places were inherited by the oldest child; in practice, they seem to have passed to the nearest male relative (either by blood or by marriage) who happened to be at hand and who continued to live at the site. Interestingly enough, in three cases (springs 55, 56, 77), ownership is said to have passed to the younger sister's son. G thought a woman might own a spring but could give no concrete example. Although a widow might "inherit" a spring from her husband, upon remarriage it became the property of her second spouse, even though he were unrelated to the deceased. Inheritance by the daughter first was reported for 75, but when questioned, G replied that "she just lived there; the spring belonged to her and her husband." This is tantamount to inheritance by the son-in-law. At springs 35-46, a son-in-law and his three brothers apparently took wholesale possession; in fact, they and their families comprised the bulk of the population.

As will be seen below, occupants of nearby watering places tended to share the same seasonal cycle, thus constituting informal local clusters, largely economic in character. These are shown diagrammatically on map 1 and will be discussed later (pp. 22-4), following presentation of specific data on watering places, their ownership, and the seasonal activities of their residents.

Springs and watering places entered by number on map 1 are as follows:

1. Kanavɨc (willow); Sheep Trough Spring?
2. Togoavac (rattlesnake water).
3. Sovipac (cottonwood water, because a cottonwood tree was nearby).
4. Siṭumpac (yellow, gray [?] water).
5. Atankwintɨ (sand stream; Canaan Spring [?]; Sapir, 1930, 553, Ata-nukwintɨ, Cottonwood Spring [?]).
6. Sovinokwint (cottonwood stream; Short Creek; Sapir, 1930, 662, Sovinukwintɨ.
7. Muɨvac (mosquito water).
8. Paganktoničˇ (cane knoll [?]; Cane Beds [?]; Sapir, 1930, 604-5, Paga-ŋkwi-ton?ninčɨ, cane valley, Canepatch Creek).
9. Oavac (salt, alkali water).
10. Mɨ?tɨŋ-wogaip-pagantɨ.
11. Mɨ?tɨŋwava (point of hill; Pipe Spring; Sapir, 1930, 570, Mɨtɨŋwa, Mɨtɨŋwa.
12. Pacpikaina (water bubbling up; Moccasin Spring; Sapir, 1930, 597, paacpikai-na, water risen).
13. Tɨŋkanivac (cave water; Antelope Spring, southwest of Pipe Spring; an exception to preceding in being located at base of Shinarump instead of Vermilion Cliffs.
14. Kacoapac (end of water; at base of cliffs, about 1 [?] mi. north of Moccasin Spring).
15. Pavuavac (Sapir, 1930, 598, pavu?a-vaac; Point Spring, about 2 mi. northeast of Moccasin).
16. Pawiavac (mud water).
17. Soviwɨnɨnčˇičˇ (cottonwood standing up).
18. Uwantičˇ (rain, because water sprays off rocks; called also Patɨtuatičˇ, water sprinkling).

19. Aŋavac (black-ant water).
20. Tiŋkanivac (cave water).
21. Skumpac (rabbit-brush water; Rigg Spring).
22. Tonovac (greasewood water; Sapir, 1930, 598, tono-vaac).
23. Samiapac, Nacɨmipac (pebble water; Cottonwood Spring).
24. Sɨivac (squawbush water; Sapir, 1930, 598, šɨɨ-vaac).
25. Sawavac (sagebrush water).
26. Kanarɨuipi (willow canyon; Kanab Creek; Sapir, 1930, 629, Kanarɨ-ʔuipi).
27. Čiakwiavac (oak [var.] spring).
28. Oavac (salt water).
29. Tɨavac (serviceberry water; has another name, which G does not remember).
30. Johnson Creek (canyon); name not recorded.
31. Naʔavac (lone spring).
32. Muiantič (said to refer to nose; a lake east of Johnson Canyon).
33. Pagawipi (cane canyon).
34. Ipa (old water; Navajo Well; about 1 mi. south of Vermilion Cliffs).
35. Tupac (black water; about 3 mi. east of 34).
36. Muʔkovac (rock [?] water).
37. Kamuwac (rabbit water).
38. Paŋwiavac (mud water).
39. Kanawaic (willow hanging down).
40. Kanarɨmpiku (knoll [?]; reference apparently to willow).
41. Tiŋkanivac (cave water).
42. Ciampivac (wild-rose water).
43. Sɨʔɨvac (squawbush water).
44. Sovpac (cottonwood water; 16-mile Spring [?]).
45. Kakarɨmpac (quail water).
46. Sovpac (cottonwood water).
47. Piki-pa (rotten water).
48. Atavac (sand water).
49. Wɨgɨmpac (vulva spring).
50. Pagarɨ (reservoir; apparently a pot-hole).
51. Tɨmpiku (rock hole).
52. Kanaŋkwicič (willow run).
53. Sɨʔɨvac (squawbush water; on east side Houserock Valley, above Kaibab Gulch).
54. Pagampacɨ (cane water; east side Houserock Valley, south of Kaibab Gulch).

55. Kankwi, Kankwic (water singing; Houserock Spring. A small spring across valley, at eastern base Kaibab Plateau called Miapi-kankwi, little Kankwi.)
56. Mukuvac (Mukwi [Mukwic] -water).
57. Wancitkunava (antelope point spring; halfway up Vermilion Cliffs).
58. Sikiava (fissure).
59. Oariŋkanivac (salt-cave water, Cane Ranch, east base of Kaibab Plateau).
60. Tumaranpaganti (from the plant timari, Stanleya).
61. Winorumpac (arrowhead water; not a running spring; "just a damp spot").
62. Uinpikavoc (pine tree pot-hole; well up on cliffs; apparently Jacobs Pools).
63. Paŋwiavac (mud water; very little water; at base of cliffs beneath 62).
64. Inantopac (badger-hole water).
65. Sovinokwicič (cottonwood running; Soap Creek).
66. Tiraupaŋkwicič (level-ground-water running; probably Badger Creek).
67. Pagampiaganti (pagampi, cane; Cane Ranch, east base of Kaibab Plateau).
68. Kwiavac (oak water; not definitely located but seemingly in the De Motte region, on Kaibab Plateau).
69. Ogontinava (water under pine tree). Sapir, 1930, 598, Ogo-ntirina-va (fir-butt spring). Sapir lists a spring called Maanavu (thorn) north of 69, at site of Coconino mining camp.
70. Paiyampaganti (water halfway up hill).
71. Pagwuiacpikanti (from Gambel oak), in the canyon just north of Mangum Spring.
72. Piačampipkwitič (locust stream); Mangum Spring; Sapir: Piaičapinukwint (oak [var.] -spring).
73. Aŋkapi (red spot); Big Spring; Sapir: Aŋkapu (reddish).
74. Mo?onticivac (owl head water); Sapir, 1930, 598, moontocivaac (humming-bird-head spring); Sapir lists this between 72 and 73.
75. Maavawiŋiti (tree in water).
76. Sinavac (coyote water).
77. Sagwogo?acpa (tobacco water).

Uninhabited or rarely used watering places may be eliminated first:

1, used only by travelers; 2-3, used by people from 4-8 only when pinenut gathering; 14, 16, formerly dry; 17, 22-24, used by transient seed-gatherers; not privately owned, but "belonged to anyone who camped there"; 28-29, normally unoccupied, occasionally visited by people from 26 and 30-34; 53, 57, used by people from 56 when camping on Paria Plateau, but not owned by them; 58, used at times by occupants of 56 and 60-61; 63, not inhabited, little water; 64, used infrequently by people of 60-62; 65, once very populous but "all dead" before informant G visited there (then occupied by 1 family: Sina?ataŋ [Sinarɨn, coyote teeth] his wife, 2 children; "Sina?ataŋ found the spring and camped there; he thought he owned it"); 66, uninhabited; 69-74, owned by Naragowocɨ, of 76, but rarely visited.

The remainder of the springs, together with an apparently unnamed series of watering places in the vicinity of Alton, in upper Kanab Canyon, I have grouped in 10 units, as follows:*

I. 4-13, springs along the Vermilion Cliffs, east to Moccasin Spring, including an isolated spring to the south, at the base of Shinarump Cliffs.

4-8, owned by Čaŋa (bull lizard), apparently a shaman. 3 camps, his own and those of his 2 married br, one of whom may have been the shaman, Mimitanavi (head bent back). In summer harvested seeds about 6; in fall, gathered pinenuts on mesa to northwest, using water from 2, 3. United with people from neighboring springs (9, 10-12, 13) for hunting trip to Kaibab Plateau.

9, owned by Oavanapun (alkali man), a shaman. 6 camps, his own and those of his 5 married s. Spring 9 occupied continuously save for annual trip to Kaibab Plateau and occasional winter or spring visit to Colorado Canyon for mescal.

---

*The accompanying material concerning settlement and household is due largely to the splendid memory of G. In retrospect [1963] I realize that a great many of the gaps might have been filled, had I been more experienced in field work and a little more insistent. Sharper definition of kinship bonds between those sharing the same camping grounds and between members of the individual domestic unit certainly would have been possible. Similarly, more complete information might have been obtainable on inheritance of springs and succession of chieftainship. In the accompanying account "camp" is used as synonymous with household. Abbreviations are: f, father; m, mother; ch, child, children; s, son; d, daughter; br, brother; ss, sister; h, husband; w, wife; o, older; y, younger; -l, in-law; gr, grand-; p, parent; mat, maternal; pat, paternal.

10-12, owned by Pačakwi (Sapir, 1930, 608, to be, get wet), local chief. G remembers 2 camps here but thinks probably there were at least 3; located at base of cliffs, either side of spring 12. With Pačakwi was his s, Tompocoaroc, a rattlesnake shaman; and in separate camp, his unmarried br, Katavɨ. 10-12 occupied less continuously than other districts, in spite of excellent water supply. Visited neighbors at 13 most of year. Wintered with them and, in spring, accompanied them to Colorado Canyon, just west of Kanab Canyon, for mescal. Camped 1 night en route, reaching rim of Grand Canyon following morning. Stayed about a month, living in caves; G does not remember about water supply. Returned to 13 with supply of mescal; remained there, living on mescal, a cactus (tasɨ), and juniper berries. Continued visit into summer, harvesting seeds along flats by 13. Toward end of summer, visitors returned to own springs. In fall (before trip to Kaibab Plateau?) gathered pinenuts on mesa on top of Vermilion Cliffs; pinyon trees scarce. In fall, united with people from 4-8, 9, 13, for month's trip to Kaibab Plateau for deer. Upon return, those of 4-8, 9, went to their own springs, but those of 10, 12 again visited 13, remaining there through winter. Actually occupied 10-12 only a short time late summer and early fall.

Introduction of agriculture altered seasonal operations somewhat, resulting in occupation of 12 during summer (pp. 39-40). Planted only at Moccasin Spring (12); 3 fields; 1 belonging to Kanavɨ (thin; error for Katavɨ [?]); another to Čaŋa of 4-8; and the third to Taŋarɨinia (crooked knee), who succeeded to springs at death of Pačakwi. With Taŋarɨinia were his w, his w's s, Wikena, and an unrelated man called Sigiki, (rattlesnake). 2 plantings, spring and summer (?). Left before corn was up, returning when about 8 in. high to weed and care for plot. After harvest went to Kaibab Plateau.

13, owned by Puɨsari (eye dog); many in his camp: his w, A?nawanc (badger breast), 4 s, 1 d; also his o ss s, an unmarried man named Ma?apituku (painted hip), who was the br of G's f; and others whom G does not remember. As noted above, 13 visited almost continuously by people from 10-12. Other frequent visitors were from an unlocated spring called Wa?akarɨ (juniper knoll; Yellowstone Spring, somewhere northwest of 13; Sapir, 1930, 598, w?akarɨrɨmpa, cedar-knoll spring). Visitors from Wa?akarɨ joined 13 in mescal-gathering and deer-hunting trips. Seasonal activities of 13 covered in preceding, under 10-12.

II. 15, 17-21, springs along the Vermilion Cliffs, from Moccasin to Rigg Spring.

15, 18-19, owned by Topɨ (white), a widower living alone; his deceased wife a shaman named Tocɨac (said to mean gray hair; perhaps the tocɨ-a-c, head-having, referred to by Sapir, 1930, 689). Spent summer at 15, fall at 19, winter at 18. Gathered seeds on flats below Vermilion Cliffs; as no woman in household, he personally gathered and prepared seeds. Joined people from 20-21 for deer hunt on top of Vermilion Cliffs; did not go to Kaibab Plateau to hunt.

20-21, owned by a shaman, Yɨnɨm?u, bald-headed (called also Nankapɨ?ia, hairy ear, and Takta [English, doctor]). 5 juniper-bark-covered houses at 20; G forgets owners of 2 of them; others belonged to (1) Yɨnɨm?u, (2) his br, Mus (English, Mose) w, 3 ch; and (3) his "half-brother" (first cousin), Sa?atkawaitɨ (doesn't eat mush), his w, s, d. Winter and spring at 20; in summer moved about; gathered seeds along base of cliffs, obtaining water at 22-24. Hunted a few deer on top Vermilion Cliffs; did not go to Kaibab Plateau.

III. 25-34, springs from the vicinity of Kanab, eastward to Navajo Well.

25, owned by Kamɨoŋšoc (tries to strike little rabbits), called also Kwičapa?aku (excrement on thigh). He and his w "stayed there all the time"; hunted deer with people from 26.

26, an important settlement with "many" camps; "so many that nobody could count them"; no statement as to ownership of stream. Can remember 3 camps; (1) Miapi (little), the chief, his w, Čaŋtuya (slashed forehead), who was a shaman, 1 ch (had others but they died); 4 other people in his camp, not relatives; cannot remember names, (2) Kipɨ (elbow), his w, 2 boys, orphaned ch of his o br, (3) Sagovonkuic (blue spot on elbow) w, 1 s, 2 d. Camps ranged along Kanab Creek, source of water supply, on site of present Kanab village. Wintered there, toward spring moving to 27 for tasiu (Peteria thompsonae Wats.) root; remained there until seeds ripe (about June), when returned to Kanab to harvest them; occasionally visited Johnson Canyon for ku?u (Mentzelia) seeds. In fall moved to cliffs above Three Lakes (Sapir, 1930, 597, pa(i)-yu(?u)gwi-či, waters-sitting) for pasɨ

(Artemisia) seeds; gathered pinenuts on mesa top of Vermilion Cliffs. In fall, sometimes hunted deer in Orderville region; often joined by those of 34 in fall trip to Kaibab Plateau for deer. Returned to 26 before snows.

30-33, owned by Mančavait (waving hand). 3 camps: (1) Mančavait, w, d, 2 s, and his br's orphaned s. (2) Aŋka?kwanu?u, (flicker, a bird), w, no ch. (3) T?oicikaipi (gray squirrel), w, no ch. Wintered at 31; in spring moved to 30, gathering what tsii (unidentified root) was available. In summer visited Alton (IV) for cičagantɨ (Balsamorrhiza sagitata) seeds, and remained to harvest other seeds. Occasionally visited 28, 29. In fall gathered yucca fruit and pinenuts on mesa top of Vermilion Cliffs; pinenuts, rabbits, porcupine found near 32. Fall trip made to Kaibab Plateau for deer; no chief; "hunted without one."

34, owned by Mu?umpi (owl eye). 4 camps: (1) Mu?umpui, w (from Kaiparowits district called Kwaguiuavɨ), 2 s, 3 d, (including informants S and A). (2) his br. Mɨanc (sour taste), w, 2 s. (3) Tukunɨmpɨ (wildcat feet, the o br [?] of Mu?umpui's w), a shaman who camped alone. (4) Aŋkak?kwanau (flicker), camped alone; not related to others; probably same person mentioned as resident of 30-33. Winter, spring, and much of summer spent in vicinity of 34. Sometimes went to Alton for seeds; visited also at 35-38, 40 (see below); and at 26 and 30. In fall returned to 34, preparatory to visiting Kaibab Plateau for deer; sometimes accompanied people of 26 to Kaibab Plateau. No chief at 34.

IV. Alton area, on upper Kanab Creek, at the foot of the High Plateaus. Individual watering places were said to have been unnamed.

District on upper Kanab Creek, near present settlement of Alton, called Paŋwavɨ (water[?] grass). Springs owned by Tɨmpinapuŋ (rock-man; called also Yɨnɨnapuŋ, bald-headed man), a shaman and "little" chief. In his camp were: his w, s (Takwasɨ, eagle tail), also a shaman, and sometimes his o ss s (Poronapuŋ, walking-stick man), likewise a shaman. Latter owned spring called Paŋwiavac (mud water), not shown on maps, but somewhere to southeast, at foot of Paunsaugunt plateau near 47. Poronapuŋ visited Alton frequently.

Because of cold, Alton people moved down Kanab Canyon for winter, staying either at 26 or in Glendale (?) Canyon, a nearby

Map 2. Sketch of Ankatɨ and adjacent country. Ankatɨ (intersection of creeks) was defined specifically as the stretch between Kanarɨmpiku (spring 40) and Kakarɨmpac (spring 45) (pp. 9, 22); accordingly, its axis was Kaibab Gulch and the upstream continuation of the gulch, called Wildcat Canyon. It is possible, however, that the name may have been applied loosely to this whole canyon district. The area here depicted was occupied by groups V and VI (map1; pp. 16-17, 22).

This series of canyons dissects the Vermilion Cliffs at about 112° 9'. At the upper left is the southern tip of Paunsaugunt Plateau. The White and Vermilion cliffs appear as two parallel lines, cut by transverse gulches. Two peaks are shown as circles; one, unidentified, is called Pikikarɨr ([var.]-seed knoll); the other, apparently Mollie's Nipple (Gregory and Moore, Pls. 1, 2), gives its name to Kaivakuwac Canyon. The latter is described as waterless and the smallest of the gulches. Kanarɨmpiku and Sovpac canyons receive their names from watering places (p. 9, nos. 40, 44) and are to be identified respectively with Wildcat and Kitchen canyons. Čunkawipi (rough creek) is Kaibab Gulch, correctly shown as tributary to the Paria River (at the lower right). Springs are entered by number (p. 9).

In major feature, the drawing agrees relatively well with the topography.

The illustration is taken from my copy of an informants' sketch in the sand. At the start, I drew the lines that correspond to the White and Vermilion cliffs, and with these as a point of departure, M and KC completed the "map." M had little talent for such graphic endeavor, but both G and KC sketched cleverly in the sand. G usually had the south farthest removed, the north, nearest himself; KC, the west farthest removed. At the conclusion of a drawing and the related discussion, invariably the sketch was erased. This, it was said, was a matter of course, not because of any associated magical belief.

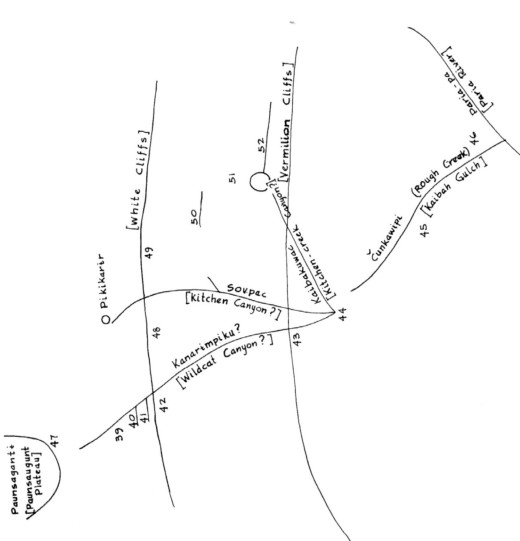

branch of Kanab Canyon. In spring returned to north, subsisting until summer on food stores hidden in caves. Remained at Alton most of summer, but gathered some seeds near 26, and there cached them for succeeding winter. In fall, hunted on southwestern part of Paunsaugunt Plateau; did not visit Kaibab Plateau.

Kaibab from Kanab (26), Johnson Canyon (30), and Navajo Well (34) (all group III) sometimes visited Alton summer to fall for serviceberries and highland seeds: pasɨ (Artemisia) and cičagantɨ (Balsamorrhiza sagitata).

V. 35-46, watering places along the Vermilion Cliffs (35-38), in Wildcat Canyon (39-44), and in Kaibab Gulch (45-46). This includes the district known to informants as Ankatɨ (map 2).

35-46, claimed by M's f, A?pɨgantɨ (horn), who came originally from Nɨnkuipi (people-killed; in memory of Apache maraud; Nankoweap Canyon); acquired springs from his f-1. M remembers 5 camps at 44: (1) A?pɨgantɨ, w (Kiačɨ, mouth open), 2 s (one, informant M), and unmarried br of A?pɨgantɨ named Tavac. Latter chief, "but not much of a one." Directed seasonal movements of camps; succeeded by his br. (2) Tukunɨmpɨ (wildcat feet), br of A?pɨgantɨ; listed previously as resident of 34 (according to G camped alone; said by M to have had w at 44). (3) Kaɨmu (from Kaɨumpuc, hawk [grouse ?]; so-named because of his nose), still another br of A?pɨgantɨ. In his camp: w and his unmarried br named Saroc ("because he talked too much"). (4) Saituŋ (white spots), some relation to A?pɨgantɨ. Said by M to be unmarried; by G, to have w and s. Camped mostly at 40; said by G to have owned latter spring. (5) Tapunapuŋ (big penis man; called also Mopuikinapuŋ, nasal-mucous-running man), who owned 47-52. Stayed at his own springs most of time, but frequently wintered with people of 35-46. He was paternal uncle of the wife of A?pɨgantɨ.

Excepting Tapunapuŋ, all camps moved in unison, spending winter and spring at foot of Vermilion Cliffs, often at 35. Gathered cacti (tasɨ, munčɨ) which grew to southeast, and unidentified seed (piki), which ripened early. In spring sometimes went to Kaibab Gulch for cacti (tasɨ, munčɨ, nɨaras); or to Nankoweap for mescal, there meeting other Kaibab from Houserock Valley (VII, VIII). In summer moved up canyons toward White Cliffs, gathering seeds (piki, cičagantɨ, akɨ, pasɨ) and, on top of cliffs, sigo?o root. Food cached in caves of Vermilion Cliffs for winter. In fall gathered pinenuts on top of Vermilion Cliffs; hunted deer either on Paunsaugunt or Kaibab plateaus.

VI. 47-52, the hinterland of Ankati, including a spring (47) at the base of Paunsaugunt Plateau, although this is outside the area informants consider to be Ankati proper.

47-52, owned by Tapunapuŋ (mentioned above as winter resident of 35-46). Camped with his br, O?oisič; latter had no w when M saw him but married later. Summer and fall spent at own springs near White Cliffs; lived in cave when camping at 48; occasionally wintered at base of White Cliffs but usually joined people of 35-46(V).

VI scarcely populated; probably should have been included as part of V; evidently the springs of V and VI once owned by brothers (p. 16). VI separated simply because no mention of deer hunting on the Kaibab Plateau nor of mescal-gathering in Nankoweap.

East of Ankati the Vermilion Cliffs swing south, then southeast, then northeast, to form the scarp front of Paria Plateau. To their west is Houserock Valley (Pl. 1, a) which separates Paria and Kaibab plateaus; and to their south is Marble Platform, through which the Colorado River cuts its gorge. Today sparse and desertlike in vegetation, this whole district is said once to have abounded in seed plants. (In spring Houserock Valley is carpeted green with Hilaria jamesii. A random sampling of flora from Marble Platform near the Vermilion Cliffs includes: Yucca, Ephedra, Atriplex, Artemisia filifolia, Gutierrezia, Fenderla or Philadelphus, and Coldenia hispidissima.) Practically all springs, and in consequence all camps, are along the base of the Vermilion Cliffs; three groups (VII-IX) are included.

VII. 54, upper Houserock Valley. (The encampment sighted by Escalante [Documentos, 1854, 515] after he crossed the northern tip of Kaibab Plateau and started the descent, may have been at this spring [called Pagampaci]: "Cogionos la noche al bajar al otro lado de una cuchilla bien alta y fragosa y de mucha guija; desde la cual vimos abajo, despues de un corto llano varias lumbres...." Undoubtedly his designation of the Indians of this area as Paganpache [Bolton, 1928, 69] derives from the name of spring 54 [p. 9]. This name identification is in Bolton's translation, but the corresponding passage does not appear in the Spanish edition of Escalante, which I have used. Some pages later, however [Documentos, 1854, 537], there is mention of pagampachis.)

54, owned by Tanui (bunion), a shaman. Only 3 camps: Tanui, Čavuiya, and Aŋtitiav. Wintered at 54; in spring, moved across Houserock Valley to lower slopes of Kaibab Plateau, to gather roots; in summer, harvested seeds about 54; in fall, to Kaibab Plateau for deer. No chief.

VIII. 55-59, lower Houserock Valley and Cane Ranch, to the south, at the eastern base of Kaibab Plateau.

55, owned by Tasɨacɨ (early morning). About 10 camps, of which G remembers: (1) Tasɨacɨ, his m (Mɨapi-magugui, little woman), his w, no ch; others in his camp whom G cannot recall. (2) Sagwoarokovac (blue tattoo), w, o s (Kwagantɨ, quiet man); several other ch. (3) Winɨtuič (setting up post; "because she stood straight"), her s (Stavɨ, a berdache, unmarried; latter was "o half br" (i.e. first cousin) of m of Kwagantɨ. (4) Taviŋwawɨcɨ (sun slope), w, several ch.

Did not winter at 55, but visited at 56, sometimes accompanying those of latter spring to 59, until seeds ripe. Gathered seeds on flats at base of Vermilion Cliffs, or at 67 (IX). For deer, went to Kaibab Plateau near Jacob Lake; camped at 1 of 2 springs owned by Tasɨacɨ: Tamavac (spring[season] water), east of lake, or Kwitɨpac (stump water), north of lake; half-day journey apart. In fall moved to Paria Plateau east of Houserock Valley for pinenuts; camped there at Wɨivac (Apocynum water), another spring belonging to Tasɨacɨ. After harvest, went to winter base at 56. Actually camped little at 55 except in summer.

At death of Tasɨacɨ, 55 became joint property of Kwagantɨ and Keno (crooked elbow), a shaman. Latter the chief; he was the y ss s of Tasɨacɨ.

56, owned by Sakɨc (crackling step). G does not know number of camps; "many"; this and 65 said to have been most populous of all. G lists following occupants: (1) Sakɨc, w; several ch, all of whom died young save a d, married and living with Panguitch. (2) Kaŋʔaŋnapiŋ ([var.] -root-man), an old man; distant relative of Sakɨc, relationship expressed as miotɨmpiaŋ (p.125, no. [32,a]). With him were: w, no ch; his w's 2 ss and several of her br. (3) Tukumɨc (wildcat whiskers), also the miotɨmpiaŋ of Sakɨc, w, "many" ch; also his 2 ss, each with h and several ch. (4) Taviŋwawɨcɨ (sun slope), listed previously as resident of 55. Camped with his w, several ch.

Sakɨc and others of 56 wintered at 59, living in cave. Made frequent trips (day's journey) to 56 for seed stores left there. In summer returned to 56, gathering seeds (Chenopodium, Epicampes, Oryzopsis), and caching them in rock shelter. Sometimes visited 67 (IX) for seeds. In late summer, to Kaibab Plateau for deer and pinenuts. In some years, harvested pinenuts and Artemisia seeds on Paria Plateau, using water from 57. When pinenut crop insufficient, went to Colorado Canyon for mescal; returned to 59 for winter.

At death of Sakɨc, spring passed to his y ss s, Kwagantɨ (mentioned previously as resident of 55), who was on hand at the time. Ch of Sakɨc all dead save married d living elsewhere. Eventually, Kwagantɨ came to own 55 (jointly with Keno), as well as 56 and 59. Latter probably inherited from Sakɨc, although notes not explicit; at least, used extensively by him. Kwagantɨ maintained same seasonal cycle as predecessor. When he owned 56, there were 2 camps: (1) Kwagantɨ and his br, Aŋikwitu (gnat [mosquito] buttocks), latter's w, 3 ch. Kwagantɨ unmarried at time, but later married Naʔanoiʔi (hooked digging stick). (2) Wɨnɨtuič and her s, Stavɨ (listed at 55).

Powell (Dellenbaugh, 1909, 326n) named Kwagunt Valley (not shown on map 1) for Kwagantɨ, who claimed "that his father, who used to live there, had given it to him." According to G, the father lived at spring 55 (p. 18); Kwagantɨ his br and ss "found" the valley when trying to hide from Apache raiders. The br and ss remained there and, after their death, Kwagantɨ claimed the site. He discouraged visitors to the valley "because he wanted to keep the sage seeds for himself"; sometimes he went there for mescal. Eventually, Kwagantɨ moved to Kanab village; chopped wood for whites; wore "clean clothes and took a bath every week"; died on Kaibab reservation. "Nobody owned the springs then."

59, probably same ownership as 56; at least, used extensively by people from there and eventually owned by Kwagantɨ, who inherited 56. People from 55 often joined those from 56; 59 the usual winter base of both.

IX. 60-62, 64, 67, 68, including springs on Marble Platform, at the base of the Vermilion Cliffs, at Cane Ranch, at the eastern base of the Kaibab Plateau, and on the latter.

60-61 owned by Nɨwarɨmpɨ (snow heel, "because his heels froze"), a shaman; 62, 64 used by him, although he seems not to have been considered actual owner. Nɨwarɨmpɨ stayed mostly at 60. Camped with his w; his 3 married s and 3 married d, all with ch, maintained separate camps. When Nɨwarɨmpɨ died "all the children moved away and nobody owned the spring." Much waiʔi (sand bunch grass) at 60; "all" neighboring Kaibab came there to gather seeds. Ownership of spring did not extend to seeds growing in vicinity.

In fall, Nɨwarɨmpɨ moved to 61 to collect pasɨ (Artemisia) and kwakwe (Epicampes) seeds, also seeds (?) of unidentified plant called pagankwakwe (cane-kwakwe). Cave at 61 called Tosapikononc (white-rock shelter). Gathered pinenuts on Paria Plateau, using water from 62. Stayed only occasionally at 64. Regular fall trips to Kaibab Plateau for deer. Kwinivac of 68 (see below), the hunting chief.

67, owned by Kɨsaici (mouth open); camped alone. In separate camps: Saitɨmpɨ (white-spot mouth), a widower, with 1 d (other ch dead), and his br Kwiuinɨmpɨ (crooked feet), also a widower, with 1 s. These 2 br were shamans. Wintered just below rim of Colorado Canyon, sometimes east of southern tip of Kaibab Plateau, sometimes crossing plateau to mouth of Kanab Canyon. In spring returned to 67 with mescal. Remained there through summer seed (<u>Oryzopsis</u>, <u>Chenopodium</u>, <u>Mentzelia</u>) harvest. Sometimes those from 55 and 56 (VIII) visited 67 in summer. In fall, hunted on Kaibab Plateau.

68, Kwiavac (oak water), not definitely located but seemingly in De Motte region. Owned by Kwinivac (stands straight), a "big" chief; was chief not only for his own spring but for people of 60-61 as well, but not for those of 56. 3 camps: Kwinivac and his br, both unmarried, but former said later to have espoused 2 sisters; Nɨaku?u (chest), his w (Čapw?uiuvi, wrinkled eyes, the ss of Kwinivac); Muiait (no nose; a woman) and her h. Camped at 68 in spring; in summer moved to east base of Kaibab Plateau, near 67, for seeds; in fall returned to Kaibab Plateau to hunt; in winter went below rim Colorado Canyon, near southeast base of Kaibab Plateau.

There are watering places on the Kaibab Plateau, but I did not record their names, and it is possible that springs, at least, were privately owned (p. 18; spring 68, above); unfortunately, I failed to clarify this point. Only one established camp (at 68,) was reported.

Along the western face of the Kaibab Plateau there are numerous springs (69-74). Said to be on the eastern side of a nameless canyon along the front of the plateau, they seldom were occupied. Although claimed by Naragowocɨ (tattooed), he habitually camped to the west, at 76, where he was a "big chief."

X. 75-77, springs at the western base of Kaibab Plateau. West of the unoccupied springs mentioned in the preceding paragraph is a spur called Na?apačaikanti (little piece of mountain), and west of this are 3 more springs. These latter seem to have supported a surprisingly large Kaibab population. Although their exact location is uncertain, they appear to be in the heads of the small canyons that drain the Kanab. At least they are described as low on the western slopes of the plateau, where juniper and pinyon give way to sage.

75, owned by Puntuwaci (swirl), an elderly widower with 2 d. Both the latter married to Kanu (sings song); each had d. Kanu originally from Moccasin district; eventually he and his wife (wives?) owned the spring. In separate camp was Ka?auc (auc, knees), alone except for woman, who "may have been his w"; at least gathered seeds and cooked for him. Also another camp which G does not remember.

76, "not owned by any one person," but supported several camps: (1) Naragowocɨ (tattooed?), a shaman and "big chief," his w, s; 4 others in his camp whom G does not recall. (2) Uipamugacɨ (creek, edge of cliffs?), w, 2 s. (3) Pa?antɨm (ˈpa?antɨwɨ, long penis), w, 4 ch. (4) Aŋkapɨi (red arm), his w (Mu?urɨ, crane's neck), 2 s, 2 d; and his w's p: her f, Ya?aičomoni (dead leaf) and her m, Panagumpɨ (metal tongue, because once scalded tongue). (5) O?oicokwasɨ (squirrel tail), w (Tɨra?atɨpɨ, one side of face), 3 s, 1 d. (6) Mu?uc (sometimes called Mu?uwic "because he threw a stone hard and it hummed"), his w (Mu?wiaitɨ, no nose "because of her small nose"), 2 s, 1 d. In addition, another camp (7), somewhat removed from others; belonged to Čopicgaikɨ ("broken ankle and foot turned in"), his w, 3 ch.

77, owned (?) by Oa?čkɨ (yellow squeeze); "or at least he lived there." Had w, 3 d; also in camp were Tai?yu (no toenails), w (Ka?ɨmuvɨ, from ka?impuc, wild turkey) s, d. At death of Oa?čkɨ, his y ss s, Mai?kacino (said to be meaningless), took over spring. About 5 camps there, but G does not remember others.

People along western base of Kaibab Plateau called Sinwɨŋtunɨwɨŋ (gravel people). Wintered "nearly to the Colorado Canyon," but not actually within it. In spring returned with mescal to own springs. Remained there through summer, harvesting seeds and burying stores for following spring. In fall went to Kaibab Plateau for deer, pine-nuts, and yucca fruit.

Seasonal Cycle and Economic Clusters

In terms of seasonal food staples, the annual cycle is quite evident. Fall was the one time of plenty; then most households made trips to the plateaus, to collect yucca fruit, harvest pinenuts, and hunt deer. Stores were cached for winter use but ordinarily ran short; late winter and especially spring were seasons of near famine. At that time, many traveled to the rim of the Colorado and several tributary canyons to gather mescal, the standby when all else failed; cacti and juniper berries also were starvation foods. With the approach of summer, the people returned to what they considered home base, at the foot of the plateaus, to resume residence at their privately owned springs. On the adjacent flats they harvested "valley" seeds, and late in summer some returned to the higher elevations, to gather "plateau" seeds and berries. A large number of plant foods supplemented those just enumerated, and small game, available throughout the year, must have been the principal source of meat.

Within this general framework, those living at nearby springs tended to share the same annual cycle, forming thereby what may be described as loose, informal economic units (map 1). These are not recognized as such by informants, although a special name was applied to the people of at least one--group X, along the western front of the Kaibab Plateau (p. 21). Far to the north, the Alton area (IV) also was named, although its individual watering places apparently were not; this is high country, presumably with abundant water.

There is one more named area that perhaps should coincide with an economic cluster. This is Ankati, said to be the country between springs 40 and 45. These fall within group V (map 1), but because springs 35 to 46 were under the same ownership, group V extends considerably to the southwest and southeast.

The 10 clusters are extremely uneven--in size of terrain and in number of watering places and of households. Group VI includes six springs, but only one camp (p. 17); group X, three springs and 14 or 15 households, each with several persons. As a matter of fact, IV and VI are so sparsely populated they should have been disregarded (as was spring 65). In some cases, the suggested clustering is open to question; 60-61, for example, have been placed with unit IX because the occupants hunted with the chief of that group. Incidentally, seven of the 10 clusters are credited with a chief, whose main responsibility was to decide when and where to move the camps and to lead the deer hunt. His functions might be called vaguely "administrative," but not authoritative (pp. 26-7).

Within the territory of the local economic units, there was considerable shifting from spring to spring; there also was a good deal of intergroup contact. Not only did those of individual camps visit neighboring economic units, but the geographical and seasonal distribution of food resources resulted in contact on much wider scale. Several households of 30-33 and 34 (III) traveled to Alton (IV) in summer (p. 14), and in winter the Alton people moved down the canyon to avoid the cold, spending some time around 26 (III) (p. 13). The one camp associated with 47-52 (VI) often wintered at 35-46 (V) (p. 16). Households from 55 and 56 (VIII) sometimes collected seeds near 67 (IX) (p. 20), and 60 (IX) was a popular seed-gathering ground for "all" the neighbors (p. 19).

The Kaibab Plateau and the fringes of the Paunsaugunt, as well as the rim of the Grand Canyon, were virtually devoid of established camps. They functioned as communal lands, exploited by the Kaibab at large. Even the flats adjacent to privately owned springs were available to anyone who wanted to harvest seeds there, although it was remarked that the individual who eventually owned springs 55, 56 and 59 (p. 19) discouraged visitors, "because he wanted to keep the sage seeds for himself." There is no indication that local terrain was exploited by non-Kaibab neighbors, except for occasional exchange visits made by the Panguitch and Cedar Paiute (p. 32) and, it would seem, in late times, annual visits by a group of vaguely identified Ute (p. 34), with whom the Kaibab were on particularly chummy terms.

People from practically all parts of Kaibab territory forgathered at the communal grounds, at least intermittently, during much of fall and winter. Under the circumstances, it is remarkable that there is no suggestion of cooperation on a band-wide basis.* For an antelope hunt, 10 men are

---

*Steward (1937, 628) defines a band as "variable in its social and economic foundation, but always entailing cooperation, some centralized political control, and a sense of solidarity among inhabitants of a well-defined territory." Subsequently (1938, 181), he again emphasizes cooperation "in a sufficient number of economic and social activities under central control to have acquired a community of interest."

It is doubtful that any of the Southern Paiute bands, as I have sketched them (Kelly, 1934), would qualify on the score of either wholesale cooperation or centralized political control. Fundamentally, they are dialectic groups, each associated with clearly defined territory, which latter in itself would seem to have political implications. Undoubtedly, there is a feeling of belonging, but this could derive from dialectic unity. I relied heavily on

mentioned; for deer, 15 or 20; for a rabbit drive, perhaps 25--numbers that could have been recruited from comparatively few households. The rabbit surround reported by Sapir's informant, with men of "one or more bands" participating, probably is comparatively recent, and so also is the "game" of hunting rabbits on horseback, with the throwing stick (pp. 51-2).

Under the circumstances, it is noteworthy that when a local chief was selected, camps from other economic clusters arrived on the scene to participate in the discussion (p. 30).

Population: Composition of Settlement and Household

"After the Mormons came, all the Indians died," and the information concerning settlements (pp. 11-21) presumably applies to the early 1870's. That is when my informants were young, when the Mormons recently had established themselves at Kanab and at scattered spots in Kaibab territory, and when the Powell parties were making their survey.

---

the latter in trying to delimit local groups and "band," as I use the term, does not have Steward's connotations.

Although I feel his points are well taken, I cannot quite abandon the notion of the Kaibab as a band, despite the notorious lack of economic co-operation and central political control. There is evident association with a given territory, and hunting gathering activities normally localized within it; it was not shared with others, apart from the few exceptions noted above. This seems significant. In the entire sketch occupied by the Southern Paiute, the Kaibab Plateau certainly was the best deer-hunting area. The Shivwits, not far to the west, claim to have had no deer whatsoever in their territory, yet there is not the slightest suggestion that they ventured to hunt within Kaibab domain.

There is specific mention in the preceding section of about 200 persons, a good many of whom are identified by name. This figure agrees pretty well with the population figure of 171, reported for the Kaibab in 1873 (Hodge, 1907, 641). (This figure is assuredly based on Powell's data. I have a note that the Powell and Ingalls report should be consulted on population. Now [1963], in Mexico, this source unfortunately is not available.) Yet both figures probably are low.

It is evident that my informants' retrospective "census" is incomplete; to the 200 individuals mentioned must be added a great number of children who escaped notice and who, in many cases, probably equaled the adults in number. Furthermore, for Kanab Creek (no. 26) and spring 56, which were considered particularly populous, only three and four camps respectively could be recalled. Spring 65, once one of the most heavily populated areas, has been counted as uninhabited (p. 11), although one family had taken possession following the death of the previous occuapnts.

With a minimal figure of 200, which evidently is far from complete, a guess of 500 seems reasonable for the population of the Kaibab just prior to white contact. The area is large, but the number is not too small for a people almost entirely dependent on hunting and collecting.

The population at a watering place frequently included relatives. Often there is mention of separate households belonging to siblings-- usually brothers (nos. 4-8, 10-12, 20-21, 34, 35-46, 67); once, to brother and sister (68); once to "half brothers" (cousins) (20-21).

Sometimes a man and his married offspring camped at the same watering place (five married sons at no. 9, three married sons and three married daughters at 60-61). In one settlement, the wife's older brother, from the Kaiparowits band, was established in a separate household (no. 34); in another, one camp belonged to the "half brother" of the wife of one resident (55). A patrilocal residence tendency is marked. Some occupants of watering places were distantly related; some, not at all; and in a good many instances information was not available.

A surprising number of households apparently consisted of a man or two men, without women folk (nos. 10-12; 15, 18-19; 34; 35-46; 47-52; 67; 68). In two instances (10-12; 67), a man and his son composed the family group; in another (67), a man and his daughter; in still another (75), a man and his two married daughters. The situation suggests high female mortality, and in some cases the man is identified as a widower. Polygyny seems to have been infrequent (p.100). At spring 75, one man was married to two sisters; a couple of additional cases of plural marriage, apparently from more recent times, were mentioned in another connection.

The family unit most frequently was formed by a couple, with or without offspring. Additional members included: the man's mother (55); his brother (35-46); his brother and the latter's wife and children (56); his two married sisters, their spouses and offspring (56); and his sibling's child, sometimes described as an orphan (13, 26, 30-33, IV). The wife's relatives in the household were represented by her two sisters and several brothers (56), and by both her parents (76). Some tendency toward matri-local residence is apparent in the composition of the family group. In some cases, G did not mention relationship; in others, he indicated it was remote; in still others, he thought house mates unrelated to either host.

Chieftainship

The Kaibab had no head chief but there were several local ones, quite independent of one another. Seven such headmen have been noted above:

Pačakwi, Moccasin Spring (group I)
Miapi, Kanab Creek (group III)
Timpinapuŋ, Alton (group IV)
Tavac, greater Ankatɨ (group V)
Keno, Houserock Valley (group VIII)
Kwinivac, Kaibab Plateau (group IX)
Naragowoci, western base of Kaibab Plateau (group X)

The last three were considered "big chiefs"; the two preceding, "little chiefs"; and of the first two, my notes contain no estimate. The distinction between "big" and "little" supposedly depended, in part, on ability; probably, also, on the size and importance of the settlement. Unfortunately, the data are too fragmentary to demonstrate satisfactorily this latter supposition. A "big" chief such as Keno addressed the people every morning:

Keno spoke early in the morning, every morning, standing by the
door of his house. He spoke loudly so all could hear from their camps.
He told the people how to hunt and where to hunt; and after a time
everybody answered, "Yes." Then they went for deer. The chief
went first, alone, and the men followed his tracks. He went to the
hills and everyone gathered around him. He had them circle about
in the timber and chase the deer toward him. Sometimes there were
15 or 20 men and each had a deer; sometimes there was 1 deer for
each 2 or 3 men. The chief stayed on the mountain until all the
hunters had left. Toward evening he came home alone. When he
reached camp everyone gave him a piece of meat. Then he spoke
again to the people.

According to Sapir, the chief sometimes mounted a hill early in
the morning and shouted directions at the top of his voice (ampa-rogoa-i,
to stand on a height and shout announcements or orders for hunting or
moving camp). At other times he cried commands from the doorway
of his camp, and his message was repeated by neighboring camps to those
out of earshot. Such addresses by a chief (or other person of prominence)
were particularly common during hunting season.

A chief (niavi) directed the seasonal movements of camps, and
usually, but not invariably, was in charge of deer hunting. He also advised
the people "to be good; not to fight; not to steal. If you find someone's
arrow, give it to him," he told them.

A chief had, however, virtually no judicial authority. In case of
theft, the victim or his relatives demanded the return of the property.
But if this were refused "nothing happened; they never really fought
over a theft." Sometimes the victim stole from the thief in retaliation.
The chief rarely intervened and then only to request the return of the
goods.

In event of murder, the chief's role was equally minor. Sometimes
the father or brother of the deceased killed the murderer; when, as
was usual, the latter fled, "all the people planned to kill him when he
returned." Accidental homicide did not call for death as retribution,
and the chief might direct that an indemnity be paid the relatives--a
large buckskin or a bow and arrows for the death of a man; nothing for
a woman or child. Murder by someone from an outside tribe usually was
unavenged: if it were a Navajo, "they could never find him." Once four or
five Utes killed a Kaibab; two or three of the murderers were killed and
the rest fled.

An aging chief nominated his successor and relinquished office voluntarily. If an incumbent died, his relatives selected one of their number to become headman, subject to popular consent. Rarely, if ever, was the successor the son. In one of the accounts to follow, a man who was renouncing the chieftainship tried to impose his son. The people demurred and selected instead the husband of the chief's first cousin. The latter, in local kinship terminology, would be called "sister," hence the choice was tantamount to that of sister's husband. No reason was given for opposition to the father-to-son sequence except that "they didn't like it that way." G demonstrated the point neatly:

> They did not want a man's son to be chief after him. [He held out his hand, fingers spread]. The thumb is the man's son, but the middle finger is the next chief. [There is strong indication that the father-to-son transfer derived from white influence.]

Most frequently, it is said, the chiefly office passed to the son of a brother or sister. There is clear statement of succession by a brother (at 35-46, p. 16) and, below, by the father's "sister's" (cousin's) husband; by the sister's son; and by the grandson.

> A long time ago, before I [G] was born, the father of Kwinivac was chief. He got to be an old, old man, and forgot how to tell the people to hunt. So he told his son that he had better be chief. But the people didn't like that and made Keno chief. [Although Kwinivac was denied the office at Houserock, he later became chief at spring 68.] Keno was married to the "half-sister" (first cousin) of Kwinivac's father.

> Then Keno died. I don't know why they waited, but for two or three years they had no chief. Then Keno's relatives called all the people to their camp to select a new chief. They sat together in the evening, almost all night. Keno's relatives talked. I was there; so was my father. He wanted his father to be the next chief. His father's name was Tapič, (string around wrist), and he was the son of Keno's sister. My father talked first. He told his father, "If you want to be chief, tell these Indians how to hunt and how to bring home their game. Then they will give you something to eat, just as they did with Keno. Tell the people in this camp to move some other place." When the people decided to make Tapič chief, he stood up and said, "It is all right for me to be the chief, but I don't know very much. Maybe I shall learn after while." He told the people to be good; to be kind to each other and to share their food: when they had deer or rabbits to give half to other camps.

Tapič told his wife to lead the other women when they went for seeds or berries. "You know where to go," he told her. She went first, as did the chief in hunting. The women did not divide their seeds with her because she gathered her own. In the morning the chief's wife told the girls, "Take the basket jar and fill it so you will have water today." If the spring were close they did as she told them, but if it were 2 or 3 mi. away the boys went for water. [One woman, not the chief's wife, supervised the pit roasting of mescal (p. 44-5).]

After Tapič died there was no real chief. The whites made my father [son of Tapič] chief; Major Powell wanted him to have the job. Then my father died, and the white people called me captain (Sapir mentions George, present Kaibab "chief"); they think I am chief. [According to informants, Powell also was responsible for the chieftainship of Frank (Chuarruumpeak; Čarɨmpipi), and one informant commented that "he could talk pretty good." Dellenbaugh (1926, 250) speaks of "Chuarooumpeak, the young chief of the Kaibab band, usually called Frank by the settlers and Chuar by his own people. ... A most fluent speaker in his native tongue, he would address his people with long flights of uninterrupted rhetorical skill." In Hillers' plates he is identified as "head chief" of the Kaibab.]

When a chief died, the relations said, "If any of you boys want to be chief, say so." After while one said he would like it. Then they called a meeting and talked it over.

When the chief was getting old--couldn't walk, couldn't see--he sent a messenger to call the people. In the morning he told them to gather at his camp, "We will have a big smoke and a big talk." They came, mostly men, and sat in a circle inside the chief's house, or outside. One man brought out a big pipe and filled it. He passed it to the man on his left. It went around the circle until it was empty and then was passed back [counterclockwise] to the owner. He filled it and started it around again. All the time--talk, talk, talk. Perhaps the old man wanted his grandson to be the next chief. Then everybody talked it over. If the chief's wife was there she listened, and when they finished she stood up and said everyone was satisfied.

In the above accounts, two points seem of considerable interest. One is the responsibilities assumed by the headman's wife, who announced the decision on a new chief and who took the initiative in gathering plant products and hauling water. The ceremonial passing of the pipe also is noteworthy. Unfortunately, my notes do not state whether it was considered an old custom or not. Powell (1961, 321) mentions such formality among the Uinkaret; the passage suggests that he may have introduced the practice.

The several chiefs seem to have been quite independent of one another. Each was concerned with his local group, whose hunting activities and seasonal movements he directed. One spring on the Kaibab Plateau, allegedly owned by a "big chief" (p. 20, spring 68), was occupied by three camps during spring and fall. Nevertheless, this chief did not lead visitors who arrived to hunt; the latter relied on their own headman or, lacking one, hunted individually.

In view of such independence, it is surprising to discover that a new chief was selected in consultation with those of other economic clusters. When one was being considered at Houserock (55, VIII), the Moccasin people (12, I) were summoned, "because they knew everything." On like occasions, the Moccasin people reciprocated by conferring with the Houserock people. Camps from Navajo Well (34, III), which had no resident chief, and from an unspecified region of the Kaibab Plateau (X?) also journeyed to Houserock to participate in the discussion. But the Alton people (IV)--a small and comparatively remote group--"didn't go anywhere." Evidently there was more unity among the several groups than is suggested by the absence of large-scale collaboration in hunting and gathering.

Although the "subsistence" chief generally headed the deer hunt, there was different leadership for other game. Antelope was of secondary importance but sometimes was taken in a simple surround, under the direction of a chief (p. 50). Still another individual supervised rabbit drives. Called kamɨn-niav (rabbit chief), he seems not to have been one of the net owners. He stood "to one side, watching." He did not call out instructions, but he gave advice on "how to get rabbits and when to get them" (p. 51).

Quite another kind of chief is mentioned as leader of the circle or round dance. This office was not inherited, and the selection of a candidate was discussed openly, as was that of the subsistence chief. "They picked the best man, someone not too old." He seems to have addressed those camped together "every evening," even when there was to be no dance. He might say, "No dancing tonight; we are tired." After such a pronouncement, "everybody goes [went] to sleep." When he decided to hold a dance, he sent advance word to neighboring camps. A messenger sallied forth unaccompanied and delivered the invitation without relying on stick, cord, or other mnemonic device.

Neighbors

The Kaibab regard themselves as indigenous; "we always have lived here as far as we know." Nevertheless, they recognize an earlier occupation by the "Mukwic" (Moqui), to whom they attribute archeological sites and pictographs. According to tradition, "the Mukwic did not like to camp one place all the time, so they kept on moving and now are across the Colorado River." G personally believed the Hopi came from the northwest but could cite no evidence.

The term for Paiute is nɨŋwɨnc, person; nɨŋwɨŋ, people; for Mormons, Momɨni; other whites, Marikac ("American"); Negroes, nɨgɨ. For other Paiute there seems to be no standard nomenclature. The Panguitch and St. George were known by group names, but the Cedar and Kaiparowits were usually referred to by local place names.

The following were recorded:

Kaibab. Kaivavituniwɨ, Kavavič-ŋɨwɨ, mountain-lying down people; Sapir, 1930, 627, kaiva-viči-ci-ŋwɨ.

Kaiparowits. Avuapɨnɨŋwɨn; Kwaguiuavi [-nɨwɨŋ], [var.] -seed-valley people; both refer to local districts in the Kaiparowits area (p. 149). The only Paiute term sometimes applied to the Kaiparowits group as a whole is derived from Kaivavič, the name of the Kaiparowits as well as the Kaibab plateau, hence practically identical with the designation for the Kaibab themselves (pp. 142-3).

San Juan. Tuyouipi-nɨŋwɨn, rock-river (Piute Canyon) people; called also Monʔkapi-nɨŋwɨn; latter said to be language of Uraivɨ (Hopi, Oraibi) and to refer to a creek, perhaps Moenkopi Wash; Sapir, 1930, 685, toiʔoipi-či-wɨ, gravel-canyon (San Juan) people.

Panguitch. Pagɨv, fish; Pagɨwaciŋ, fish people; Sapir, 1930, 638, pa(a)gɨɨi-ci-wɨ, fish people.

Cedar. Kurkwit, Kurkwi; Kurkewek-nɨŋwɨn, meaningless, probably name of a specific locality. Paruguna-nɨŋwɨn, purple (?)-lake people, at Parowan and Paragonah; Sapir, 1930, 607, Paruguna-nci-ŋwɨ, Indians of Parowan Lake. Kanarɨnɨŋwɨn, willow people, at Kanarraville; Sapir, 1930, 598, aŋka-pa-nukwi-či-či-ŋwɨ, red-water-flowing people, near Cedar City.

Uinkaret. Yuinkariri-niŋwin, pine-mountain (Mt. Trumbull) people.

St. George. Tuŋkwint-niŋwin, black-rock-[basalt] stream people; reference is to Santa Clara Creek.

Shivwits. Sivic; Sapir, 1930, 656, sivi-či-ŋwi.

Gunlock (?). Uitiniwin, intersection-of-creeks people; said to be near Mountain Meadows.

Paranigat (?). Paranigi-niŋwin; Sapir, 1930, 597, pa(a)-ra-n?igi-ci-ŋwi, people-who-stick-their-feet-in-water.

In addition, Sapir (1930, 575, 586, 651, 549) adds the following:

Moapa. muurii-ci-ŋwi, bean people.

[Las Vegas]. niva-ganti-ci-ŋwi, snowy-mountain [Charleston Peak] people.

[Beaver]. kwi?u-mpaa-ci-wi,(?) – water people, formerly west of Sevier Lake. [From Kwiimpuc, site of Beaver.]

aŋka-kaniga-či-ŋwi, red-cliff-base people, formerly in Long Valley. [Latter within Kaibab territory; perhaps a local place name.]

With their Paiute neighbors, the Kaibab seem to have been on friendly terms; there are specific, if infrequent, references to marriage with Kaiparowits, San Juan, Panguitch, and Cedar groups. Moreover, a certain amount of trade was reported (p. 90).

Probably relationships fluctuated somewhat from time to time. There was a complaint that the Panguitch Paiute, as well as the Koosharem Ute, came to Kaibab country to steal children for sale to the whites. Nevertheless--but perhaps decades later--the Kaibab sometimes visited the Panguitch area to fish, and the Panguitch, in turn, came to hunt deer on the Kaibab Plateau. A similarly reciprocal visit was made by some of the Cedar Paiute, when the Kaibab collected berries in their territory. In no instance does such travel outside Kaibab limits form part of the normal seasonal cycle.

Sapir's informant described an occasional skirmish, only half serious, between two bands. An enterprising man assembled his friends--as many as 50 or 100, which number implies residence on reservations--and arrived on the scene to capture a girl. Local men rallied to defend her, and the opponents fought with their fists, not to kill. If the intruder won, the girl belonged to him, and he might settle down and remain with his newly acquired wife's parents. There were no hard feelings.

It is difficult to guess how much communication there may have been with the more distant Paiute groups in early times; even now, informants are vague about the country south or west of Moapa. Indubitably, intercourse was stimulated by the introduction of the horse and, decades later, by the opening and improving of roads and by residence on reservations. As early as 1901 (p. 95), for the celebration of a "Cry," some 300 men and women assembled--Paiute from the Kaibab, St. George, Moapa, Cedar, San Juan, and Kaiparowits groups, as well as some Shoshoni from western Utah.

Nowadays, Paiute from Moapa to Moccasin forgather for "big times"; there is a good deal of informal visiting and intermarriage and some patronage of extra-band shamans.

Bounded on three sides by fellow Paiute, and on the fourth by the Colorado River, the Kaibab seem to have had comparatively limited contact with other tribes. There is only one slight hint of territorial aggression (on the part of the Apache, p. 35) and no indication whatsoever of war. An occasional murder by Ute or Navajo seems to have been accepted passively, and, despite plaintive comments to the effect that Ute and Panguitch (Paiute) sometimes stole children, the Kaibab apparently attempted neither resistance nor retaliation.

North of the river, relationships seem to have been exclusively with the immediately adjacent Ute. "In the old days we didn't know the 'real' Ute, only the Koosharem." The Ute enjoy enormous prestige: "They know everything. They know the bear dance and the sun dance. They know how to make buckskin dresses and gloves and how to make beadwork."

With the Koosharem, the Kaibab feel close affinity. In fact, G pronounced them predominantly Paiute "because many Circleville people [Panguitch Paiute] moved to Koosharem and now think they are Ute." Moreover, by some the Panguitch and Kaiparowits are considered Paiute; by others, Ute or "half-Ute." The latter was defined, not very helpfully, as "a man who dressed like a Ute and who wore his hair in two braids." Language differences are said to be slight: "Some Utes use our language, but the voice is different. It is low; ours is light."

In other words, there is no very clear distinction between Ute and Paiute, and the cultures probably would be quite similar if the Ute were stripped of the horse and a number of obvious Plains traits. Some of the latter, incidentally, the Kaibab have acquired from the Ute: tipi, travois, presumably smoking of buckskin; perhaps also braided hair among the men. A very few years before my visit, the skin-covered board cradle had appeared, inspired specifically by Koosharem example.

As will be seen below, there is some doubt concerning the identity of a group, presumably Ute, which visited the Kaibab frequently. G speaks of them thus:

The Paiute were always friendly with the Utes, and they used to come here to visit. [Statement to the effect that visits not reciprocated.] They used to come here to hunt and then joined these Indians in a circle dance. Their leader was called Walker by the whites; Wakarɨ his Indian name. He was a Ute and it was his people who came here.... There were about 12 or 13.... They came almost every fall ... and returned before winter. Brought horses, knives, and guns to trade for bucksin. Brought [used] tipis of elk skin. Used the oravɨ [travois] too.

G was unable to say where these Ute came from but "thought they were camping somewhere the other side of Provo." At the time, I assumed, somewhat doubtfully, that reference must be to the famous Walker's band. It now appears that a nearby Ute group may be involved, perhaps even the Koosharem; and one statement by Sapir's informant appears to identify the latter with the Kaiparowits (Escalante) Paiute on East Fork. In Sapir's notes, under Ute, the Koosharem are placed "in Grass Valley (chief named Oakar: yellow) (not on reservation)." However, his dictionary (1930, 643) identifies the group as "Paiute band at Grass Valley." The latter does not appear on my maps, but Sapir's informant reported that, in 1910, the surviving Panguitch were living there. This apparently agrees with G's statement, cited above, that Circleville (Panguitch) people joined the Koosharem. There are other scattered references in Sapir's notes. One describes the Koosharem as "Utes affiliated with the Paiute"; another places them on East Fork, within Kaiparowits (Escalante) territory and identifies them with the latter band. The situation is inconclusive, but the Koosharem evidently were very close neighbors, presumably Ute; the name of their chief links them with the unidentified Ute visitors. These details demonstrate the borderline fuzziness between Ute and Paiute. It would be interesting to have expressions of opinion from the Koosharem and from Ute less closely identified with the Paiute.

An incomplete list of Ute groups follows:

Koosharem. Kusarɨmpi; Sapir, 1930, 643, kušaa-ru-mpɨ, "trousers-string, rope; Paiute band at Grass Valley."

Uintah. Yuwinta (pine valley); Sapir, 1930, 725, yuvi-ntɨi-ci-wɨ, pine-canyon-mouth people.

Whiterocks. Pariagaivɨ (elk mountain).

Ouray. Sapir, 1930, 574, mogwataviŋʔwa-nci-ŋwɨ.

Unidentified. Pagɨmwac (fish-river-side?). Perhaps Lowie's (1924, 194) Paguwadziu, "west of the Uintah."

There was limited knowledge of tribes across the Colorado River:

Havasupai (Kuʔinina, meaning not known). Lived on far side of Grand Canyon; scarcely known; no trade relations. G denied their visiting, much less owning Powell and Kaibab plateaus (cf. Spier, 1928, 94, Fig. 1), saying they were afraid to cross the river. He had seen one Havasupai at Tuba City and two who had managed to cross the Colorado near Mt. Trumbull; no others.

Apache (Muwinakac, nose "earring, because they wore nose ornaments"). Likewise little known. G once saw one at Cameron. Had heard of an Apache raid, which occurred before his grm was born and which is the only hint of aggression against Kaibab territory reported.

"Just for fun" and because they wanted Kaibab Plateau, Apache forded the Colorado (point of crossing not known) and at night came upon Kaibab camp. With handled-stone weapons, hit each sleeping Kaibab on the head, killing all but one woman who escaped to Moccasin. Kaibab "never got even with them." Nankoweap (nɨnkoipɨ, people killed) canyon on eastern scarp of Kaibab plateau named for this massacre.

Navajo (Pagaŋwicɨn, cane-knife people, "because they stood straight and tall"). In post-horse days, extensive trade with Navajo (p. 91); apparently little contact in earlier times.

Hopi (Mukwic, Tɨŋwanc, Uraivɨ "were all alike"). Tɨŋwanc spoke the same language and lived between the other two. G saw one Hopi near Tuba City. Little contact (p. 91). G had heard they had houses "like the Navajo," describing them as earth-covered sweat houses with roof hole. Had never seen a Hopi blanket but thought they were like the Navajo. S remembered one Hopi trading party; M said his uncle once visited Hopi villages, there witnessing pottery making (pp. 77-8).

In addition to the above, Sapir's informant--young, educated, and traveled--reported the Walapai as Oaaripaiaa-acciŋw (yellow-breast people); they were not known to G. Sapir also lists Aiato as Coconino, possibly Havasupai; this is the name by which the Mohave are known to the Shivwits and Moapa Paiute. The Shoshoni (Kɨmancciŋw, strangers) appear in Sapir's notes, as do the Sioux (Sugucciŋw) and Arapaho (sariitikaniʔ dog eaters), but his informant could give no name for Apache or Zuni. Of these, only the Arapaho was known to G; he had seen one when he visited the Southern Ute at Bluff, Utah.

Subsistence

The Kaibab were almost entirely dependent upon wild foods. About the middle of the past century, a limited form of native agriculture reached them (pp. 39-41), as a consequence of which three fields were planted at Moccasin (12) and one near the present site of Kanab (26). Other Kaibab did not plant "because there was not enough water at Ankatɨ; it was too cold on Buckskin [Kaibab Plateau]; and the Houserock people were too lazy.... They wanted to eat corn but did not plant it." The introduction of agriculture could not have altered very materially the subsistence of the group as a whole.

The seasonal cycle has been summarized previously (p. 22). Of vegetable foods, seeds were the mainstay; they ripened in summer and early fall. Yucca fruit and pinenuts were enormously important in autumn, particularly because they could be stored for winter and spring, when food regularly ran short. Mescal, various cacti, and juniper berries were winter products, available when all else failed. Several different kinds of berries are listed, but they and acorns were minor items; nor were roots of major consideration.

Deer was the chief large-game animal and was hunted on the plateaus in late summer and fall; antelope and mountain sheep were much less plentiful. Small game was taken throughout the year. Rabbits and an assortment of rodents were most important, but large-scale rabbit drives were held only in winter Birds, eggs, locusts (?), and "green caterpillars" were welcome, but certainly not basic in the diet. There was no fish

Details on the preparation of specific foods are given in the pages to follow Techniques included parching (pp. 41-2) grinding, boiling, roasting in the ashes and baking in the pit oven. All cooking was done in the open, not inside the house or beneath a shade. Men and women ate together, twice daily, morning and evening.

Cooking equipment was simple. The fire drill is described elsewhere (pp. 76-7) as is the variety of baskets used in food preparation, for which there were parching and winnowing trays, cooking baskets, and food bowls (pp. 78-83) In stone boiling, heated pebbles were lifted between two sticks, dropped into the contents of the cooking basket, and the mixture stirred with any stick at hand. This technique had been abandoned before the birth of my informants. A very few families seem to have cooked in an unfired clay vessel (pp. 77-8), set directly on the coals; the tripod kettle support shown in a Hillers' photograph (Steward, 1939, Pl. 13, b) probably is of late introduction.

The mealing stone (marac) was an unsquared slab collected "in the mountains" and pointed slightly by the woman (Pl. 2, d-f; Hillers' plate no. 1600, a [not reproduced by Steward]). Steward (1939), in Pls. 10, b and 13, a shows other metates; that in Pl. 10, b is somewhat troughed. The mano (mu?ac) invariably was picked up at an archeological site. Grinding on the slab was always from the same end; "a woman could tell by the wear." One surface was used for hulling and grinding seeds (pp. 41-3) and pinenuts; the other, for crushing berries (pp. 42-3) The stone was washed upon occasion but no special brush was used to clean it. In Hillers' plates, the woman sits on the ground, her legs stretched out before her, and the stone slab between them (Powell, 1961, 319); grinding posture has changed since those days (Pl. 2, d-f).

A woman made spoons (agoc) by smoothing the "back of a deer skull" with a stone, and the Powell and Palmer collections (Fig. 1) establish the use of horn spoons and ladles in some unspecified part of southern Utah, in the 1870's.

Surplus products were dried and cached against future needs. Food was wrapped in cliffrose bark or placed in fawn-skin sacks, sinew-sewn, and deposited in bark-lined pits (not jar shaped), dug in the floors

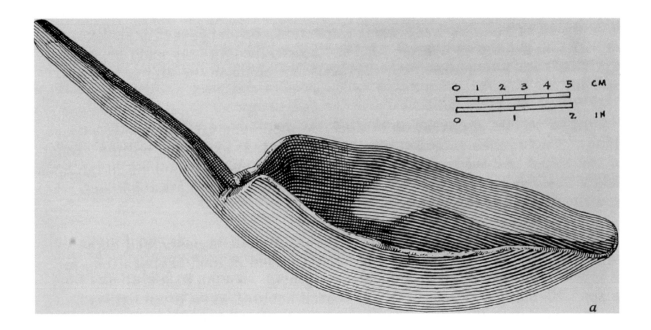

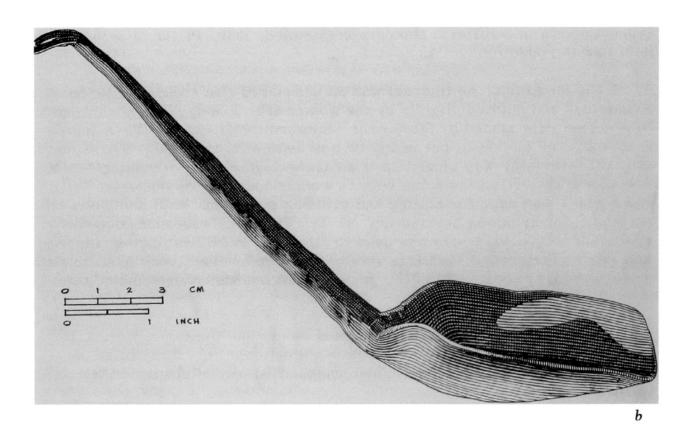

Fig. 1. Horn spoon and ladle. a, PM 9427. b, mountain sheep horn; PM 50666. a, Palmer collection, 1875. b, Powell collection, 1873 or 1874. Both are from southern Utah, band provenience unknown.

of caves or rock shelters. The cached products were covered with layers of bark, poles, earth and stone. Each family had one or more such deposits, often in widely separated places. The people from Moccasin, for example, did not attempt to bring home the products of their hunting and gathering trips to the Kaibab Plateau, but stored them in caves or rock shelters along the western slopes of the plateau. Then, as the need arose, they journeyed there to draw upon the stores. The Alton people (group IV) cached food for winter consumption at their winter base, near the town of Kanab, and for spring consumption, at their home camps.

Agriculture

Kaibab learned to plant from the St. George Paiute. Gave them small buckskin for sack of corn about 2 ft. tall. Corn called aŋwivɨ; nowadays, kumi; latter said to be quite different from native corn which had (Sapir) smaller cobs. 4 colors of corn (white, tosagarɨ; blue, kwike, smoke-fire; yellow, oakarɨ; red, aŋkagarɨ); all colors equally good; mixed on cobs.

Other crops: paraŋwar, a squash or pumpkin with "black" rind; and a plant called mukwiɨkɨ (said not to mean Hopi sunflower, but thought to be same as the sunflower grown today, which is Helianthus annuus, cultivated).

Another seed plant, unidentified, called kumutɨ. Described as 3 ft. tall, with black seeds 5 in. long; said to be different from wild plant of the same name. Sapir was told of a cultigen called tuu-puwi-vi (black-seed). (A wild seed of similar name (tupuipi) proved to be Amaranthus blitoides Wats., and wild kumutɨ was identified as A. retroflexus. This is suggestive. The Kaibab description does not sound much like an Amaranthus, yet the 5 in. seed might refer to the seed head and the "pod" (p. 41) to the husk. A cultivated kumutɨ was reported by Shivwits, St. George, and Moapa informants; there is some hint that their reference may be to sorghum.)

Beans not grown by Kaibab, although known as a crop among St. George neighbors, from whom all cultigens were obtained.

Agriculture reached Kaibab after death of Pačakwi, chief at Moccasin (spring 12; p. 12), and before settlement of country by whites; evidently about middle of last century. 3 fields, each about 200 ft. sq., planted just below Moccasin Spring. Plot nearest the spring belonged to Taŋarɨinia (crooked knee), who owned the watering place after death of Pačakwi; almost adjoining it to southeast was field of Kanavɨ (thin); and to northeast, that of Čaŋa (bull lizard), ordinarily resident of 4-8, but with field at Moccasin. Main ditch led to field of Taŋarɨinia, laterals to other plots. Owner of spring irrigated first; others waited 2 days before using water. Irrigated at about 10-day intervals. One other field, at 26, owned by Kipɨ (elbow). Planted in bed of Kanab Creek, then not so deeply trenched as now.

Planted "about June first, when the morning star (tasɨantupucipi) appeared in the east"; (Sapir: planted May or June); crop ripened middle of August. 2 plantings, one spring (June evidently considered such) and another summer. Men prepared fields, burning brush and grubbing roots. Ground watered before planting; latter done by man or woman; no prayers. Corn planted in hills, arranged in rows. (Sapir: did not plant in rows, but in pit about 3 ft. dia. and 6 in. deep; rain allowed to collect; water brought from nearby springs. Informant thought planting in rows due to white influence.) Hole made with stick "flattened like a shovel"; about 6 in. deep, 2 ft. apart. 3 kernels dropped in; sprouted 5-7 days. People left before corn was up, returning when it was about 8 in. tall to weed and tend plot; remained through harvest season. Both sexes worked in fields; weeds pulled by hand; no hoe; no fertilizer. Fields unfenced; brush waved in air morning and evening to frighten birds; surrounded fields with fire or went about morning and evening with smoking brands to frighten rodents.

Ears of corn gathered by men; stacked in pile about 5 ft. high; carried to camp in burden basket by women. According to Sapir, owner of field invited whole camp to assist in picking; assigned particular rows [sic] to neighbors; latter kept what they gathered; owner himself picked all his own corn.

Green ears roasted in ashes; never boiled; sometimes kernels cut off with knife; ground, unparched; made into mush; called kumi-tusupɨ (corn-ground). Ripe corn parched, ground, made into mush; not mixed with anything. Corn spread on grass until dry; then kernels removed from cob with a twist; stored in buckskin sack. Some of each color kept for seed.

Sapir describes several methods of preparing corn. Roasted in husks under ashes for half hour; or burnt in blaze 5 or 10 min. until husks burned out; or husked, roasted near fire about 15 min., being turned from time to time. Boiled corn sometimes removed from cob, dried, shriveling in process; stored; boiled again. No "paper bread."

Cornstalks occasionally used as covering for house or shade; no other utility.

Squash (or pumpkin?) planted between rows of corn, at same time; about 3 ft. apart. Ripened in fall, later than corn. Blossoms boiled; sometimes with young, green fruits; S used to cook blossoms with pasɨ seeds. Squash roasted whole in ashes; sometimes split in two, seeds extracted, and halves set against fire to bake, or (Sapir) buried under ashes overnight. To dry, squash was peeled, cleaned, allowed to dry slightly; then cut spirally, strung on pole, and hung beneath roof of shade. Dried squash boiled.

Sunflowers planted (in row?) to one side of corn. Seed heads picked, spread on ground to dry, pounded with stick; seed winnowed, parched, ground, made into mush.

Kumutɨ planted alone, broadcast, in plot about 25 ft. sq. ; irrigated. One planting only, in spring; ripened in fall. When ripe, women broke off tops in burden basket; spread heads on ground to dry. Rubbed between palms over tray; winnowed. Dried seed made into gruel. Sometimes eaten fresh as mush; then "ground on the metate, pods and all."

Wild Plant Products

Seeds.--Regarded as chief vegetable staple. "Valley"seeds are those growing at lower elevations (at base of Vermilion Cliffs; Kanab Plateau, Houserock Valley, etc.); "plateau" seeds, those found at higher elevations (top Vermilion Cliffs, Kaibab, Paria plateaus). Former ripened mostly in summer; latter, toward fall.

Seed preparation shown in Pl. 2. Nowadays, seeds gathered with basketry beater (Pl. 4, b) in canvas-covered frame (Pl. 2, a); formerly, in close-twined, conical basket. Hillers' plates indicate clearly that both coiled and twined burden baskets once used by Kaibab (pp. 79, 81).

Some seeds, such as Oryzopsis, harvested by cutting off tops. Seeds hulled, if necessary, on metate; winnowed in circular coiled basket (Pl. 3, e) or in close-twined, fan-shaped tray (Pl. 3, d). Parched with charcoal, formerly in basket tray, nowadays in metal receptacle. Tray shaken first in one hand, then in other; rolled gently counterclockwise, bringing coals to far side of container; light coals blown off, heavier ones poured out.

Parched seeds ground on metate. Both hands on mano, which barely accommodates them; stone worked back and forth with considerable pressure and without being lifted from grinding surface. Seeds deposited at near end of metate, brushed in path of hand stone, and ground products accumulated at far end, in close-twined, fan-shaped tray. Some seeds (e. g., Mentzelia) pastelike when ground; usually mixed with water and made into mush (Sapir: mush, sɨʔapi).

"Valley" seeds include several grasses; waʔai (waʔaipi; Oryzopsis hymenoides Ricker), tops cut off into burden basket, piled, ignited to burn off hulls, winnowed, ground, eaten as flour or mush; kwakwe (kokwevi; Epicampes rigens); monɨmpɨ (Sporobolus cryptandrus). Other valley seeds: wara (Sapir, 1930, 713, wara-ˢ) (Chenopodium album); kovɨ (Chenopodium fremontii); tupuipi (Amaranthus blitoides Wats. (Sapir, 1930, 623, tuu-pʔui-vi, black-seed; vine-like plant [sic] with black, oily seeds. Sapir: heads cut, piled on hide, beaten with stick). Akɨ (tansy mustard, Descurainia) made into mush; sometimes mixed with snow as confection: Kuikumpɨ (cakurɨmpui, Sphaeralcea marginata) regarded as edible by one informant, inedible by another. Kuʔu (Mentzelia albicaulis); a specimen near M. multiflora called tusawaiyav by one informant, who regarded seeds as edible; called kuʔumaivi (friend of kuʔu) by another who said seeds not eaten. Akɨmpɨ (Helianthus annuus; Dutton, 1882, 105, noted fields of H. lenticularis, now called H. annuus, between Pipe Spring and Mount Trumbull); according to Sapir, sometimes mixed with crushed roasted pinenuts or with pumpkin and made into mush. Pakɨmpuipi (Gilia inconspicua). Seeds of saŋwavɨ (Artemisia tridentata) formerly eaten in time of shortage.

"Plateau" seeds; kumutɨ (Amaranthus retroflexus); cičagantɨ (Balsamorrhiza); pasɨ of several kinds (Artemisia dracunculus, A. wrightii Gray [A. vulgaris wrightii, Hall and Clements]), the most important plateau seed. Tuʔpuipi, unidentified;(same name as the valley seed, but said to be a different plant).

Berries.--Found chiefly on higher elevations--some by Alton, some on plateaus; in recent times, at least, gathered on High Plateaus east of Cedar City (outside Kaibab territory). Some berries (juniper, currant, raspberry, etc.) eaten fresh; others (serviceberry, squawbush) dried. Ground on metate, stroking away from body, not back and forth as with seeds; mano lifted each time. Usually ground pulp stirred into water and drunk "like canned tomatoes."

Wa?apɨ (Juniperus utahensis); "berries on some trees sweet"; on others, "strong; used to go about testing them." Gathered winter, spring; crushed on metate, seeded, eaten raw; not mixed with water. Wiyɨmpipi (Mahonia fremontii?); found lower slopes Kaibab Plateau; ripe late summer; eaten raw. (Sapir: sometimes ground and made into mush). Pogompɨ (currant, Ribes aureum), eaten fresh. Berries of another currant, kai?apipi (R. cereum) sometimes eaten by children; thought to cause headache. Tɨvi?isi (wild strawberry). Nagawantapapɨ (mountain-sheep-penis; raspberry, Rubus leucodermis Dougl.). Tɨwampɨ (serviceberry; the shrub, tɨav; Amelanchier pallida Greene); those growing at higher elevations edible; gathered fall; dried; ground on metate; mixed with water. Kwičuapɨ (Peraphyllum ramosissimum Nutt.) starvation food. Tonopɨ (chokecherry, Prunus melanocarpa Rydb.). Sɨiwimpɨ (squawbush, Rhus utahensis) ripe in summer. Eaten fresh or dried; ground and mixed with water. U?upɨ (Lycium, either L. andersonii or L. torreyi, probably the latter) ripe in summer; eaten fresh or dried; Sapir: "considered best berry of all." Another Lycium, probably L. pallidium, called sɨna?aupip (coyote-berry); not eaten. Kunuk?wi (elder, Sambucus melanocarpa) boiled. Pagau?upi (buffaloberry) not found in Kaibab habitat; known from Panguitch region.

Pinenuts, acorns.--Pinenuts (tɨv) harvested in fall, on Kaibab, Paria plateaus and top of Vermilion Cliffs. Some women claimed certain pinyon trees; latter not marked, "but they knew the place." Quarreled if anyone gathered cones from their special trees. Men, sometimes girls, climbed tree and broke off branches. In recent times knocked cones from tree with hooked pole (uinki) of mountain birch. Said to have learned this from "Nevada people"; nowadays travel by auto to Utah-Nevada border for pinenuts. Women gathered cones in burden baskets. Sagebrush fire built on ground between 2 long poles (Sapir: fire built in center of hollow-like wood pile shaped like eagle's nest; wood thick on sides). Cones dumped on fire; stirred by shaking the 2 protruding poles. Whole covered with ashes and earth and allowed to bake a couple of hours to force opening of cones. Latter removed, cracked on top with flat rock to open. Loose nuts shaken out; others plucked from cones with fingers. Spread in sun to dry. Shelled with light stroke on "seed side" of metate; winnowed to remove hulls. Meats parched, ground; greasy, "like peanut butter"; "taste the same same as Mentzelia seeds." Local pinyons (Pinus edulis) all have greasy nuts; but Nevada pinyon nuts said to yield a meal suitable for mush. Dried pinenuts, unhulled, stored for winter in buckskin bag.

Acorns (tɨmɨmpipi, tomɨmpi) eaten "all the time" but not a staple. Obtained from 2 kinds of oak: tocampipi (Quercus turbinella Green) and kwiavɨ (Q. gambelii). Gathered in fall; black when ripe. Shelled; roasted in ashes; brushed with leaves to remove ashes. Not leached.

Yucca. -- Usi (fruit of broad-leaved yucca, presumably Yucca baccata) gathered in fall, chiefly on slopes Kaibab Plateau. An important staple. Not eaten raw. When "real" ripe, made into cakes. Green fruits tossed into fire, stirred constantly with forked stick. Removed when brown; allowed to cool. Broken open, seeded, dried. Stored in sack. Dried fruit boiled (Sapir: warmed and darkened by burning on charcoal; boiled into mush). Flowers not eaten "because they taste green."

Blossoms of čamavipi (narrow-leaved yucca; evidently Y. baileyi) baked in ashes and eaten. Base of stalk (čuari) also eaten. Plant cut off at base with wooden chisel; leaves broken off; head roasted in ashes. This is a spring food. Fruit not eaten.

Mescal. -- Agave (nanta) available year-round but gathered mostly in winter, spring, when short of food. Found in Kanab Canyon and just below rim of Grand Canyon (including Nankoweap area). "The women fixed nanta every day they camped near Grand Canyon; the men hunted rabbits and sat around." Plant cut off at base by pounding with stone. About half each leaf cut away with sharp stone knife, leaving head "like a cabbage." Fig. 2 shows a bone mescal knife from the 1875 Palmer collection; from southern Utah, but precise provenience unknown.

Fig. 2. Bone knife for gathering mescal (Agave); PM 9410. Palmer collection, 1875, southern Utah, band provenience unknown.

Cut leaves sucked to extract juice; discarded. Heads brought to camp in burden basket. Roasted in pit oven. Women dug hole about 3 ft. deep (Sapir: 8 to 10 ft. dia.); 1 pit for whole group. Stones put in; large fire kindled; ashes spread evenly to form bed. Each woman gathered mescal individually; dumped it into communal oven. No means of separating individual piles. Placed in oven at night, covered with hot rocks, grass (Sapir: a tall, bunched grass called tunuugwivɨ, growing on sand hills) or juniper bark, and earth. Appearance of low mound. No steam vent. Left to roast 2 nights and 1 day; then 2 women trenched to test cooking. If ready, earth removed with hands; otherwise, opening closed, to allow further baking. Whole roasting procedure in charge of 1 woman, (not the chief's wife) who "told them how to do it."

Leaves peeled from cooked mescal. Hearts pounded into sheets and spread to dry on bed of grass; a yellow-brown color, "like pumpkin." Sweet to taste. Could be eaten directly or dried, which required 5 days. Pieces of dried mescal broken off, soaked in water, squeezed in hand, mixed with tansy mustard (meal?) and drunk. The removed leaves were dried, pounded and ground, resulting in meal "like corn flour." Saved for winter. Made into mush or mixed with cold water for beverage. Dried mescal carried to home camps and cached for future use; women carried it in burden basket; men in "sack" (carrying net?) slung on back, tumpline across chest.

Mescal fruit not used; G thought blossoms not eaten; but according to S, were gathered in large pile, roasted 2 days and 2 nights in oval earth oven. Sapir: mescal stalks roasted in spring when fresh and juicy.

Cacti.--Blossoms of certain cacti, fruit of others, and fleshy core of still others considered edible. Latter eaten mostly winter and spring, in times of stress. No cactus products dried. Blossoms of wɨsarɨmpɨ (Opuntia whipplei Engelm. and Bigel.) eaten, boiled (?). No other parts edible. Fruit of iuwavimpɨ (Opuntia engelmannii Salm-Dyck) and wɨsuyuavimpi (thornberry; Echinocereus engelmannii [Parry] Rümpler) eaten fresh, late summer. Fleshy leaf of latter cactus also eaten in former times; tossed into fire to remove spines and skin. Core of manavimpɨ (Opuntia rhodantha Schumann.) eaten any time of year; roasted in ashes. Core of nɨaras (Coryphantha arizonica Engelm.) tossed in fire to loosen spines; removed, and spines scraped off with stick; core then baked in ashes. Tasɨ (Phellosperma tetrancistra Engelm. B. and R.) collected in large quantities any time of year, usually when gathering mescal by Colorado Canyon. Carried by roots and deposited in fire to remove spines. Flesh eaten without further cooking, or roasted overnight in ashes. Blossoms eaten raw; fruit roasted overnight in ashes. Ovagovɨ (Echinocereus coccineus Engelm.) considered inedible; Sapir: uvagu?uvɨ, a cactus, said to be poisonous; if eaten, makes person "crazy." No mention of fermented beverage of cactus fruit (Powell, 1961, 318).

Roots.--Limited in number; found mostly on higher plateaus. Dug by women with serviceberry stick (poru) having handle crooked "like a cane." Point sharpened with stone knife and hardened in fire. Special kind "hooked stick" called na?anoi?i used for corms of Oreogenia.

Sigo?o (mariposa lily, Calochortus flexuosus [?], C. nuttallii) dug in summer, Kaibab Plateau and (recently) on "Cedar Mountain," the plateau east of Cedar City, Utah. Not dried. Usually boiled or roasted in ashes; spread on grass to cool. Sometimes used special kind earth oven called pasui (described, p. 154, for Kaiparowits band). Wičuna (Oreogenia linearifolia Wats.), spring, summer; on "Cedar Mountain"; none on Kaibab Plateau because of "too many deer." Dug with stick; skinned between palms; roasted or boiled. Tasiu (Peteria thompsonae Wats.), a winter food; grew "everywhere on the hills" (i.e., top Vermilion Cliffs). Tuberous rootstock baked overnight in earth oven. Unidentified roots; ci?i, ka?anc.

Miscellaneous. -- Haws of wild rose (ci?impipi) occasionally eaten raw. Tu?u (Orobanche fasciculata) grew around base of sagebrush; another kind broomrape around base of Chrysothamnus viscidifolius. Latter sweet, tastier. Gathered spring, boiled. Few greens eaten old days. Leaves of timari (Stanleya pinnata [Pursh] Britt.) gathered in spring; boiled; drained; boiled again. Poured on grass to cool. Squeezed into small balls with hands; allowed to cool further; eaten. Now cooked in frying pan with grease. Leaves of kwivavi (Rumex hymenosepalus) boiled in spring, when young; nowadays cooked with sugar. Pigweed leaves not eaten formerly. Sapir mentions green called timpicugu, said to taste like dandelion. Blossoms of locust (piasičampipi, čampipi, thorns; Robinia neomexicana) boiled and eaten. Young stalks of ci (Sonchus asper) eaten raw; found near springs. In summer ate root of to?uivi (Typha latifolia); seed heads also eaten.

Beverages made from utupi (Mormon tea; Ephedra torreyana Watson) and pagwananimpi (Mentha canadensis). A sweet (aphis?) "like brown sugar" obtained from cane leaves. Hide placed on ground, plant beaten with stick. Substance eaten without further preparation. Sap of aspen tree (siavi) gathered summer. Bark removed, sap scraped off with deer cannon bone; deposited in basket. Eaten without preparation. "Spots" on roots of saŋakovi (Stephanomeria exigua) chewed, "like chewing gum."

Tobacco. -- Plot "anywhere" burned in fall; following spring, tobacco grew plentifully. Seed not planted; plot neither watered nor weeded; crop belonged to individual who did burning. Tobacco (sagwogwoapi; Nicotiana attenuata) gathered in fall; whole plant pulled; dried near fire. Not mixed with anything in old days; S claims dried leaves ofararimpip (Arctostaphylos) mixed with commercial tobacco; learned this recently "from north," from Ute.

Tobacco never drunk; sometimes chewed, plain; no particular effect. Smoked "any time," especially by old men and women. Boys did not smoke until adult.

Pipes made by men. Of stone, some white; but most a gray-blue-green color obtained in cave of Grand Canyon near river. Stone brought home, worked into shape, drilled with stone-tipped shaft. Shape not well described; not tubular; apparently cup-shaped, with cane mouthpiece.

Hunting

First-game observances.--Boys killed small game, usually in following order; squirrel, cottontail, jackrabbit, and eventually deer; "then could hunt any animal." A's father and M's uncle made them bows and taught them to hunt. M had simple bow first; when about 12, (his presumably paternal) uncle made him sinew-backed one. Took him deer-hunting early in morning; told him how to hold bow; to keep eyes on deer. He led and M followed, walking slowly behind trees. When deer was shot, uncle showed M how to skin and butcher it. M carried home 1 shoulder; uncle, the rest. After this M hunted alone.

Boy not allowed to eat any game he killed until grown, "old enough to marry"; gave it to old men or women; not to young women. If latter ate of kill boy would be lazy; according to Sapir, women could tell immediately if game killed by boy because tasted "weak, like water," no matter how cooked; might make woman sick and boy lazy and weak. Small girls could eat such game; so also could other boys, hence (Sapir) lads traded game with each other.

Boy told to get up early and travel eastward. Killed deer, leaving it there. Returned to camp to tell father. Ate "breakfast," then both went to deer. Father skinned and butchered, boy assisting with latter. Each carried half home. Son told not to eat first deer lest he be tired and lazy; "eat it when you are grown." Even though he killed several deer could not eat them. A ate rabbits before deer. When about 16 told his father he wanted to eat cottontail. Father had him eat handful of ashes first, then cottontail meat. Still too young to smoke.

Large game.--Deer, antelope, mountain sheep; no elk. No bear (kwiac; called also kagunaipiaŋ, mat grm). G had heard that bear was a chief who told other bears to kill people. Had not heard of formal address to bear.

Deer found on higher plateaus, particularly Kaibab; a few on top Vermilion Cliffs. Hunted year-round, although winter snows precluded much plateau traverse; principal hunting season late summer, fall. No hunting fences; no firing; no deer nets; no individually owned hunting preserves.

Deer stalked by lone hunter, who sighted quarry and approached slowly, dodging behind trees. In summer put leaf in mouth, inhaled heavily, imitating fawn's cry (Sapir: in spring; using aspen leaf). Hunted naked; no disguise; nothing rubbed on body to kill scent. No prayers or magical procedure before hunt; continence not requisite (as among Havasupai and others, Spier, 1928, 120). 2 or 3 might join in hunt; 1 remained stationary, usually in hole or blind near trail; others circled about, chasing deer toward him.

Technique similar when several hunted together under direction of chief; latter addressed people, telling them how and where to hunt. Chief left first, alone, and hunters followed tracks. Had them circle about in timber, chasing game toward him (or other marksmen) (p. 27).

Chief sometimes stationed men near watering hole or other favorable spot; others drove game toward stations. Meat divided evenly; hide to successful marksman; cut in pieces if quarreled over it.

Sapir gives following data: hunt leader (tinaa-tigaari) not necessarily same as ordinary chief, but anyone with knowledge of country and habits of game. He addressed hunters; later, small fire built at meeting spot, apparently for no particular purpose. Chief assigned several hunters particular stations (e.g., "divides" or hollows in ridges where deer apt to rush when pursued). Others went through timber to round up game. Chief might be with either division of party. Most deer killed at stations. Chief permitted to help himself, even though he killed nothing. Meat shared on spot, and subsequently by women at camp. Hide went to killer. Because of dense timber party could not keep together; returned to camp at irregular intervals; occasionally got lost.

Deer skinned and butchered on spot. If lone hunter got 2 deer, left part cached in tree for later trip. Apparently 2 methods of transport. A said flesh piled on hide; forelegs tied together; hind legs tied together. Front legs slung over head of hunter as tump line. According to M, hunter wore rope about waist for packing. Attached one end to tied forelegs of deer; other, to hind legs. Burden placed on rise of ground; hunter squatted below it, placed rope across chest, and stood up; sometimes "pretty hard." If 2 hunters, other helped hoist deer to shoulders. Horns thrown away; entrails and head taken to camp.

Sapir gives following account: deer sometimes carried to camp in one haul; if too heavy, hind quarters and hide taken first; rest suspended high in tree. When whole packed, head turned inside; each pair legs roped together separately, then turned in and roped together, the skin covering all; carried directly on back and shoulders without further assistance.

Men butchered; women cooked. Fat meat preferred. A considered rib meat best; M preferred hind leg because "plenty of marrow"; (Sapir: usually threw bones away, as did not care for marrow). Rib meat (gawantampɨpi) eaten first; boiled; roasted over fire on stick; or roasted on large heated stone. No boiling in carcass (Kelly, 1932, 92). Head eaten next, baked overnight in earth oven. Liver, heart, lungs, kidneys baked same way but shorter time. Removed from oven and set aside; eaten cold. Stomach boiled. Brains used only for tanning. Entrails washed, roasted in ashes or boiled; sometimes filled with blood, which thickened when cooked. "Knee" and "ankle" joints pounded into sort of pemmican, called čogopiek; boiled; eaten immediately. Shoulders and legs boiled or impaled on sticks and roasted. Sometimes cut in strips, dried over pole set between 2 branches of tree. Turned to ensure even drying, which took "quite a time." Sapir: sometimes meat put on wood-rest, placed horizontally on ground near fire; turned around from time to time. Meat not smoked except summer "when flies too thick"; never smoked in house. Sapir: meat dried about 3 days, often roasted slightly each side. Then pounded on rock to break fibers; dried again; sometimes mixed with chopped fat from around stomach. Dried meat stored in buckskin sack; cached high in a tree; not buried until well toward winter, about November.

Antelope apparently much less important than deer; found on flats of Kanab Plateau and Houserock Valley-Marble Platform. Stalked; no disguise, but held tuft of rabbitbrush in front of body. 1 or 2 hunters sometimes hid in hole by trail or sat on knoll, while others drove game toward them.

No antelope "charming"; no firing. A described a straight sagebrush barrier about 500 ft. long, with opening in center; antelope driven toward fence and shot as passed through opening. This presumably applies to Navajo Well (Spring 34) vicinity; circular corral not used there. For Houserock Valley, G reported sagebrush piled closely in half circle, with wings. 1 hunter stood by entrance and shot as others drove game. Could be done any season of year. (Kaiparowits informant, L, claimed to have seen remains of circular stone corral near 64, vicinity of Marble Platform.) Had also simple surround, with perhaps 10 hunters under direction of chief. Latter given head and lower part of trunk; hide went to killer, who divided meat.

Mountain sheep (nag) hunted any time of year but difficult in snow. Found along rim of Grand Canyon and region of upper Zion Creek. Camps near Kaibab Plateau hunted in first-mentioned area; those near Moccasin Spring, in Zion district. 2, 3, or more men went to latter place; all-day trip each way; carried food, weapons; camped "anywhere" en route.

Sheep found among rocks, sometimes in rock shelters. Never driven over bluff. Hunter hid near trail or at base of rock slope, while others chased quarry toward him. Sheep prepared same as deer; horns usually thrown away because of weight; some saved for bow.

Small game.--Most small game available year-round. Rabbits most important; cottontail (tavuc) and jack (kamɨ) considered equally tasty. Shot on sagebrush flats. In winter, tracked in snow; pulled from hole beneath sagebrush with straight stick twisted in fur. In spring, hunter attracted rabbits by smacking lips in imitation of young.

Rabbit drives held in winter; rabbits the only game taken in nets (wana). Latter of twisted outer fibers of w?ivi (Apocynum cannabinum) manufacture took about month. 3-5 nets strung in straight line, sometimes in arc. Each net supported by about 10 3-ft. stakes. No sagebrush wings. Each man stood by own net; 10 to 20 others, with bows, drove rabbits toward nets, shooting. Did not beat brush; sometimes fired it, cutting off retreat. Rabbits entangled in net killed by wringing neck or by running fingers down sides of body with considerable pressure (Sapir: stroked sides strongly between thumb and index finger, causing heart to burst). "Rabbit" chief (kamɨn-niav) evidently not net owner; stood "to one side, watching." Did not call instructions. Was someone who "liked that job" and could tell the people "how to get rabbits and when to get them." Drive continued all morning, net being moved from time to time. Kill carried over shoulder, strung on wand thrust through front legs. At end of drive, rabbits divided by "boys who chased them," presumably including net owners. Chief usually given 2 or 3 rabbits.

Sapir describes simple surround, in which all males of 1 or more bands participated. Bow barred in favor of rabbit stick (Fig. 3) (latter said by my informants to be late introduction; see below). Kill was individual property; no collective sharing. Sapir also describes modern hunt in which several men participated. Fire built and hunters practiced target shooting (at rock, or other conspicuous object) prior to hunt; then chased and shot rabbits. If spring, imitated sound made during mating season by holding thumbs straight up against lips and producing peculiar smacking or sucking noise. Each man kept own kill; if needy in camp, women saw that they received meat.

Fig. 3. Rabbit stick. Scale not indicated; presumably model made by Tony Tillohash, Sapir's Kaibab informant, 1910. Sketch with Sapir's field notes.

Rabbit stick (Fig. 3) said to have been introduced same time as horse; source unknown; used mostly in competitive game on horseback, of which Sapir gives following account: Kamunarɨr-uʔpu, a game played in spring. Firearms and bows prohibited; rabbit stick used; each man had 2 or 3 so he need not retrieve after each shot. Thrown with downward off movement, thin end in right hand (Pl. 7, c); care taken to hurl stick ahead of spot rabbit sighted to allow for progress of latter. Sticks thrown from horseback; considered more difficult than afoot. All rushed after rabbit, each participant trying to hit animal and head off other contestants; no partnership, although housemates might assist one another. When rabbit killed, all gathered at spot; dismounted to rest horses and pick up outstanding sticks. If rabbit ran into hole all rushed on foot to burrow; first there thrust arm in hole and pulled out animal. Held it in left hand, hind legs down; clubbed on nape with stick. Sole purpose of game to catch as many rabbits as possible.

Rabbits roasted about an hour in ashes; in summer, baked in skins; winter, skinned and pelt preserved. When removed from fire dusted off with tuft of rabbitbrush. Ribs, backbone, legs sometimes pounded on stone (mortar [?], found on hills; called čokomoran). Rabbit meat not dried.

Assorted rodents important. Marmot (ya?ampuc) shot in summer on High Plateaus; plentiful about Alton. Roasted in skin; sometimes boiled. Squirrel (o?uicic); 3 kinds described: intokwoščim (grayish-brown-black mixture; found in pine trees, Kaibab Plateau); tavarinkwic (same color but smaller; found at foot of cliffs; probably rock squirrel); ogontavac (white-tailed; Kaibab Plateau; hide, with hair on, used as moccasin soles). Whistled to attract squirrels; shot; laid in row in ashes, heads all same direction; roasted in skins about 2 hours; removed, skins peeled off.

Prairie dog not found in Kaibab habitat; recently Minnie Frank, young Kaibab woman, made unsuccessful effort to introduce and breed them near Moccasin. Chipmunk (oncopi) found on Kaibab Plateau; roasted in ashes. 2 kinds of rat: tavac (on sagebrush flats; nest often under cacti) and kaac (found in timber, presumably juniper; nest at foot of tree). Shot, or long straight stick jabbed in nest. Latter sometimes fired, roasting rats in process. Rats usually baked in ashes, unskinned; sometimes skinned, cleaned; never boiled.

No raccoon. Porcupine (yiŋimpic) available year-round; hit on head with stick as it climbed tree. Tossed into fire; removed; quills scraped off; gutted. Badger (inampici) not hunted, but found on desert. or along rock cliffs. Hit with stick; occasionally shot in head. Meat boiled, drained 3 times; otherwise "tasted strong." Hide for moccasin soles. Wildcat (tukupic) shot on emerging from rock hole; not trapped.

Flesh roasted overnight in earth oven, never directly on coals. Hide used for cap.

Many kinds birds eaten; most unidentified. Usually shot; not hunted with jacklight. Sapir describes use of bird call: light cylindrical piece of wood held lightly close to mouth, not quite touching it, in horizontal position. Breath blown against it in high pitch, producing melodious rapid tremolo with changing pitch; effect melancholy owing to chromatic intervals. Birds attracted; shot as soon as lit on trees. Precedent for this established by Coyote. If birds flew away, boy called "č+č+"; invariably impelled their return.

Most birds taken from blind, a dome-shaped affair covered with juniper bark; built near watering place; birds roosted on 2 crossed poles emerging from top; shot through roof of blind by concealed hunter. Pačakwi (chief, springs 10-12) owned blind at unoccupied spring 14; used early spring and summer mornings; others in camp allowed use in turn; no payment. Keno (chief, spring 55) owned 3 such blinds near unlisted spring not far from 55.

Birds plucked, cleaned, cooked in ashes; not boiled, as "would not taste good." Following, an incomplete list of edible birds: ka?kari, kakari (quail); iyivi (mourning dove); aŋ (blue, no crest; nest in junipers, lower slope hills; 3 eggs, white with brown spots; probably pinyon jay); sa?gwatoink (blue, crested; near Moccasin and on Kaibab Plateau; 2-3 eggs, white with brown spots; Steller's jay?); čoinki (large blue bird); aŋ?kakwanawanc (red-shafted flicker); wii?ac (small, gray; found mostly in sagebrush on low hills; 2 white eggs); pi?ipiwinc (a woodpecker; young birds taken from nest; not shot at blind as "never came to water").

Ciča?a (sage grouse?; gray, with white spots; black breast; long tail; does not fly; "walks like a chicken; gobbles like a turkey"); found near Alton; shot January, February. Occasionally shot from blind; hunter usually dug hole, waited in it for birds to gather. Not taken in net. Plucked, roasted in ashes; occasionally boiled (exception to most birds); not dried. Ka?impiciŋ (dusky grouse?; all gray, not spotted; "looks like black and white chicken; yellow eye, like an owl"; slightly smaller than preceding; short tail; "stays on Cedar and Kaibab mountains"; nests under sagebrush). shot while roosting in trees; prepared same as preceding.

Čɨʔkaŋ (ducks) found at Three Lakes and lake (p. 9, no. 32) east of Johnson Canyon. Several men hunted ducks in spring; no chief; game divided evenly. Shot from shore; hunter waited for wind to blow catch to bank; did not enter water; no boats, balsas. Duck not dried.

Following birds not eaten: atapuc (crow); tokopavi (a woodpecker, red and white head) although considered edible by 1 informant; pepiwɨns (blue; pecks like woodpecker; Kaibab Plateau; 2 blue eggs); itoc (meadow lark); tukwaʔsukuvi (gray; Kaibab Plateau; 3 bright blue eggs); yampa (gray and black, "kind of white wings"; 2-3 white eggs) considered edible by 1 informant.

Eggs of quail, grouse, and of bird called monopokwic (white spotted; size of quail; bird itself not eaten) eaten in spring. Grass piled, eggs placed on top; pile fired, roasting eggs; seldom boiled. Sapir: duck eggs boiled. Menstruating woman does not eat eggs.

In spring ate locusts (?)(kɨvɨ) and "green caterpillars" (probably what is known locally as tomato worm). Former gathered in baskets by both sexes; picked from Chrysothamnus nauseosus. Dry rabbit-brush stacked; locusts poured on top; pile fired, stirred; locusts eaten when blaze died down (Sapir: locusts parched in tray). "Caterpillars" found in desert and along hills. Gathered in basket; head twisted off; body squeezed between fingers to clean. Twisted into sort of braid, bodies crossing one another, with new caterpillar inserted each time. Roasted between 2 flat stones that were "red hot."

No fish in Kaibab country; nowadays some in Zion Creek. Sometimes visited (perhaps only since introduction of modern transportation facilities) Panguitch band, spring, summer, to fish where creeks enter Panguitch Lake; did not fish in Sevier River. Used hosts' fish traps; latter called wana (same as net); twined, of willow. 1 man stood either side of trap, holding it. Catch dumped on shore, hit with stick. Fish "kind of red"; boiled. Dried: cut open, hung on pole; not smoked; kept well; dried fish boiled; never pounded.

Game not eaten.--Three kinds of skunk (poni): little spotted skunk; Arizona skunk; and a third, whose description suggests marten, except for habitat, or possibly mountain weasel. Described as size of small house cat, brown fur, lighter underparts; lives among rocks. Skunks hunted for sport, by men and boys. Hunter sits behind a rock and waits for animal to emerge. Or builds fire to smoke out prey; latter pulled out with long hooked stick. Pelt not used for blankets because of odor; sometimes served as sole for moccasin. Fox (ɨncet), coyote (šɨnavi) shot; no deadfall; hide for quiver but not for headgear. Wolf (piav-šɨnavi; avata-šɨnavi; big dog, coyote) not killed. Cougar (apparently 2 names; tukumumuc, piarukɨ) shot for skin, used as blanket, quiver.

Gopher (muiyɨmpɨc) shot "for fun" upon emerging from hole; skin not used. Mouse (puičac) shot or hit with stick; no utility. Grasshoppers, ants, ant eggs not eaten.

Pets, dogs.--Children kept birds, squirrels, other small animals as pets. Sapir: boys used to catch young sparrow hawks because "it was fun to hear them fly way up in the air and screech." His informant's uncle once caught a young coyote; tamed, but eventually ran away.

No dog in old days (p. 86). Dog (saric) formerly called šɨnavi (coyote, the animal; Coyote, mythical being, called Šɨnawavi). Dogs used for hunting rabbits; did not bear packs; not eaten.

Salt

"Dark-colored" salt called tɨmpi-oavi (rock-salt); obtained from Grand Canyon.

Shelter

The preferred site for a semipermanent camp was at the base of a scarp or on its lower slopes, adjacent to water and to juniper stands. In winter, there was little dependence on springs and water holes, for snow could be melted:

Large stone set against fire to heat; hole dug to one side. Snow gathered in burden basket, dumped on hot stones, and water drained into cavity; stored in basket water jar. Melted snow called nɨwa-va (snow water).

There was no set arrangement of houses; usually they were scattered about the spring or, in the case of Kanab Creek (26), they were on either side of the stream. The type of shelter varied with the season. As will be seen below, a cave sometimes provided a snug retreat in winter, and there were several kinds of winter houses, occasionally earth covered. Shades and circular windbreaks were used respectively, in summer and fall. By the turn of the century, a canvas-covered tipi had been copied from the Ute. Information concerning the sweat house is scanty; sweating was not an established local practice.

The winter house was owned "by the man and the woman" and was the product of joint labor. The man set up the frame; the woman collected the bark. The structure took about half a day to build and was left standing when camp was broken. Sometimes it was reoccupied but generally was built anew; the bark covering lasted barely one winter.

Visitors entered the house without warning or salutation and might sit anywhere; there was no place of honor. Guests were not offered food but might be given tobacco to smoke.

Winter Dwellings

Some sites (66, for example) had caves that were occupied in winter. Floor covered with cliffrose bark; branches of green juniper stacked across the mouth to a height of 3 or 4 ft., with opening left for doorway. Storage pits handily located in floor of cave.

Usual winter dwelling (kani; Sapir, 1930, 629) was circular in ground plan; overhanging limb of tree served as ridge pole. Specified for Moccasin, Ankati, Houserock, and western slopes of Kaibab Plateau. Size varied according to number of occupants; some dwellings housed 10 people. Height sufficient to permit entrance without stooping, although Hillers' plates suggest essentially low structures.

Description as follows. Ground beneath horizontally projecting limb of juniper smoothed with stick, to serve as floor. Latter flush with ground; no excavation. No ax; dry juniper for poles felled by being struck with large stone. Poles (oravɨ) stood (not set in holes) in three-quarter circle and leaned against projecting branch above. Opening of circle at opposite side from trunk of tree; left thus as doorway. Frame covered with upright layers of bark stripped from junipers; not woven into mats; not tied on; impermeability dependent upon thickness of covering. Cliffrose bark spread on floor; occasionally substituted for juniper "thatch." For warmth, a fire built in doorway; no firepit. Occupants slept with feet to fire; no ill consequences if position reversed. Cooking done outside. Personal and household chattels hung on walls of house or stored at base of posts; by day, bedding rolled or hung outside on a tree.

Another style winter house built by people from western base of Kaibab Plateau when camping in Colorado Canyon. Actually a half cone; ground plan semicircular; entire front open. Skeleton of 3 forked poles of cottonwood; 2 interlocking poles framed doorway; braced from rear by third pole. Frame closely overlaid with lighter poles; whole covered with a grass (wavɨ) gathered on plateau, or with brush; not made into mats. Sometimes earth covered. Basic structure that of house type photographed by Hillers (Steward, 1939, Pl. 21, a, b) in St. George area.

Dellenbaugh (1926, 177-8) describes house near Kanab as about 7 ft. high, merely cedar boughs set in three-quarter circle, to form conical shelter with opening toward south. Elsewhere (MS) he speaks of the house as roughly dome shaped, with the south-facing entrance about one-quarter of the whole.

Sapir's account differs considerably. For 12-person dwelling, house 40 ft. in dia.; poles 30 ft. long, of cedar trunk, usually with bark left on; inserted in pits about 4 in. deep. Floor of packed earth, some 6 in. below ground level; earth banked at base of poles inside and outside. Spaces between poles filled with small cedar branches; whole covered with cedar bark; sometimes with added covering of earth. Smoke hole at top, above a circular hoop attached somewhat below extremities of poles; always open despite weather. No firepit; fire in center floor, beneath smoke hole; kept burning all the time; banked with ashes when occupants left camp. Horizontal bar tied on outside across 2 poles that framed entry (cf. Hillers' photos in Steward, 1939, Pls. 9, b, 13, a); space above filled with branches; that below, used as doorway. Doorway covered by old blanket, usually worn rabbit skin robe. Robe tied to crosspole; 3 sticks run horizontally through weave at top, bottom, middle of robe. Weight sufficient to keep door close to opening, without tying or pegging. To enter, one grasped middle stick, thrust blanket up and to one side. Sapir's proportions exaggerated when compared with Hillers' photos and descriptions given by my informants.

Less Substantial Structures

Sometimes arbor or shade (avagan; Sapir, 1930, 550, ava-gani), a flat roof on posts, built near house. This was a common summer dwelling; not walled, according to my informants. Sapir has a more detailed description: 4 cedar uprights, bark left on, along either side; set in holes about 1 ft. deep; banked at base. Crosspoles 20 ft. long rested in crotches of uprights. Roof covering of willow branches, other materials. Sides of shelter covered with matting of interlaced willows.

Sapir reports another style of shade (called also ava-gani), used chiefly for sleeping. Apparently dome shaped, 8 to 9 ft. high. Willow branches stuck in pits around circle at 2-ft. intervals; bent over in "round" outline, all meeting at top. Intertwined; sometimes tied with willow withes. Doorway formed of 2 willow branches. No fire used in this structure, hence no need of smoke hole.

Circular enclosure (witokwanovi, around circle; Sapir, 1930, 720, wituko-novi-pi, witoko-novi-pi, wind-protecting cover?) of brush or pine boughs, the usual fall shelter. Served as wind break without cutting off warmth of sun. Opening in "any direction," presumably to leeward. Sapir: cedar branches piled in near-circle about 4 ft. high; fire in center; used when traveling.

Tipi

Photograph of S's dwelling taken in 1904 (in possession of Mrs. Maggie Heaton, Moccasin, Arizona) shows Plains-type tipi (kaniv; Sapir: kanivu). Learned from Ute in "late" times; precise dating not established. Brush lodge still used at time of Powell survey. Informants recognized advantage of tipi's being portable. 4-pole frame; 6 additional poles for body; 2 more for flaps.

Sapir has considerable detail concerning tipi. Poles longer than for "wickiup," but slanted more steeply, resulting in smaller floor space. Set up by women; 4 poles tied together with buckskin thongs, rope; 2 front poles for doorway set close together; 2 rear poles farther apart. 6 other poles laid against the frame; all rested on surface of ground, not set into it. 2 flap poles held by own weight, without peg supports. Buckskin covering undecorated; held to framework in 2 places. 1 pole was added last; it was attached by thongs to middle of skin cover, then leaned against the frame. Skin brought around either side of frame and roped; pinned together above doorway with wooden pins thrust through pairs of holes in hide. Skin covering further secured by strings, held down by wooden pegs. Doorway covered with separate piece of skin; 3 crossbars attached to inside of it, projecting about 5 in. either side. In storm, tipi roped around, secured to a tree.

Sweathouses

Kaibab informants (A, S, G) denied use of sweathouse (Sapir, 1930, 630, nasa?a-kani). Kaiparowits informant had heard that Kaibab used sweathouse only once. Said that Čarɨmpipi ("Chuarruumpeak," S's h) learned of sweating from San Juan Paiute. Introduced practice at Moccasin; built lodge; entered first; died. San Juan informant (J) had heard of incident; claimed that lodge built directly against rock cliff, which reflected heat and caused excessive temperature. No details of construction; perhaps suggestive that G described Hopi and Navajo as living in earth-covered sweathouses.

Sapir's informant denied regular, standing sweathouse, but implied at least intermittent use. Sweated mostly in spring; not necessarily curative. Interested person built small conical frame, 4 ft. high, 5 ft. dia. sufficiently large for 2 men; women did not sweat. Crawled through opening; poured water on hot stones; remained about 10 min. Structure destroyed at conclusion.

Dress

Considerable variety in costume is reported. In my informants' youth, skin clothing was common, "but the old people wore cliffrose bark" and used yucca sandals. This suggests that buckskin may have been a recent style and that the conservative element clung to an older, more or less generic Basin type of costume.

The Hillers photographs give the impression that the Kaibab were dressed from stem to stern in buckskin in the early 1870's. But Dellenbaugh writes (personal communication) that by that time they relied almost entirely on cast-off garments of the white settlers, adding that "Powell employed the Paiutes of the Kanab region to make buckskin garments of the olden time, and he had them photographed in those costumes." There is, however, some possibility that these models may have been influenced unduly by Powell's familiarity with Plains raiment. Certainly the elaborately decorated shirt consistently worn by "Chuarruumpeak" (Steward, 1939, Pls. 10, a, b, 11, 17, b, 18, a) is not likely to have been of local manufacture, and the feather headgear, prominent in many of the plates, is highly suspect. (In fact, Julian Steward has heard that Powell carried Ute clothing from Green River and dressed the Paiute in it for the photographs. Dellenbaugh[personal communication, November 17, 1933]writes: "Thinking over the Pai Ute costume, I believe the feather head dress is all right--real local manufacture and tradition, for they made one for me in 1875. I am very dubious about the shirt heavily beaded that Chuar is wearing in some of the [Kaibab] photographs. I never saw any of them wear beaded garments of that type, hence I think it is Ute. Patnish's gang [San Juan Paiute] dressed in plain buckskin; and so did the Red-Lake Utes we surprised in the Henry Mountain region" [later, he places these specifically between the Aquarius Plateau and the Henry Mountains, adding that they were "pure Utes"]. The correspondence with Mr. Dellenbaugh gives no suggestion of wholesale importation of Ute costumes by the Powell party.)

Body Clothing

Old men usually naked; sometimes used belt with fringe of cliffrose bark (inapɨ; Cowania stansburiana) front and back; called kwasun; said to have been a double-apron effect similar to woman's garment, but scantier. Knee-length leggings twined of same bark also common. Models (AMNH 50.2/3460, MNM, 9913/12; not illustrated) made by S have buckskin loops along side for lacing.

When G was grown, a man wore buckskin breechcloth (pikotaiyapi, pikuča?aipɨ); full-length leggings (wičakusa), fringed on sides and attached to belt (pičamuku); and buckskin shirt (tai?ɨ). "A man had 2 shirts."

Shirt described by S as poncholike affair of single hide (neither smoked nor painted) with center hole for head; side seams sinew sewn, bottom fringed. According to G, shirt composed of 2 hides, 1 front and 1 back, head end of skins uppermost. Shoulder seams fringed, sinew sewn. U-shaped tab, fringed on edges, added front and back about head opening (Fig. 4). Rectangular pieces of hide sewn to shoulders for sleeves. Fringed seams from wrist to elbow and from bottom of garment to breast height; underarms open (J, San Juan informant, wears calico shirt open thus). Bottom of shirt cut straight across, not fringed. Hillers' plates seem to show shirts of both 1 and 2 skins, heavily fringed; cf. Havasupai account (Spier, 1928, pp. 183-5).

Women wore twined skirt of cliffrose bark; usually a double apron, open on sides. Sometimes a "wrap-around," closed on one side, with pairs of braided strands tied together along other side. Both types reached just below knee. Half day required to gather sufficient bark for skirt. Twice the finished length measured and bark cut off; more easily worked when damp. Bark doubled over the strand to serve as foundation belt; caught in simple twined stitch (left to right); number of rows of twine varied from specimen to specimen. One informant thought belt and weft usually of Apocynum cord; stronger. Woman crushed double apron between legs when seated, leaving thighs bare. Models of each type apron essayed from traditional description; makers had never seen such garments and results unsatisfactory.

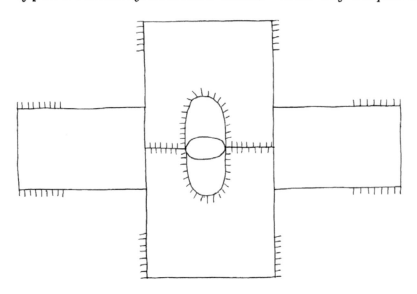

Fig. 4. Pattern of man's buckskin shirt. Redrawn from a sketch by Kaibab informant G.

Skins not used for woman's apron. However, G remembers having seen a skin butcher-apron dress, with bib-skirt front, apron back; apparently similar to Havasupai (Spier, 1928, 185-6); not common among Paiute.

Some women wore a dress (tɨiatai) of antelope or buckskin, not smoked; this the only woman's costume known to Ankatɨ informant M. A skin hung from shoulders, 1 front, 1 back; disagreement as to which end of hide upward; sometimes a third skin used for gores. Hides measured against body, marked with red paint; bow not used to shape sides. No separate sleeves; no yoke. Straight piece, fringed, sewn to bottom "to make the skirt hang well." No clothing worn beneath dress.

Some Hillers' plates (Steward, 1939, Pls. 14,b, 18,b, 19,b) show heavily fringed garments, apparently 1 skin front and 1 back; attached at shoulders; open down sides. Held in place by broad skin girdle, terminating in long fringe and constituting almost an overskirt. Unfortunately, I had not seen these photos when in the field, hence did not ask concerning overskirt; no mention by informants.

Plains-type dresses, apparently with bead trim, appear in several Hillers photographs (Steward, 1939, Pls, 8, 10, b, for example). In fact, same dress, or one with identical ornament, seems to be worn by different individuals (Steward, 1939, Pls, 15, a, b, 16, a, b). Buckskin evidently plentiful among Kaibab (p. 87), but bead trim unlikely. Informants report no decoration except fringe. However, women said sometimes to have used a buckskin belt sewn with undyed porcupine quills; this the only use for quills. No such belt apparent in Hillers' plates.

Skin clothing said not to be copied from elsewhere; "they [the old people] learned it themselves." Cut out and sewn by either sex, but men usually made fringe.

Uncertainty concerning woman's leggings. Some declared that none worn; others, that knee-length leggings consisted of a straight piece of skin tied about leg. Fig. 6,b shows a woman's moccasin with double-width cuff; perhaps latter sufficed to protect leg.

Footgear

Old people wore yucca "shoes" (usi-pač) that "gave out quickly if you walked around much." Narrow-leaved yucca more serviceable than broad-leaved. Worn mostly in snow and considered durable for such use. Hide moccasin preferable for summer wear.

Yucca footgear of 2 types; sandal and "moccasin." Model of former illustrated, Pl. 4, g, Fig. 5, a, b. Made as follows:

Butts of several yucca leaves pounded, scraped. Butts doubled over foundation leaf (Fig. 5, a) and caught in twine stitch (left to right, upward twine); weft of pounded yucca leaf. Twined across face; turned, and second row of twine added. Foundation leaf bent parallel to warps, incorporated in second row of twine; wefts tied at end of second row. On third row, twine abandoned and checker weave begun. Another model has 4 rows of twine before start of checker. Latter continues left to right; specimen turned at end of each course. Old wefts secured at selvage; new ones inserted, butts left hanging, to be incorporated into selvage on next course. When length sufficient, last 2 rows of checker work pulled tight. One model (MNM 875/12) has last 2 rows of twine instead of checker. Warps divided, those on right bunched and bent to left, at right angles, and vice versa, forming heel rim. Edge of sandal encircled by 2 entire yucca leaves; whole overcast (coil stitch, right to left). Sandal held on foot by mesh of yucca strands across instep (Pl. 4, g). Bark pad sometimes placed on upper surface of sandal to cushion foot.

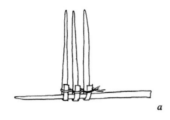

Fig. 5. Yucca-fiber footgear. a, start of yucca sandal and moccasin. b, section of yucca sandal, twine and checker; AMNH 50.2/3441.

Yucca "moccasin": M not familiar with sandal just described, but from his directions model yucca "moccasins" (Pl. 4, f) made; probably not accurately, as maker had never seen such footgear. Model illustrated starts with twined stitch; main body checker; another model twined throughout. Latter made as follows: for warp, 4 leaves of broad-leaved yucca pounded, narrow strip peeled from convex surface. Start at heel: butts of 3 warp leaves pared thin, doubled over fourth leaf, which serves as foundation (Fig. 5, a); 3 leaves and butts caught in simple twine stitch (left to right, upward). Foundation strand bent parallel to warps and incorporated in twining for half length of sole. Twining continued to end of warps, equal to length-and-a-half of average foot. Loose ends of foundation strand now pulled tight, cupping heel; ends tied together at what eventually becomes inside toe of moccasin. When nearly to end of warps, wefts tied. New leaf placed across warps at right angles; warps bent back over it, tucked into twined stitches of preceding row; 1 more row twine added. Whole rim now overcast (coiled stitch). Last third of finished fabric bent back 180° to form instep of moccasin; edges lashed to rim of sole. Moccasin held on foot by buckskin thong tied over instep.

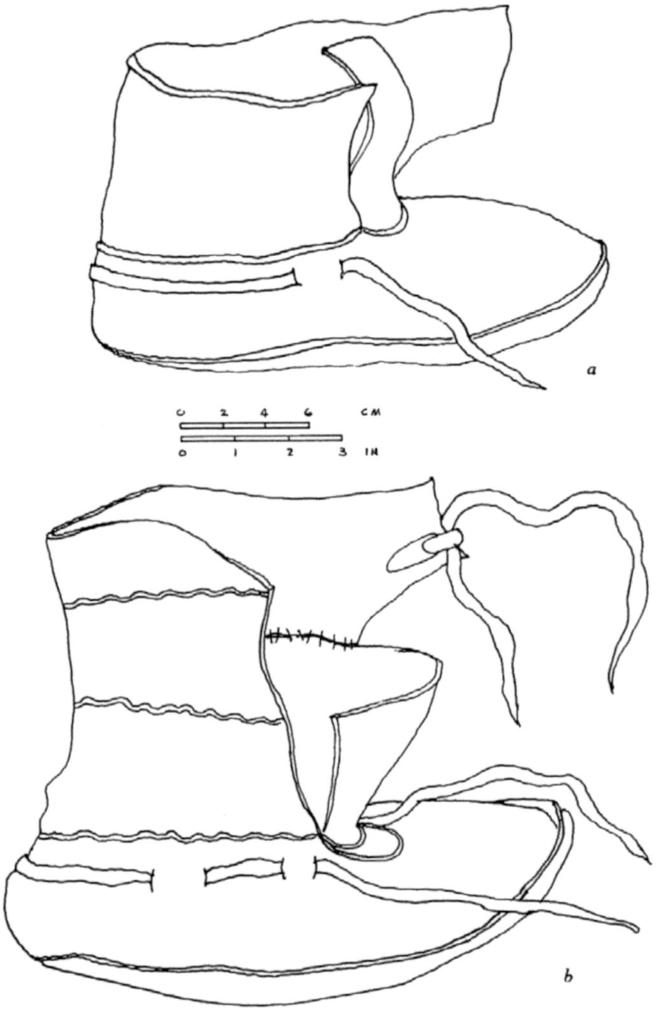

Hide moccasin (pač, pačan) usual summer footgear; when worn in winter stuffed with cliff-rose bark; or cottontail pelt, hair inward, wrapped about foot. Moccasins made by women; by man if no woman in household.

Fig. 6. Moccasins. a, man's style. b, woman's style, with double cuff. AMNH 50.2/3464, 50.2/3451. Both models made by Sarah Frank, Kaibab.

Moccasin pattern resembles Wissler's style no. 4 (1910, 141). Parts: sole, upper, cuff, tongue, no trailer (Fig. 6,a). Sole from neck part of deerhide, mountain sheep; or badger, white-tailed (Kaibab?) squirrel, tanned with hair on outside of sole; rawhide soles in recent times only. Dellenbaugh (MS) mentions "moccasin of the raw-hide sole variety." Uppers of buckskin, mountain sheep hide. Outline of foot traced for sole; for upper, hide placed over instep, cut off even with ankle bones, slashed down center to pass either side of foot.

-64-

Seams sewn with sinew; back sinew best; rolled on thigh; nowadays some use doubled linen thread. Right sides of hide placed together, with lightweight welt between to prevent pulling out. Welt an old trait; cut off close when seam completed. Sewing on wrong side, left to right; seam formerly overcast; now, simple running stitch. Awl formerly of bone or of a white stone; needle used today. Heel seamed first; upper placed on sole, tacked at toe, heel, and either side. Sewing starts just forward from heel, inside of foot, and proceeds left to right. Moccasin turned, tried on; slash for tongue marked. Tongue inserted; U-shaped, never pointed. Cuff attached. Fig. 6, b shows woman's moccasin with double-width cuff; some said to have reached halfway up calf. In figured specimen, one side of cuff brought around over tongue. Finished moccasin filled with damp earth; seams flattened by placing stick against inside of seam and pounding outside with stone. Moccasins undecorated.

Definitely unusual moccasin for Basin people seen on Kaibab reservation; bead ornament. Pattern similar to Wissler's no. 11 (1910, 144), but without trailer. Exact provenience uncertain; owner claimed purchase from "Paiute at Cedar City," apparently in hope of making sale. Style regarded as foreign by Kaibab.

Hairdress and Headgear

Hillers' photos show most men with hair hanging loosely over shoulders. Central part, or none; "Chuarruumpeak" seems to use parting on left side. Extremely few men appear with braids.

In contrast, informants claimed men wore hair in 2 braids, or tied behind "like the Navajo." Braids usually associated with the extravagantly admired Ute (p. 33).

Sapir's informant likewise described braids, saying men used a central part, 2 main braids. From forehead to shoulder, 2 smaller braids which joined main ones. Latter wrapped with beaver skin (later times, red flannel) from shoulder to within few inches of tip. He also described an elaborate hair ornament; strips of parallel, horizontally disposed oblongs of buckskin or rawhide, connected to each other by 2 or 3 sinew strings wrapped with porcupine quills. Usually worn on left side. More recently, tin or silver rostels or discs used instead.

Women's hair hung loose from central part; about shoulder length. Cut at mourning. Fillet apparently not used, although common in Hillers' plates for both sexes, especially women. Seems particularly prominent in elaborately posed plates. Hairbrush of dry mescal fiber; suds from peeled root of narrow-leaved yucca for shampoo.

Men usually bareheaded; for warmth, some wore wildcat-hide cap. Made by man; skin encircled head, covering ears; Sapir's informant reported it worn above ears. Sewn on top with sinew; tail thrown away. Statement that "some people stuck a feather in the hair" is nearest approach to the impressive feather headdress so common in Hillers' plates; no suggestion in my data that head surrounded by upstanding feathers. Sapir mentions a single eagle-tail feather "sticking straight out from back of head."

Women wore basketry caps (sɨʔkaičogo), especially for protection from tumpline. Twined, usually undecorated; specimens in Hillers' photos seem consistently mammiform. Sapir's informant described cap as coiled (p. 83).

Adornment

Small girls strung wild rose haws; a few "beads" (kind not specified) traded from Navajo (recently?); small hide exchanged for short necklace. Several necklaces, apparently commercial beads, in Hillers' plates.

Mother punched ears of children of both sexes at adolescence (while girl in menstrual lodge), using sharp piece of rabbitbrush. Stick worn in aperture. No earrings except Navajo silver (apparently late), although S mentioned turquoise. Source unknown to her; presumably Navajo.

No tattooing; considered a Shivwits trait. Naragowocɨ (tattooed), of springs 69-74, said to have "been born that way"; name evidently referred to birthmark.

Some use of paint. A red pigment (ompi) looked "just like red earth"; obtained in Ankatɨ district and near Grand Canyon; a deposit known from "near Escalante" (in Kaiparowits territory), but not visited by Kaibab. Mixed with water; not heated; drained; stored in cake form, tied in buckskin. Used to prevent chapping, sunburn. Also for decoration; men painted faces every day "if they liked it."

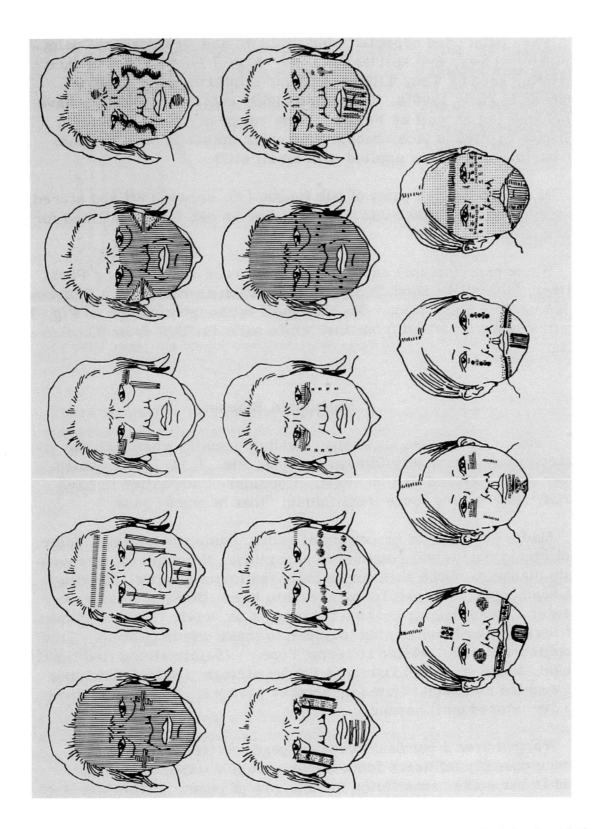

Fig. 7. Face painting seen by Sapir's Kaibab informant, Tony Tillohash, 1910, at "squaw" dance attended by various Southern Paiute (Kaibab, Shivwits and Cedar, latter including individuals said to be from Parowan). Red, vertical hatch; blue, horizontal hatch; yellow, stipple; black, black.

Face paint used especially for "squaw" and bear dances; paint frightened away evil spirits (p. 141). Fig. 7 shows types of face painting seen by Tony Tillohash (Sapir's informant) at "squaw" dances in early 1900's. Gathering highly composite and may have included Ute as well as Paiute. Wide range of colors indicated. Grease applied to face, background color smeared on with hand; superimposed colors applied with small stick.

M reported a red paint of oak fungus (?); scraped off and stored; not used on face (other use?). Sapir has an oak fungus utilized for face paint.

Black paint (turupɨ) came from "little rock caves" along Paria River; "looks like sand." Same preparation as red paint. Charcoal also used as black paint. No blue paint (although common in Fig. 7); yellow pigment traded from Ute; white paint (avimp) from Koosharem Ute.

Rabbitskin Blankets

Used by both sexes as wraps, bedding; usually worn with fur warp running vertically (Steward, 1939, Pls. 7, 11, 13, b); placed over shoulders and tied on chest. Considered attractive to have tails, feet hanging loose from fabric; "that is pretty good."

Made of jackrabbit or cottontail skins, sometimes mixed (Sapir: not mixed; jackrabbit considered superior). No other skins woven into blankets. Open skin cut spirally (with stone knife), starting at head, encircling pelt to tail, back to head, thence spirally to center. Resulting strip 5 to 6 ft. long, 2 in. wide. Several (Sapir: at least 15 per blanket) tied together to make one long strip. This doubled on itself, twisted to form "rope." (Sapir: string tied tightly about looped end, held firmly in hands; strings tied to 2 free ends of doubled strip and twisted by another person). Twisted fur hung to dry; stored until needed.

Warped over 2 parallel rows low pegs; or (according to MT, hence possibly influence from Cedar group) a wand, tied at each end to low stake, substituted for one row of pegs. Latter warping shown in Fig. 8. Warping completed, worker sits on ground before row of pegs; starts twine with _Apocynum_ weft (nowadays, strips of cloth) at left side of near edge. Twines across (MT: downward twine, left to right); at right-hand selvage, reverses direction and twines back (MT: upward, right to left on return course). Twining continuous throughout near half of specimen. When necessary, old wefts

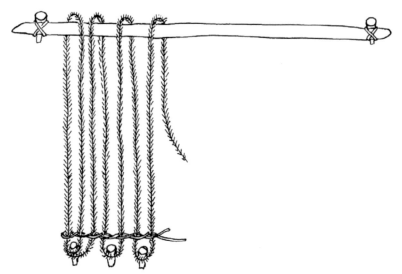

Fig. 8. Start of rabbitskin blanket: warping and first row of twine. Field sketch based on technique used by Minnie Tom, 1932, by birth of Cedar band, but long a resident among Kaibab

tied; the new one looped over a warp, to make a double weft. When blanket half finished, worker moves, sitting before opposite side of frame. Twines as before until work meets in center. If blanket large (Sapir: maximum size 5 by 7 ft.), worker sits on fabric to complete central part.

Crafts and Manufactures

There is no tradition of fine craftsmanship among the Kaibab and their neighbors, but the descriptive detail to follow should be placed on record, because, a few years hence, it may be difficult to find informants who remember even the occurrence of these traits, much less the specific techniques. Today, for example, the horn bow is known only through hearsay.

From the viewpoint of cultural change, some of the data associated with crafts are of considerable interest. Thus, smoking of buckskin was considered an innovation, introduced "when they learned to make gauntlets, from the people to the north." Presumably reference is to the Ute, who have exerted a profound influence on the Kaibab and adjacent groups, particularly, it would seem since the introduction of the horse.

What amounts to an eyewitness account of the introduction of pottery among the Kaibab was given by M, an Ankatɨ (springs 40-45) informant, who claimed that a few years before the arrival of the Mormons, his uncle visited the Hopi country and, on his return, "made about five pots, which he gave away" (pp. 77-8).

The Kaibab were the easternmost of the Southern Paiute to make pottery. Kaiparowits and San Juan groups had no ceramic tradition, but all Paiute north and west of the Kaibab used clay vessels, and most manufactured them. Except for the Las Vegas and Chemehuevi, where Mohave influence was strong, there seem to have been two ceramic complexes, more or less mutually exclusive. One, characterized by a fired or semifired vessel, conical or sub-conical, occurred among the central bands; typologically, the Palmer specimens in Peabody Museum, from southern Utah, belong to this tradition. The other complex was represented by a sun-baked, unfired pot, flat bottomed, with straight sides, either vertical or flaring. The latter was reported for Kaibab, Panguitch and Beaver bands; Cedar informants spoke of both types. It is difficult to reconcile with this distribution the circumstantial account (pp. 77-8) of a Kaibab man who, a few years before the coming of the whites, visited Hopi country and, upon his return, tried his hand at making unfired, flat bottomed pots. Perhaps he traveled north rather than southeast and was inspired by the Panguitch Paiute rather than the Hopi.

An inspection of basketry styles demonstrates drastic cultural change during the past 60 years. There is scarcely any recollection of the conical burden basket, in coiled stitch, strongly reminiscent of Basketmaker tradition. Nevertheless, it was in common use in the 1870's, as attested by the Hillers plates. Moreover, at that time, coiled ware included a cooking basket, food bowl, water jar, and winnowing-parching tray. Nowadays, none of these are made, except for an occasional plaquelike tray (Pl. 3, e).

Modern coiling is pretty much limited to the production of decorated baskets made for sale. Traditionally, Kaibab specimens had a minimum of ornament. The new style--with geometric figures in Martynia and with "fancy" rim finishes (Pl. 4, d, e)--is intrusive and may trace ultimately to Moapa influence. KC and her age mates learned to make baskets of this kind about 1907, when they were in a (presumably Indian) school in Panguitch. The school brought two women to teach basetry; one, named Sally Rice, was originally from Moapa, but had lived some time among the Shivwits; the other, Nora, was of unknown provenience. This formal instruction apparently started the new trend in coiled basketry among the Kaibab, and doubtless among other groups whose children attended the school.

The cradle also has changed demonstrably since the early 1870's. Subsequently, it acquired a skin covering, presumably owing to Ute influence. Now, it looks as though the basketry body might be abandoned. At least, a large board cradle, with buckskin cover, was made for KC's youngest child, about 5 years old at present. She declared it copied from the Koosharem Ute, and the style is roughly similar to that of the Ute specimen figured by Lowie (1924, Fig. 33, b).

Tanning

Men skinned; women tanned. Skinning: cut around hoofs (Sapir: legs cut off below hocks, thrown away); skin slit up inside front, hind legs. Cut around horns, leaving ear skin intact; cut from top of head over nose, continuing with full-length ventral cut.

Tanning: fresh hide placed over slanting post; flesh side scraped with cannon bone from deer foreleg (later times, horse rib; Sapir: late times used flesher with iron blade riveted to grooved wooden handle, Fig. 9). Hide soaked overnight; de-haired same process as fleshing; rinsed in hot water; brains rubbed (not sprayed) on.

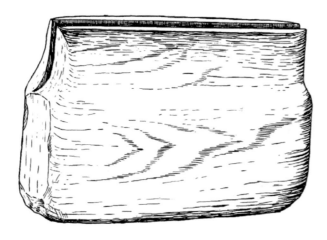

Fig. 9. Handle of skin flesher, presumably of wood; scale not indicated. Probably a model made by Tony Tillohash, Sapir's Kaibab informant, 1910. Sketch with Sapir's field notes.

Tan prepared previously; marrow pushed from spinal canal with long stick; mixed with deer (nowadays, beef) brains, set by boiling or frying; mixed with hair; stored. Softened with water before application to hide.

Brain-smeared hide hung 2 to 3 days to dry; then soaked, worked in water. Wrung: head of hide passed around post, folded in and twisted with rest of hide, thus holding skin securely to post. Hind legs tied together, stick thrust through and twisted. Hide unfolded and worked (i.e., rubbed, pulled, in hands) 2 to 3 hours until dry. Brains again applied, usually to hair side, sometimes both sides. Hung up about 10 days, then, dry, worked all day. Formerly skewers used to assist stretching. Sapir mentions but does not describe stretching frame. Skin now soft, ready to be smoked.

Hides not smoked until "they learned to make gauntlets, from the people to the north" (probably Ute). Hide folded lengthwise, hair side inward; sewn into sacklike form. Hung from tree limb, with open lower end pegged, or weighted down with stones, over hole containing smudge fire of clean wood chips. Sapir reports hide hung from tripod over hole 2 to 3 ft. in depth, containing smudge fire of green cedar branches, dried manure. His informant also mentioned leaves of wiampipi (<u>Mahonia fremontii</u>?) for smudge. Hide smoked right side only, perhaps 15 min., depending on shade desired.

Badger, wildcat hides tanned with hair on. Skin fleshed, dried. Brains applied to dry hide; rubbed in, hide worked. Buried short time in damp red earth to soften.

Rawhide not an old trait; used "recently" (at least as early as 1870's, as mentioned in Dellenbaugh, MS) for moccasin soles, rope.

Weapons

Simple bow (ač) used mostly by boys, by few for deer; sinew-backed bow (taŋakainak, Sapir, 1930, 667, tanŋa-ʔačɨ) most common; horn bow with sinew backing scarce, considered best.

Wooden bow of locust (A: strongest wood); scrub oak (Sapir: "slow"); serviceberry (Sapir: best, most plentiful); juniper (A: preferable, if no locust; S: broke easily). Branch (Sapir: or stalk growing from roots) selected; broken off with sharp rock. Allowed to dry thoroughly; length not measured. Rubbed with sandstone; tapered in width and thickness toward ends. Notched for string.

Self bow either simply bent or recurved (Fig. 10, a; 2 recurved specimens visible in Steward, 1939, Pl. 19, a). I have no description of manufacture, but Sapir gives following account. If bow to be simply bent, wood left to dry completely before being strung. The recurved bow tapered, notched, but not smoothed; held rigid on ground between 5 pegs; 3 in line, 1 at either end and in middle. Two pegs (1 each side, between center and end pegs) forced wood to bend away from initial alignment. Released after week or so, when completely dry. Thought to have "better shape" than simply bent bow. Illustrated model (Fig. 10, a) about 45 in. long, of locust; inside flat; outside markedly convex. Grip not constricted; pair of notches either end for string; latter of 2-ply sinew

Sinew-backed bow: sinew from leg of deer or other animal applied along back with horn glue; (Sapir: with pinyon gum; said by my informant not to stick well). Deer horn cut (?) in 2

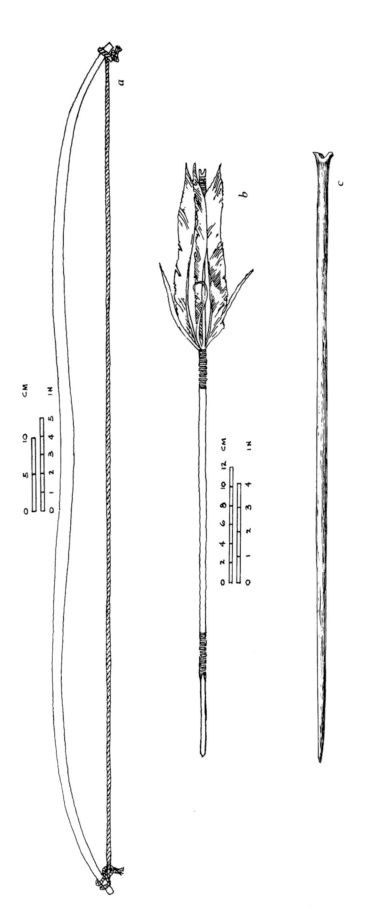

Fig. 10. Bow and arrows. a, simple, recurved bow, of locust; length, 45-46 in.; AMNH 50.2/3467. b, serviceberry arrow, eagle feathered; point made from a nail; length, 26 in.; AMNH 50.2/3468. c, blunt arrow for small game; scale not indicated. a, b, models made by Albert Frank, Kaibab; c, sketch with Sapir's field notes; probably model made by Tony Tillohash, his Kaibab informant, 1910.

pieces; soaked, boiled overnight; "sticky" the following morning. Rubbed on back of bow. Sinew applied; tapped gently with stone to make wide, flat strip; 1 application; bow dried 3 days in sun; grip tied with buckskin.

Horn bow: shot farther than others; scarce, brought 2 to 3 buckskins in trade; made locally; sometimes bartered from Kaiparowits. Description of manufacture unsatisfactory. Butts of 2 mountain sheep horns overlapped; in old days, tied with buckskin; post-white times, nailed. Horns set against fire; when hot, pounded gently between 2 large stones; whole flattened; splice more or less fused. Juncture further secured with pinyon pitch, buckskin wrapping. Sinew backing added.

Bowstring 2-ply sinew from back or leg; ordinarily 1 end of string permanently attached with pinyon gum; other end loosened in wet weather. Bow braced against foot or, if man seated, against knee to string. Release primary; arrow held between thumb, index finger, with thumb superior; (Sapir: if great strength needed, 2 or 3 fingers pulled below on string, as in Pl. 7, a); when bow held vertically, arrow rested on clenched fist to (marksman's) left of bow. Subject, Pl. 7, a, b, evidently left-handed. Wrist guard of buckskin.

Often inside of bow smeared with pinyon gum, over which red paint spread; no property marks; each knew his own bow. Sapir: to prevent cracking during cold weather, bow warmed slightly before hunting.

Arrows of serviceberry (tɨav) or cane (Sapir: cane swift, but easily broken; sometimes used currant, wild rose, which cracked easily, had to be greased when dry). Length of arrow measured from forefinger to chest, but with elbow crooked (Sapir: arrow, length of arm). Specimen (Fig. 10, b) 26 in.; comparatively short; "too long an arrow did not shoot straight."

Serviceberry wands cleaned (Sapir: dried about a week); stuck in hot ashes; straightened between teeth. Some used wrench (kuyuik) of antelope, mountain sheep horn; 3-holed; A does not know old manner of piercing horn; in his youth, used heated wire. Shafts smoothed between 2 stones (grooved through use) "of any kind," probably red sandstone. Nock (Sapir: ukušigi?a; nock ends pointed or square-cut; nocked at switch end of branch to give equal balance when feathered;

shaft beveled, sanded to allow for feathering [?]). Shaft beneath feathering painted red; no property marks; (Sapir: blue or red earth paint applied from nock over half distance covered by feathering and again below end of lower feather attachment). Shaft below feathering grooved, with incisions sometimes straight, sometimes wavy. M reported 3 such grooves (spopiakɨ, mark down); G, 2 straight grooves the full length of the low feathering; A, single straight groove painted red and running from feathering to half length of shaft. When "wavy," knife (drill point, found archeologically; Sapir: formerly had special flint implement for purpose) held stationary in hand and arrow twisted (Sapir: arrow lightly twirled in left hand while instrument run perpendicularly down shaft). Grooves said "to look nice"; (Sapir: arrow not complete without them); purchased specimens are ungrooved.

Feathering: tail or wing feathers of eagle, flicker used; latter for smaller game. Unfeathered arrows "wobbled"; (Sapir: model [Fig. 10, c] a small-game arrow, unfeathered, simple shaft sharpened at 1 end, nocked at other). Some arrows 2-feathered; if so, vanes not split, and 2 whole feathers applied opposite sides of shaft with pine gum, sinew. Usually 3-feathered. Feathers about 5 in. long, cut off at tip to proper length. Vanes split, trimmed; quill stripped of feathers along section to be covered by sinew-wrapping. Latter extends from nock about 1 in. along shaft and again at base of feathers. According to Sapir, tip ends of 3 (split) feathers applied equidistant about nock; wrapped with damp sinew; allowed to dry before butt ends quills attached. Wrapping of latter somewhat longer than at nock end. Fig. 10, b shows feathers trimmed save at butt ends, where wisps of full-width feather escape just above wrapping; other specimens (not figured) have feathers trimmed full length.

Points of stone or greasewood (tonovi, Sarcobatus; considered harder than serviceberry; used even for deer) inserted in cleft at tip of shaft, secured with pinyon pitch, sinew wrapping. Late times, nail used as point (Fig. 10, b). Stone (flint?) for points found on desert; manufactured points found archeologically also used. Some points long, thin, "like a drill"; others (Sapir: triangular, or rounded at base, i.e., heart shaped. Both latter had serrated stem, which was smeared with heated gum, thrust into shaft, wrapped with sinew).

Cane (pagampɨ, <u>Phalaris communis</u>?) arrows differed slightly. Straightened on large flat stone heated in fire. Cooled; serviceberry point inserted in hollow stem, secured with pitch, sinew wrapping. Sapir describes serviceberry foreshaft 8 to 10 in. long with stone point; not mentioned by my informants. Cane arrows nocked at joint; reinforced with pine gum, sinew; butt not plugged. Feathering normal (Sapir: cane arrows occasionally not feathered; swifter so, suitable for small game). Cane arrows not grooved, nor painted.

No arrow poison; fresh (deer) blood rubbed on deer arrows "for fun." Care taken to recover arrows; each hunter recognized own. Sapir: arrows repaired from time to time by refeathering or by replacing point.

Quiver (uguna) of wildcat, ringtail, fox, coyote, lion or fawn skin. Sometimes skin removed as cylinder, without ventral slash: cut around legs, head, nose, peeled skin off; required only end seam to become quiver. Man made the quiver; sewn with buckskin; if ventral cut, light serviceberry wand sewed in seam as support. Head at bottom; "looked nice"; receptacle wider at top; tail usually cut off; buckskin drawstring around top could pull quiver closed. Quiver hung at left side by means of line over right shoulder; arrows removed with right hand.

Other weapons: no spear; sling a toy. Informants deny warfare, trophy-taking; claim Ute scalped; but Dellenbaugh (1926, 170) says Paiute (presumably Kaibab) with Hamblin killed and scalped a Navajo.

Fire Making Equipment

Fire made by drill, percussion methods; former more common. Latter declared by A to be pre-white; 2 "black rocks" struck together over shredded cliffrose bark. A claimed to be unfamiliar with drill, although latter known to S, his sister.

Drill shaft usually not composite (as in Steward, 1939, Pl. 19, a); simple shaft made from stalk of narrow-leaved yucca; composite, from length of cane into which yucca stalk point inserted. According to S, hearth 3-holed, also of narrow-leaved yucca; according to G, 3 or 4 holed, usually of dry wood of sagebrush (Artemisia tridentata). Models by G (AMNH, 50.2/3463; MNM, 9921/12): straight shaft of yucca, one 15.5, other 19 in. long; hearth, 7.5 in. long, of sage wood, 3 holes, equispaced.

Juniper, sagebrush, cliffrose bark used as tinder, according to convenience. Sand not used to increase friction.

Slow match (kosovɨ) of shredded juniper bark, wrapped with same material. About length of forearm; carried in hand when traveling. Sapir: when fire needed, lighted end waved or blown on. Juniper the usual fuel; tree burned at base, dragged to camp.

Pottery

Pottery manufacture is said to have started a very few years before the Mormon occupation and did not become general. Although clay vessels did not replace cooking baskets, it is difficult to believe that ceramic production was as evanescent as seems indicated by the following statement from M.

Some Ankatɨ people had clay pots (wiav-pampuŋ, clay pot), which they made themselves. My father's brother, Tavac, visited across the Colorado and learned from the Mukwic [Hopi]. He came back and made about 5 pots, which he gave away. The women watched him make them, but he did not teach anyone. I think none of the other Kaibab made pottery. This was when I was about 5 years old, before the Mormons came around here.

Pots were easy to make. The clay came from near Sovpac [spring 46]; it was a red mud which was mixed with dirt [containing temper?] and water; nothing else was added; the dirt made the clay harder. The clay was put on the ground or in a pan [?] of some sort; then it was pounded with any kind of stone and the dirt and water mixed in. It was pounded and pounded. Then a piece was flattened for the bottom; then some clay was rolled in the hands and put around the edge [walls evidently concentric rather than spiral]. My uncle kept dipping his hand in water and smoothing the pot inside and out. The pots he made had straight sides and were 8 to 12 in. tall; they were a reddish color, undecorated. When he finished, he stood the pot in the sun for 5, sometimes 6 days. When it was dry he put it right on the coals and cooked in it [informant insistent on nonfiring aspect]. It did not crack; but it did not last long, not more than a few weeks.

-ooo-

S remembered that her people (spring 34) used to have pottery. Nothing was mixed with the clay, and she, too, described the vessels as flat bottomed and sun dried. She made two miniature models of unfired pots, such as children used as toys; these had a conical base, of a single lump of clay, and the sides were built by adding sausage-like rolls.

Sapir's informant had heard of an old type earthenware pot (pampuni) without handles. It was used for boiling meat and was placed directly on the ashes and a fire built around it.

Basketry

Kaibab basketry may be considered more or less typically Great Basin, with techniques both coiled and twined and with such representative forms as the conical burden basket, the fanlike winnowing and parching tray, the spoon-shaped seed beater, the pitch-covered water jar, and the woman's basket cap. In addition to these almost standard Basin specimens, the Kaibab and adjacent bands made use of a wrapped-stitch carrying frame, technically similar to that of the Mohave (Mason, 1904, 231, Pl. 17). There are no detailed accounts of its manufacture, but Kaibab informants claim it was similar to that described (pp. 162-3) for the Kaiparowits (Pl. 3, a).

Basketry both coiled (yɨŋapɨ) and twined (čagapɨ). Coiling proceeds right to left, perforations made with awl of bone or white stone; twining invariably left to right. Squawbush (sɨiwimp, Rhus utahensis) used almost exclusively; willow, considered inferior, could serve as unsplit rods (i.e., coil foundation, twine warps). Squawbush found in canyons; best said to come from "below Zion Canyon," from Long Velley, and from St. George country to west. Gathered mostly in winter; this season essential for splint material (i.e., sewing strands or twine wefts); less so for unsplit rods. Basket materials buried to keep them pliable.

Rods for coil foundation or for twine warp scraped with knife held across palm; ready for use. For splints, squawbush shoot split in 3 sections, from each of which inner wood stripped; bark scraped off later, formerly with knife, nowadays by running strand through hole punctured in tin can. Splints soaked overnight before being used.

Traditionally, Kaibab basketry little decorated; food bowl might have simple design formed by light green inner bark of squawbush. Twined burden basket in one Hillers plate (Steward, 1939, Pl. 13, b) has 2 bands of darker material. Basket cap occasionally had simple design in <u>Martynia</u>, obtained from lower country to the west.

<u>Coiled baskets</u>. --Coiled ware little used now except for decorated specimens made for sale (see below). Nevertheless, Hillers' photographs show a preponderance of coiling, including conical burden basket, cooking basket, food bowl, water jar, winnowing-parching tray.

Coiled burden baskets an interesting parallel to Basketmaker specimens (cf. Steward, 1939, Pl. 11, at right, and Hillers, no. 1603, left foreground, not included in Steward; Guernsey and Kidder, 1921, 61, Pls. 23, k, l, 24, e, f). Informants scarcely remember this type; in recent years, completely replaced by twined burden containers. Hillers' plates indicate both in use in 1870's.

Cooking basket (koc) bowl shaped; 2 sizes, the larger about 12 in. deep (one apparently shown in Steward, 1939, Pl. 11, at knee of woman wearing rabbitskin robe). Coil closely sewn; cold water allowed to stand in new receptacle, to make it watertight. Food bowl smaller; same shape; same name as cooking basket.

Winnowing-parching tray coiled, plaquelike. One observed in field has foundation of 2 rods, arranged vertically; concave surface smeared with pinyon gum.

Water jar (oc) had globular body; base rounded to flat; neck straight sided; handles of horsehair, formerly of braided sinew, added during manufacture of walls. No tradition of a twined, pointed-base water vessel. Most specimens in Hillers' photos (no. 1600, a; Steward, 1939, Pls. 9, a, b, 11, 12) obviously coiled, but one (Steward, 1939, Pl. 13, b), flat bottomed, apparently with diagonal design, is of indeterminate technique.

Model (Pl. 3, f) has single-rod foundation at start; changes to 2 rods, arranged vertically. Exterior the work surface; awl inserted between 2 stitches of previous row. Dry dung or root of narrow-leaved yucca rubbed well into interstices of finished vessel; red paint smeared over surface. One account (KC) has yucca root soaked overnight, pounded with a stone, and applied, apparently after red paint; probably should precede paint. Jar dried; coated with pinyon gum, boiled "until it strings, like molasses." Gum and hot pebbles poured inside; well shaken; excess gum poured out; hot pitch then applied to exterior with swab of skumpɨ (Chrysothamnus nauseosus). Placed in shade to dry. Another account: gum poured inside, swabbed with tuft of brush; then applied to exterior with flat stick. Wad of sagebrush bark used as stopper.

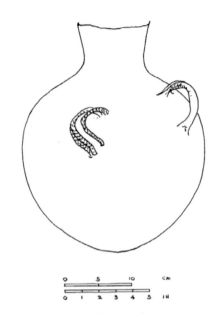

Fig. 11. Water jar, coiled basketry, pine-gum coated; AMNH 50.2/3466. Model by Sarah Frank, Kaibab.

Decorated coiled ware (Pl. 4, d, e) not known when KC was a child; she and age mates learned style about 1907, in Panguitch school (p.70). Women, even of older generation, now make such baskets for sale. S claims to copy some shapes, designs, from Moapa; included is a tall jar, more reminiscent of Apache than Moapa. Some women say they take motifs from Navajo rugs.

Following traits may be associated: decorated coiled ware, oval and other exotic shapes, "fancy" rim finishes (as in Pl. 4, d), and possibly 3-rod foundation. All these seem to have been learned at same time. Kaibab decorated baskets of good workmanship, but coarse; typically with black Martynia designs on natural squawbush ground.

New materials introduced with decorated coiling. Formerly had only green inner bark of squawbush and, very rarely, Martynia, imported from country to west. With development of decorated ware, seeds of Martynia (tuusupɨ, Martynia proboscidea) obtained from St. George, planted locally. "Horns" soaked in water 2 nights, split into strands. Vague references to a red material, apparently little used. None seen on Kaibab baskets at time of my visit. Said by S to be yucca root, dug out, buried in ground, removed strand at a time, soaked in water; Sapir's informant thought squawbush boiled with red earth. Another material, yellowish brown, obtained from Moapa; a sort of "water grass," looking "like straw"; soaked, split into 2 to 4 strands, according to desired fineness.

Twined baskets.—Twined technique used for conical burden basket; winnowing-parching tray; seed beater; woman's cap; awning, body of cradle. Conical burden basket (ais), close twined, used formerly for seed gathering; twine assuredly diagonal, although no specimens available (cf. Steward, 1939, Pls. 10, b, 13, b). Nowadays, seeds gathered in conical canvas-covered container (Pl. 2, a); 2 heavy rods of oak, serviceberry crossed at right angles, bent upward to form conical frame; attached at top to encircling hoop; not clear if this is modern substitute for seed basket or if it has old prototype (i.e., skin-covered frame).

Open-twined conical burden basket (yantu-ais) for fruit, pinenuts, etc. 2 sizes: larger deposited at convenient spot near scene of gathering; contents of smaller basket, carried by worker, emptied from time to time into large container. Model started by S begins on 6 rods, crossed in 3's (Fig. 12, a); diagonal twine, upward, left to right, exterior the work surface. After first few rows warps swing away from direction of work, producing spiral effect (cf. Steward, 1939, Pl. 9, a); informant thought this resulted from dampening squawbush. Last twined row usually 3-strand; said to prevent stretching. Top encircled by hoop, attached in coil stitch. Hide cap often applied at base for reinforcement or repair. Burden basket supported on back by tumpline of buckskin or Apocynum cord.

Winnowing-parching tray (takweu, takwuiyu) diagonal, close twined; fan shaped. Concave surface smeared with yucca fruit (nowadays, flour paste), rarely with pinyon gum, to seal interstices. Seeds parched; winnowed by tossing and blowing (Pl. 2, b) or by pouring. This type of tray used also as receptacle for meal ground on metate (Steward, 1939, Pl. 13, a). Miniature model made by S as follows: start shown Fig. 12, c. On third row new warp added (not bent over encircling rods); stitch changed from simple to diagonal twine. Last row 3-strand; "tightens," encourages slight concavity, and prevents stretching. Specimen shown Pl. 3, d has row of 3-strand about

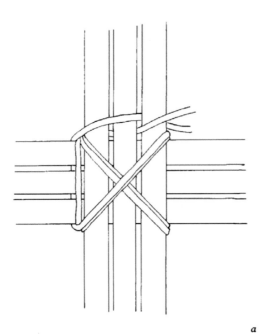
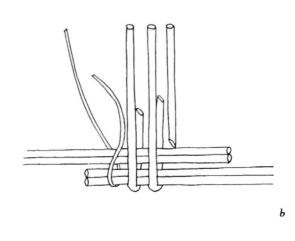
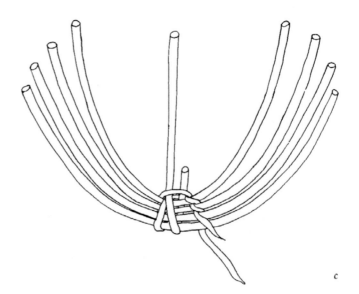

Fig. 12. Twined-basketry techniques. a, start of conical, twined burden basket. b, start of infant's first cradle (cf. Pl. 5, b). c, start of close-twined tray. Sketches from Kaibab field notes, 1932.

2 in. from top and again last row. Warps shredded, thinned close to last row; shreds bent to worker's left, whipped to top with remaining length of weft; several rods added about rim, and overcast.

Tray similar to above, but open twined (Pl. 3, c) used for winnowing berries, pinenuts. Sometimes cloth covering added to permit use in winnowing small seeds.

Seed beater (tɨkanɨmpɨ) spoon shaped. Modern product (Pl. 4, b) indistinguishable in shape, technique, from one in Hillers photo (Steward, 1939, Pl. 9, a); sketch in Mason, 1904, 492, probably also Kaibab specimen. Elongate shape and squared tip of beater shown in Pl. 4, c said to result from error in manufacture; same specimen also atypical in being downward twine.

Miniature model seed beater made by S. Tips of 2 encircling rods overlapped; warps placed against them at right angles, and butts bent back on themselves, enclosing encircling rods. Similar to start of sandal (Fig. 5, a), except for additional foundation rod. Twined across face; turned; on second row, new warp added every stitch. Twine open, diagonal, upward. When body complete, alternate warps raised; encircling rods from either side passed beneath lifted warps and brought around body, to enclose entire rim; overcast. Warp rods bundled, caught together in twine stitch to form handle. A length of oak split, sharpened, to serve as blade; bent, and tied at intervals about lower part of bowl (Pl. 4, b). Nowadays metal blade, wired in place, has replaced wooden one.

Basketry cap (sɨkaičogo) no longer used; worn mostly to prevent chafing by head tump. Specimens in Hillers plates are mammary shaped. Usually undecorated; rarely, simple pattern in *Martynia*. Sapir's informant described cap as coiled. Probably incorrect; specimens in Hillers photos indubitably twined; informants speak of this technique alone; and it is characteristic of basketry headgear of other Southern Paiute.

Cradle. —The cradle type current in the 1870's is established definitively by views in several Hillers photographs (for example, no. 1603; and Steward, 1939, Pl. 15, a, b) and by a similar specimen (Pl. 5, a) collected by Powell in southern Utah. An oval frame supports a basketry body, which consists of about a dozen sizable rods, disposed longitudinally, and held together by widely spaced rows of twining. At either end, the rods extend beyond the oval frame. The awning is trapezoidal, of open twine in zigzagged rows. Hillers' photographs show a pad, evidently of bark, for the infant's head.

The style has changed materially. Nowadays, a child has 2 cradles (kon). The first, for a newborn, is small and light. In contrast to the cradle used by an older child, it has no heavy frame, no skin cover, and no tump. When outgrown, it is torn apart and left in a tree.

A model first cradle (Pl. 5,b) made by S. Start shown in Fig. 12,b. Willow warp; squawbush weft. Two warps are bent over 2 pairs of overlapping rods, and their butts doubled back on far side; a third warp is added, but not doubled. Twining begins at the left and incorporates the folded-back butts. Sketch somewhat misleading, for twine is upward. Subsequent warps added in pairs. When length is sufficient, row of 3-strand twine added to help preserve shape. Except for a few warps at either edge, all are broken off and their splinters bent at right angles across top; 3 rods are added to them, and the whole overcast. The outer warps, together with additional rods, bent to form arched handle. Handle and body of cradle enclosed by heavy encircling rod of currant or snowberry; overcast. Twined awning attached damp to cradle and arched support; tied with sinew and allowed to dry bent. Buckskin loops along sides for lacing; mattress pad of loose cliffrose bark placed beneath infant. Umbilical cord attached "anywhere."

A larger, more substantial cradle (Pl. 5,d) made for an older child. Rigid wooden frame with cross slats, to which twined body attached. Illustrated specimen is diagonal, upward twine, with rows paired. Last row apparently finished as in model described above. Whole, including arched handle, buckskin covered; canvas or ticking sometimes substituted. Loops along front for lacing; tump attached. Awning twined. Sometimes shape nearly triangular; sometimes sides relatively parallel; no sex indication on awning.

In recent years, large board cradle, skin covered (called ovon-kɨn) copied from Koosharem Ute (p. 70). Made for KC's youngest child but not, as yet, widely used among Kaibab.

Miscellaneous basketry techniques.--Wrapped-stitch carrying frame (kaŋavɨ) once current. Said to have resembled that of Kaiparowits, described below (pp.162-3; Pl.3,a). No mention of wickerwork seed beater similar to Kaiparowits specimen (Pl. 4, a).

Musical Instruments

None, at one time. A rattle (Pl. 7, e, f; Fig. 13, a) associated with the "Cry" ceremony (Sapir) (p. 95) of relatively recent introduction; evidently a substitute for the gourd rattle that, farther west, is associated with the mourning ceremony.

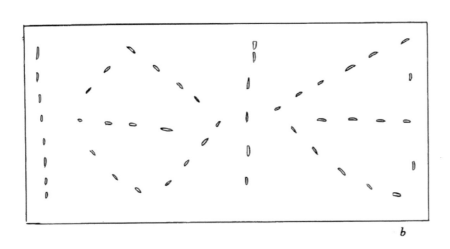

Fig. 13. Rattle used in "Cry" ceremony. a, tin can filled with shot; scale not indicated. b, development of rattle design. Sketches with Sapir's field notes; probably models made by Tony Tillohash, his Kaibab informant, 1910. Cf. Pl. 7, e, f.

The rasp (Pl. 7, d; Fig. 14), also of late introduction, as accompaniment of bear dance (pp. 104, 107-12).

Fig. 14. Rasp and rasper used in bear dance; evidently of wood; scale not indicated. Sketches with Sapir's field notes; probably models made by Tony Tillohash, his Kaibab informant, 1910. Cf. Pl. 7, d.

Communications and Trade

The Colorado Canyon was an effective barrier to communication south and southeast. With the Havasupai and Walapai, informants claimed literally no contact. They also indicated that extremely few Kaibab crossed the Colorado, although one man who journeyed from Ankatɨ (map 2) to the Hopi country a few years before Mormon times, allegedly brought back knowledge of pottery making (p. 77) and another, who visited the San Juan Paiute, returned to build the first sweathouse in Kaibab territory (p. 59). In contrast, the Navajo were frequent visitors, at least after the introduction of the horse. Then, too, contact with the Ute seems to have become intensified.

North of the Colorado, trails led to Ute country and to that of other Paiute groups. Unfortunately, I collected little information on routes, but a great deal could be accomplished by going over the land with informants, the accounts of early travelers in hand. Escalante seems to have followed established trails (Bolton), and so also did later travelers, including the Powell parties and, presumably, the Mormon pioneers.

On trips, a woman carried provender and household effects in a conical basket or frame on her back, a small child sitting atop the load. The mealing stone seldom was taken on seasonal moves, for one was cached in the neighborhood of a frequently visited campsite. A woman ordinarily used a head tump of buckskin or Apocynum fiber, but one Hillers plate (Steward, 1939, Pl 16, b) shows two seed gatherers whose burden baskets are supported by a chest tump. The chest tump normally was utilized by a man to carry loads in a "sack." I neglected to ask specifically, but reference probably is to the carrying net, which is faintly visible in two of Hillers' plates (no. 1600, a; and Steward, 1939, Pl. 13, b, although not discernible in the reproduction).

The dog was a late acquisition and was not used in transportation. It reached the Kaibab from the north, about the middle of the past century. The first one on the local scene may have been that brought by a man of spring 68, on his return from a visit to the Parowan (Cedar) area. The Ankatɨ (map 2) Kaibab apparently had no dogs prior to the Mormon occupation, when they were obtained in trade from the Panguitch Paiute and the Koosharem Ute. At first, the dog was so esteemed that a child was given in exchange, yet its utility seems to have been limited to guarding the camp and to chasing rabbits. Dogs were not eaten.

There is difference of opinion concerning the introduction of the horse (p. 89), but it seems to have been surprisingly late. Precise dating should be sought in other sources. Its acquisition by neighboring peoples must have changed the local situation considerably. The earlier isolation came to an end and, intermittently, Kaibab territory became a thoroughfare for stock-raiding parties, particularly Navajo. They crossed from east to west, en route to "California" and returned with large numbers of animals; they also raided nearby Mormon settlements. There must have been a good deal of local turmoil, yet informants, correctly or not, depicted the Kaibab as passive and nonaggressive, sticking close to home base, and taking advantage of the new and lively trade opportunities (pp. 89-91).

In post-horse days, contact with the Ute also became closer, and a group, perhaps Koosharem, perhaps not (p. 34), took to coming annually, traveling with horse travois and tipi. Eventually, both these Plains elements were adopted by the Kaibab. When KC was a child, presumably in the late 1890's, the travois (oravɨ, house poles) was being used, and a photograph taken in 1904 shows a Kaibab tipi (p. 58). In 1910, Sapir's informant was able to give a detailed description of the latter type of dwelling (pp. 58-9).

In all trade, the chief Kaibab commodity was buckskin, a fact that gives validity to the abundance of skin clothing shown in Hillers' plates. Children also were bartered. To a considerable extent, the Kaibab operated as intermediaries and passed along to their neighbors Navajo rugs and horses they themselves had received in trade.

Routes

A few obvious references to trails in Kaibab country may be cited from the literature:

Powell--and probably Escalante before him--used an old route from the mouth of Zion Creek, along the base of the Vermilion Cliffs, to Pipe Spring (map 1, no. 11) (Powell, 1961, 297). Traverse comparatively easy at foot of these cliffs; doubtless a far more important line of communication than my data suggest.

From mouth of the Paria, Powell party used "old Navajo trail" skirting the Vermilion Cliffs of the Paria Plateau, to Houserock (Dellenbaugh, 1926, 158-60, 213).

On authority of Hamblin, Dellenbaugh (1909, 93) has an old route down Kanab Canyon, crossing the Colorado into Havasupai country.

Nevertheless, my informants declared no contact with latter area, and Dellenbaugh himself (1926, 244-5) had difficulty ascending the Kanab by "a trail worked to some extent" by prospectors.

Paiute trails in Nankoweap and Kwagunt valleys, which descend to the Colorado from the eastern front of Kaibab Plateau, also mentioned by Dellenbaugh (1909, 326).

The principal routes reported by informants clearly incomplete; evidently many local trails within the territory of individual economic clusters (latter in Roman numerals on map) and connecting these with one another. A summary follows:

Pipe Spring (map 1, no. 11) to Mt. Trumbull, "west, across the desert"; traveled by Powell party (Dellenbaugh, 1926, 186).

Short Creek (no. 6) along Vermilion Cliffs, to Hurricane area.

Moccasin (no. 12) to Cane Beds (no. 8), across mesa spur.

Antelope Spring (no. 13) to Colorado Canyon; direct line, coming out just west of mouth of Kanab Canyon; camped one night en route.

Kanab (no. 26) to Alton (map 1, IV), via upper Kanab Canyon.

Kanab (no. 26) to Navajo Well (no. 34), along base of Vermilion Cliffs, "where the road is today." Undoubtedly extended southwest to Moccasin (no. 12) and northeast to Ankati (nos. 40-45). Escalante may have followed latter route, turning off on false trail which took him across northern tip of Kaibab Plateau.

Kanab (no. 26) to Kaibab Plateau, "straight across the desert." Navajo Well (no. 34) people could have gone directly south to Kaibab Plateau, but "usually went first to Kanab, so as to go with the rest of the Indians."

Moccasin (no. 12) to Kaibab Plateau also described as "straight across the desert," to northwestern face of plateau; from there, several trails up side canyons to summit. One continued across plateau to Houserock (no. 55) (Dellenbaugh, 1926, 164); another, along western front, to Grand Canyon; a branch to the southwest reached canyon just east of mouth of Kanab Creek.

Kaibab Plateau to Houserock (no. 55) a day's journey, "starting early in the morning." From Houserock, a trail undoubtedly skirted base of Vermilion Cliffs, communicating with springs to east, but not mentioned in my notes. In upper Houserock Valley (probably near spring 54), Escalante heard of route to Colorado crossing.

Pagampagantɨ (no. 67) to Grand Canyon; trail apparently ran along eastern side of Kaibab Plateau, encircled a peak, and continued to winter camp, just below rim of Colorado gorge. This might be the route Dellenbaugh (1909, 92) says comes "down from the north, reaching the river a few miles below the Little Colorado."

Travelers--principally Navajo--said to have crossed the Colorado at Parovɨ (crossing), upstream from Lees Ferry. Presumably Ute Ford, called also Crossing of the Fathers (cf. p. 165); not within Kaibab territory. Described as wide, chest deep, frozen in winter. Lees Ferry (called Parɨ, intersection of rivers, undoubtedly referring to confluence of the Paria with the Colorado) uninhabited.

For the Kaibab, water transport need not be considered; no opportunity to use craft of any kind.

Commerce

Conflicting accounts regarding first horses in area. None attributed introduction to the Navajo, although general agreement that latter had animals before the Kaibab did.

One informant declared horses received first "from Mexicans across the river" and Spanish-derived name for horse (Sapir, 1930, 632, kavaa-^{S}) suggests such derivation not unlikely; another, from "the first whites"; still another specified Mormons. An Ankatɨ (map 2) man claimed horses introduced first by Utes, who traded an animal for a child. Another reported horses seen first at Ankatɨ about 10 years before Mormon settlement; at that time, about 10 men, "wearing blue overalls," arrived from the west with band of horses. Tried to barter animals; ate with Ankatɨ people. Requested a guide; continued across Paria River into Kaiparowits country. Accompanied by a Paiute whose speech sounded as if "he came from Nevada."

In time, Kaibab received animals from Panguitch and Cedar Paiute and from Ute and Navajo; in turn, traded horses to these same groups. Standard price seems to have been a child, 5 blankets (Navajo) or 5 buckskins for an animal.

Firearms (tɨmpiu, gun) received from first whites, some time after introduction of horse.

Trade with Paiute.--Kaiparowits people crossed the Paria, trading bows, arrows for buckskin. Bows of serviceberry and horn. Latter prized; brought large hide in exchange. Not exclusively a trade article; made also by Kaibab.

Some commerce with the San Juan Paiute, who crossed the Colorado to Kaibab Plateau, to offer (presumably Navajo) rugs for buckskin.

Panguitch group traded same articles as Ute; mentioned below, with latter group.

Some, not all, Kaibab obtained agricultural products from St. George Paiute--possibly also from Shivwits and from Cedar people near Toquerville; somewhat dubiously, from Moapa Paiute. One buckskin exchanged for about 50 lbs. [sic] of maize, beans. Kaibab at Navajo Well (spring 34) "heard they had corn and sometimes squash at Moccasin [12] but did not know how it looked; we thought they got it from the Mukwic." The latter implies some knowledge of the Hopi as farmers.

An informant of the Toquerville district remembered that the Kaibab used to come there, bringing pipes to trade; they were "the best pipes" of the entire region.

Trade with Ute.--Vigorous commerce with adjacent Ute, at least after acquisition of the horse. Ute made frequent trips to Kaibab territory; apparently these not reciprocated. One group, not well identified (p. 34) brought horses, knives, guns, yellow paint to trade for buckskin, horses. Koosharem Ute offered horses, buffalo robes (thought to be from Uintah originally) in exchange for buckskins, horses, Navajo blankets. New buffalo robe equalled a horse in value; an old one, 2 saddle blankets. Koosharem also traded white paint for moccasins, woman's skin dress.

From them (and from Panguitch Paiute, whom some regarded as more Ute than Paiute), in post-Mormon times, Ankatɨ Kaibab obtained dogs, knives, firearms. Allegedly an even trade: dog for a child. Both Panguitch and Koosharem said to have stolen Ankatɨ children for sale to whites.

Commerce with other tribes.--Navajo sometimes came to Kaibab area on foot; swam the Colorado "other side" of Lees Ferry. Brought blankets to exchange for buckskin, horses. Rarely visited Ankatɨ without trading. Often showed up on Kaibab Plateau, to offer blankets for buckskin; blankets traded subsequently by Kaibab to Cedar and St. George Paiute. Eagle feathers also trafficked, but reference ambiguous.

Brisk Kaibab-Navajo horse trade, in which a blanket and a buckskin considered of equal value. Navajo gave 6 to 8 blankets for a good animal. They also offered horses to Kaibab, in even exchange for a child. Girl, 4 to 5 years old, usually preferred, "but sometimes they wanted boys." It was believed the girl later married a Navajo; boy's fate unknown. KC remembered "an old woman around here who had been traded as a child to the Navajo. They made her herd sheep. She got so lonesome she ran away. She said they were pretty good to her but made her work all the time."

Little reference to traffic in silver (p. 66), although today Navajo continue their visits, bringing silver and blankets. Maggie Johnny gave a tanned deer hide for a small diamond-stitch blanket, later selling it for $3.00. Recently, KC accepted 2 medium-sized, poor-quality rugs for a buckskin vest.

No basketry traded to Navajo; "Paiute" basketry among latter (Franciscan Fathers, 1910, 291) probably attributable to San Juan Paiute (pp. 173-4).

With the Hopi, G believed there was no contact. Had never seen a Hopi blanket, but thought it similar to the Navajo. S remembered only one Hopi trading party, which brought both Hopi and Navajo rugs to exchange for horses; 10 small rugs offered for an animal. She remembered Hopi textiles as of wool, finer than Navajo.

Property and Inheritance

Springs were private property (pp. 7-8); land, not. A man who fired a plot to encourage growth of wild tobacco considered the crop his(p. 46) but presumably not the ground. Women claimed certain pinyon trees(p. 43) and quarreled with anyone who harvested from them. However, seeds might be gathered on flats adjacent to occupied springs, regardless of the ownership of the latter.

There were no hunting rights in the sense of a preserve and, in fall, for example, virtually all the Kaibab hunted deer on the plateau of that name. However, if a man went to the trouble of constructing a bird blind (p. 53) it was considered his, although he allowed others to use it without payment. Some blinds were mentioned specifically as property of local chiefs (p 53).

A well developed sense of property was associated with eagle (kwananc) aeries. They were privately owned, by right of discovery or inheritance, and quarreling followed unauthorized exploitation.

Aeries were found "anywhere on the cliffs," and claimants usually were residents of nearby springs. However, there were no nests along the west front of the Kaibab Plateau, and group X (map 1) obtained feathers from those of spring 59 (VIII), giving buckskin in trade. Others without source of supply also traded for feathers; a bundle 2 to 3 in. in dia. brought a buckskin in exchange.

The following list of aeries and their owners was provided by G:

(1) 2 nests west of Moccasin, (spring 12) near Yellowstone Spring; owned originally by Ma?apituku, br of G's f (spring 13); inherited by sons and, on their death, by G. (2) Nest near Moccasin owned by Katavɨ (spring 12); inherited from f. (3) Nest east of spring 15 owned by Miapi (spring 26); thought to have been inherited from f. (4) Nest west of 26 owned jointly by Takta and Mus, brs (springs 20-21); previous owner unknown; "maybe their father." (5) Nest east of Kanab Creek (26) owned by Sagovonkuic (26); inherited from f. (6) Nest near 34 owned by Mu?umpui (spring 34). (7) 2 nests in Ankatɨ (map 2) belonged to A?pɨgantɨ (spring 44); "nobody owned them before." (8) Nest near spring 55 owned by Keno, of same spring. (9) One east of 60 owned by Nɨwarɨmpɨ (spring 60). (10) One near 66 owned by Kɨsaɨcɨ (spring 67); "when he died nobody owned it."

Exploitation was described thus:

Aerie inspected every 2 or 3 days in summer, to keep track of birds' growth. When barely able to fly, eaglets removed; no danger from old birds. Sometimes 1 man stood on top of cliff; another, at bottom, beneath nest. Burning brush dropped from above, or a lighted slow match let down on end of a net. Blaze frightened birds from nest. They were picked up at base of cliff; feet tied together; taken to camp. Sometimes several men lowered a boy from the cliff; net tied about his waist and between legs. Lad collected the small birds and was hoisted up, together with cargo.

Once in camp, birds placed in nest of piled sticks (Sapir: in wooden cage, or nest in tree). Not tethered (Sapir: string tied to 1 foot); allowed to walk about; did not escape if fed meat. Owner or other member of household provided rabbits twice daily, sometimes more often.

No ceremonial observances; no address; no need to feed bird before owner ate. When grown, feathers suitable for arrows were plucked; birds either freed or necks wrung and bodies thrown away.

Ownership of aeries usually passed from father to son. Three such cases (nos. 1, 2, 5) appear above and two more (nos. 3 and 4) were thought perhaps to have been similar. The first nest mentioned passed from the original owner to his sons and later to his brother's son. Inheritance by a grandson was mentioned but no example give. In the absence of a near male relative, the mother or the wife inherited and thereafter delegated someone to steal the young birds.

It will be convenient at this point to summarize other information concerning inheritance, for the father-to-son succession is weak or denied. Although ownership of watering places was said to be transferred to the oldest child, specific examples indicate that they went to a male relative--by blood or marriage--who happened to be on the spot (pp. 7-8). Three cases of inheritance by the younger sister's son and two, by the son-in-law, accord with a statement that matrilocal residence prevailed (p. 99).

A new chief was chosen from among the male relatives--again, by blood or marriage--but selection of a man's son was opposed. Four known cases include transmission to the brother, to the father's "sister's" (cousin's) husband, to the sister's son, and to the grandson (p. 28).

-93-

Because of the destruction of personal property at death, there usually was little to inherit. Some buckskins and a horse--provided the deceased had two animals--were spared for the use of "relatives."

Life Crises

On the whole, Kaibab practices associated with life crises are reminiscent of the Great Basin. The chief aspects are summarized here, and details are presented below.

A parturient was secluded; used the "hot bed" and the head scratcher; and avoided eating meat and drinking cold water. Perhaps through oversight, there is no mention of the "tooth stick," a small bit of wood held in the mouth; this trait is common among the central and western bands. Some restrictions applied to the child's father, and he also performed certain tasks--fetching wood and water--so as not to become "lazy." A birth regularly was attended by a shaman, in addition to a woman who acted as midwife; other Southern Paiute called the shaman only in difficult cases or not at all.

Puberty observances for a girl were similar to those associated with childbirth. Little formal attention was given a boy, but it is possible that, at this time, the ears of both sexes were pierced.

Blood relationship was the only bar to marriage, and cousin marriage was prohibited. The sororate and levirate were practiced. Polygyny seems to have been infrequent, perhaps because of economic limitations; in two of the three cases reported, the husband was a chief, who normally received gifts of meat from fellow hunters (p. 27).

Although matrilocal residence was said to prevail, this is not confirmed by the fragmentary data for either composition of settlement or of household (p.25-6). With respect to the former, the informant obviously thought in terms of the male head of the family and thus might have neglected to mention relationship through the wife. Nevertheless, there are a good many specific instances of both patrilocal and matrilocal residence. Perhaps the couple remained with the wife's family for a time and established later residence according to convenience and inclination. There was no parent-in-law tabu.

It already has been noted (p. 26) that a surprising number of households were described as without women folk; one widower (springs 15, 18-19; p. 13) was said specifically to have gathered and prepared seeds. Polygyny was not sufficiently common to explain a dearth of women. Moreover, slave-trade incursions were mentioned casually and in connection with children, and it is unlikely that they decimated the female population. Despite the apparent shortage of women, there is no report of polyandry.

A corpse was deposited in a rock shelter and covered with stones; only a chief received true burial. Cremation was reserved for a little-esteemed person.

Women mourners wailed and cut the hair. Personal property was deposited with the body, and a horse was killed, either at the grave or elsewhere. It is likely that at one time a relative was dispatched to accompany the deceased; although this was denied by Kaibab informants, Gunlock, Shivwits, and St. George informants claimed it to have been their former custom. The dwelling was torn down and rebuilt elsewhere, and the name of the dead was not mentioned thereafter.

Toward the end of the century, an attenuated version of the Colorado River mourning ceremony reached the Kaibab, via the St. George Paiute. Sapir has an excellent and detailed account of the introduction, with dates, locations, preparations, participants, and procedures. (His material should be published in full, and we should know something of the subsequent development of the "Cry." The present report, prepared in 1934, terminated the description of death and mourning with a reference to Sapir's data. Now, in 1963, I have looked through my original field notes but find no mention of the "Cry.") The first "Cry" (yaagapɨ) attended by the Kaibab, together with the St. George and Cedar Paiute, took place in 1894, between "'Cain Batch' and Rockville" (?). The last "Cry" mentioned by his informant was in 1909, near Cedar City; on this occasion, "all bands" except the San Juan apparently participated, as did some Shoshoni. The "Cry" of 1901 was sponsored by Kanab residents--originally, it would seem, of the Escalante (Kaiparowits) area, and probably with Koosharem ties. It was held at East Fork, in country that might have been either Kaiparowits or Koosharem Ute (pp.34,145). The actual performance was in the hands of people from St. George and Moapa, and some 300 people assembled (p. 33).

A "Cry" lasted five days and nights; was ostensibly to "show respect" for the dead; and involved burning of considerable property and slaughtering of horses. There were four song cycles--roan, coyote, bird, and mountain sheep (Sapir, 1930, 347, 529, fn. 9). The words, unintelligible, presumably were in Mohave language. Apparently all songs had rattle (Fig. 13, a) accompaniment. Not only was there highly emotional demonstration of grief, but likewise opportunity for major diversion in the form of the circle dance, gambling, card games, foot races and arrow-target competitions.

Birth

Birth did not take place in the usual menstrual hut, but in a special structure called tɨakani. Might be a miniature dwelling or, presumably in warm weather, a circular brush enclosure, with fire inside. When no longer needed, demolished, not burned.

Husband fetched wood and water, running, so as not to become lazy. He built fire, heated water, and prepared "hot bed" (tɨarupa) inside the hut. "Bed," an excavation filled with hot stones, ashes; covered with brush and rabbitskin blanket. Following delivery, parturient "sat" on this--according to Sapir, for a week. Morning and evening, stones replaced with newly heated ones, by attending women or by husband. Parturient remained in hut until discharge ceased; 7 to 8 days for a boy; 5 to 6 for a girl; a boy said to'have more blood." During this time, husband bathed each morning in cool water.

Head scratcher used by woman for an unspecified time, perhaps also by husband. Described by S as "any kind of stick"; but model (Fig. 15) by Sapir's informant is shaped and painted. No drinking tube; no mention of "tooth stick."

No food tabus during pregnancy; "let the woman eat what she wants to; some don't want meat." Following delivery, both

Fig. 15. Menstrual scratching stick, with red paint. Scale not given. Sketch with Sapir's field notes; probably model made by Tony Tillohash, his Kaibab informant, 1910.

parents avoided drinking cold water and eating meat. Woman ate principally mush. She ate no meat for a month; her husband, for shorter period. He might hunt, but gave kill to others. He also gave away (did not trade) clothing. Same observances for stillborn.

Several persons, including husband, assisted at birth. Shaman attended, singing; sometimes inside hut, sometimes outside. Midwife (tiapogint; tia, birth; puaganti, shaman) said to be "like a doctor," but presumably any woman with skill, experience. Not paid for services. Parturient squatted, supported by 2 persons in front and 2 behind; sometimes husband assisted thus. When tired, she stood, clinging to a post set up for the occasion. If labor prolonged, woman held beneath armpits and shaken.

Cord cut with stone knife; tied with sinew. Saved and tied to cradle; no ill consequences if lost. Afterbirth buried, in "any position"; consumption by coyote or other animal not considered dangerous.

Child put to breast when milk came; until then, given warm water. Milk squeezed from breast to heated stone, to insure plentiful supply. Children nursed until about 2 years old.

No contraceptives; no means of inducing pregnancy. Did not reckon duration of pregnancy. Intercourse ceased during (latter part of?) pregnancy and perhaps "one and a half months afterward, when [until] the baby was big enough." No devices for determining sex of unborn child. Dual births unknown to S. Girls said formerly to have married younger; had easy time at birth "because their bones were soft." Had 6 to 8 children, "but most died."

Here follows a sumary of Sapir's material:

Parturition hut, tuwakani (child-house) said to resemble menstrual hut; destroyed after use. Women attending lifted, shook parturient to facilitate delivery; precedent said to have been set by Coyote, who hung on limb and shook himself. Immediately after birth, mother lay face down on hot, dry bath; pit about a foot deep, same width, long enough to accommodate body. Filled with flat stones heated in fire, covered loosely with earth, then blankets. Used for a week after delivery.

Woman remained in hut a month, doing own work but nothing for others. During pregnancy, might eat meat; but it, fish, and probably "all living things," including grasshoppers, forbidden for a month after birth. On one occasion, Sapir's informant said meat barred both parents month before and after delivery. Woman did not eat prohibited foods for fear of being derided by other women. Meat-eating thought not to injure infant but to cause heavier bleeding at next delivery. Cold water not drunk by woman for about 2 weeks; head scratcher used 2 weeks to month. Precedent for warm water, head scratcher, but not for meat tabu, established by Coyote (cf. Sapir, 1930, 377).

Husband's restrictions less exacting. For month after birth, but not before, he gave away meat or fish he killed or caught. Did not eat meat for several days, generally a week after birth; [thereafter?] might eat meat but generally did not, because sight of it sickened him. Man did not share tabu on drinking cold water; did not use head scratcher. Copulation banned for month after birth and at least a month before.

Adolescence and Menstruation

Apparently no special observances for boy at puberty, although G remembered that his mother pierced his ears.

No singing, dancing associated with girl's puberty. She withdrew to menstrual hut (časkani) built by her mother. Lay on "hot bed" as in childbirth. For 5 days drank warm water, direct from container, without tube. Avoided animal food; meat, fish (fresh and dried specified by informant, although none available in Kaibab territory), even birds' eggs.

Careful not to touch face, eyes and hair; latter tied behind head. Otherwise would age quickly and hair turn gray. Used scratching stick (Fig. 15). Face not covered; no special clothing.

Girl remained alone in hut, prepared her own food. At end, presumably of 5 days, mother punched her ears with Chrysothamnus twig. Girl bathed; painted face and top of head red; returned to family dwelling. Paint remained until it wore off; not applied subsequently.

Girl usually married soon after puberty, in former times, at 12 or 13 years. During later periods might occupy menstrual hut jointly with 1 or more girls or women.

Sapir gives the following data on mentrual observances:

Hut built when required by women, about 25 ft. from dwelling. A man who approached hut was twitted; people said he wanted to sleep with one of the women. If he talked with menstruating women or smelled blood would become lazy and unable to walk swiftly. Woman remained in hut until menses ceased, meanwhile avoiding cold water and eating no meat--the latter, probably because game animals might take offense. Used head scratcher, otherwise hair always would be mussed, even though just combed.

Marriage

Girl married soon after puberty. "Some married for good looks," but S preferred a husband who hunted deer. No exogamy; no cousin marriage. Groom might be an age mate or someone considerably older. To attract one of opposite sex, KC had heard of small purple flower growing at higher elevations; wrapped in "a tiny bit of buckskin" and presumably carried; "don't tell anyone about it." Sapir's informant said that to win girl's love, one sought small, brownish bird that stays under the rocks; shot and carried, without being skinned or otherwise prepared. He had intended to try the dried heart but had no opportunity. Love charms and love songs unknown to G.

Latter reported occasional marriage with Panguitch, Kaiparowits, and San Juan Paiute in former times; none, with Ute, Navajo, or Paiute bands to west. Nowadays "they marry anybody." At present, several men and women from comparatively distant Paiute groups (Panaca, Paranigat, for example) married and living with Kaibab. Inter-band marriage by "capture" described by Sapir's informant (pp. 32-3).

As a rule, marriage arrangement casual. Boy attracted to a certain girl went to her camp to sleep with her. If her parents disapproved, they sent him away. According to Sapir, if they offered him mush, they favored the union. Parents might persuade a daughter to marry against her wishes. Residence said to have been matrilocal, but evidence conflicting (pp. 25-6, 93-94, 100)

No formal bride price, but eventually girl's parents received gift from the groom--horse, buckskin, or Navajo blanket. No exchange gift; in case of divorce, property not returned to husband.

Polygyny not common. Chief and occasionally others might have 2 wives, usually sisters. G recalled only 3 cases: Kanu (spring 75) and Kwinivac (chief, 68), each married to 2 sisters; and "Chuarruumpeak," Powell-appointed chief, espoused to 2 unrelated women. Both wives in 1 dwelling. No polyandry.

Barren wife sometimes abandoned. S had heard that Moccasin (spring 12) women might desert their husbands; she, living at Navajo Well (34) had no first-hand knowledge. After a quarrel, "the girl would run away to her parents"--a statement scarcely consonant with matrilocal residence. After a time, the husband went for her. Wife's father said nothing; did not interfere even if she were beaten.

In case of infidelity, aggrieved husband assembled friends and fought with wife, lover, and latter's friends; the chief might participate, on side of husband. "Sometimes the man got his wife back," but if she left again, he let her go. Sometimes "she wanted to go back to her husband." Similarly, if husband unfaithful, women rallied and fought over the man. Vigorous struggle, but "for fun." When men fought on such occasions, likewise used fists, not arrows; no fatalities. Paramour not killed; no indemnity.

Widow usually married the brother of her deceased husband, younger or older; if he already had a wife, "she married someone else." Similarly, widower married deceased wife's sister. After death of a spouse, usually waited half year before remarrying.

Rape carried no formal penalty but occasioned upbraiding from girl's mother. Illegitimate child raised by girl and her parents; sometimes the child's father made a gift. Such offspring no bar to subsequent union.

Herewith a few oddments concerning sex abnormalities. Among occupants of spring 55, a berdache (tawanaverɨm), who lived with mother; "used to go around and grind sage for the women." About 20 years ago, a 15-year-old boy made himself a dress; "married" a Koosharem lad, but Indian Service authorities separated the couple. Today, a girl about 12 years old said to be "half a boy; she plays with boys all the time... and works in the field with her brother."

In one of the tales recorded by Sapir, "idle Coyote" used for female purposes; "after badger-wives came, they didn't care for him." Sapir's informant had heard that in "southern California" girls have row of holes around the vagina, with drawstrings attached. A woman who wants to kill a man allows him to copulate with her; then, from behind her anus, she pulls strings, holding man's penis firm until he dies.

Same informant also had heard following narrated as true: Somewhere northwest of Kaibab territory lived 2 pretty unmarried girls, great friends. Once they went far from camp and sat down. Said one, "Let us do something." Replied the other, "What shall we do?" First one said, "Let us play with each other. You lie on your belly and I shall lie on top of you like a man." The girl consented, and the first girl began to copulate with her; she discovered thereupon that the friend had a penis as well as female genitals.

Death and Mourning

Both cremation and burial reported. Former not standard procedure; according to G, "They burned a 'mean' man; a good one was buried." Sapir's informant denied cremation, yet Dellenbuagh (MS) heard "that the corpse was burned in the wickiup." M claimed a corpse was left in the dwelling, which was torn down and abandoned. As a rule, dead apparently interred in rock shelter; cremation reserved for reviled individual. Only a chief received true burial in a grave, 4 ft. deep, lined with cane.

Koosharem Ute and "other Indians to the north" said to have killed relatives, usually wife and daughter, when a man died. Vigorously denied by informants as local practice; nevertheless, several Mormon residents maintained it was former Kaibab custom and cited one actual instance. Both versions probably biased, but immolation of relatives mentioned by several other Paiute groups.

Expiring individual left alone in dwelling to die. Immediately following death, women gathered, wailing. Corpse not bathed; wrapped (by relative or nonrelative) in buckskin or in blanket of cliffrose bark, together with personal effects. According to Sapir, belongings first destroyed so as to be of no further value. Body borne on litter of 3 lashed poles; deposited in a rock shelter and covered with stones; no particular orientation.

House torn down and location shifted, even if deceased a child and if death took place elsewhere. With a man were buried his bows, arrows, buckskins; with a woman, her baskets, buckskins. Mealing stone broken, thrown away. Ordinarily some skins retained for use of family. Horse of the deceased might be strangled (Sapir: or shot), either at grave or elsewhere, "in the hills." If needy, relatives ate the sacrificed animal as a matter of economy. If 2 horses, one might be killed; other spared for use of relatives, but its mane and tail docked. No necessity of trading such a horse for another.

Mourners, especially women, cut hair. Amount shorn not in direct proportion to degree of relationship to deceased. In former times, no other public expression of grief; no slashing; no application of ashes; no ban against bathing. Late introduction of "Cry" ceremony noted above (p. 95).

Suicide unknown. Name of dead avoided; "just forgot it." According to Sapir, any animal or object after which the deceased was named, no longer mentioned directly, but by circumlocution. After death, soul "went away"; no particular abode specified; Sapir's informant thought it wandered westward. Milky way apparently not considered road of dead.

Diversions

Dancing, games, and recitation of folk tales are mentioned as diversions.

A man, usually an elderly one, was the raconteur of the tales, but in dancing and games, women participated to a considerable extent. They danced, either with the men or by themselves, in the traditional circle dance; for it, a woman might even be the principal singer, although probably never the dance chief. Both sexes performed jointly in the bear dance, which was intrusive in comparatively recent times. Although women did not share the target games with which men and boys amused themselves, they might organize all-women teams for shinny, and they were not barred from playing the hand game.

Two recreational activities were limited to winter, when snakes were not in evidence. Then only, with impunity, could the (rabbit-skull) ring and pin game be played and could folk tales be related. Indulgence out of season might result in snake bite.

Kaibab diversions were geared to the small number of families that camped together in an economic cluster. There are specific indications that the circle dance usually was performed by comparatively close neighbors-- although, in post-horse times, a dubiously identified Ute group took to visiting in the fall, to hunt on the Kaibab Plateau and, on these occasions, joined in the circle dance (p.34). The bear dance, it is said, did not attract visitors from other groups.

In fall, there was a general exodus to the Kaibab Plateau to hunt deer and, in winter, to the edge of the Grand Canyon, to gather mescal. Accordingly, during several months of the year, intermittently at least, people of the various economic clusters might well have camped in reasonable proximity. Nevertheless, there is no more indication of bandwide sociability than there is of bandwide collaboration in economic pursuits (pp. 23-4).

It is almost certain that large gatherings--attended by most of the Kaibab, as well as by other Paiute--are a relatively late development. They may date from the turn of the century, with the introduction of the "Cry" (p. 95). In fact, the "Cry" perhaps will prove to have been the forerunner of the "big times" (kiapɨ) (p. 33) of recent years, when large numbers of Paiute and neighboring peoples assemble, to sing and dance. Unfortunately, I recorded no information on either "big times" or the eventual fate of the "Cry." Indubitably, inter-band sociability was facilitated through concentration of the population on reservations and through the development of modern communications; it probably was not part of the native social scheme.

Dances

The only traditional dance among the Kaibab was the circle, round or "squaw" dance; others were introduced relatively late, roughly within a decade of one another.

The "Cry"--which derives ultimately from the Colorado River mourning ceremony--has been mentioned in connection with life crises (p. 95). It was known to the Kaibab in 1894, according to Sapir's informant, and his statement suggests more or less the same dating for the ghost dance. At the time of the latter, he was about 5 years old; if he were 20 in 1910, when he worked with Sapir, the middle 1890's would be indicated. He did not relate "Cry" and ghost dance, despite their common focus on the dead and apparent contemporaneity. In 1910, he reported the ghost dance discredited: "they do not like to sing those songs, for they claim the dances 'ate up' the people; all the prohets died"--as Sapir comments, "probably from over-exertion" (see below).

The bear dance seems to have been introduced from the Koosharem, but possibly from the Cedar Paiute, in the early 1900's. KC said it was not known when she was "a little girl" but was adopted while she was at school (in Panguitch), "about 25 years ago." That would mean 1907. However, Sapir's informant was 8 or 9 years old when the bear dance reached the Kaibab, and this suggests introduction about the turn of the century. Perhaps specific dating could be established through the records of the United States Indian Service. Both G and one Tom, who was instrumental in launching the dance, noted that the appearance coincided with the building of the school at Moccasin.

The scalp dance was mentioned by Sapir's informant, who considered it more Ute than Paiute. Presumably he had witnessed the dance. At least, he described clockwise movement to the accompaniment of a drum; the scalp hung on a pole inside the house; hitting of scalp with a stick carried by dancers. It is difficult to associate the scalp dance with the apparently pusillanimous Kaibab, yet there is one report of a scalping in 1869-1870 by a "friendly" Paiute (presumably Kaibab) who accompanied Hamblin in pursuit of Navajo raiders (Dellenbaugh, 1926, 170). Moreover, Sapir's informant reported that on one occasion "some drunken Paiutes" sang the scalp dance preparatory to getting even with an enemy, who was, at the moment, engaged in a round dance. "At a given signal they all... pounced upon him, but other Indians held them in check and tied them... until they... sobered."

Circle dance.--Round dance (kwinunɨp, apparently literal translation; Sapir, 1930, 648, kwinun?nu-, to revolve) held "any time, day or night, winter or summer" (Hillers' plates in Steward, 1939, Pls. 7, 8). Both sexes participated; sometimes, women alone, hence name of "squaw" dance. No musical instrument; no masks; no special paraphernalia or raiment. Faces painted with "all kinds of designs" (Fig. 7); but some painted face daily, hence not necessarily embellishment exclusively for dance.

Circle-dance leader (p. 30) chosen more or less as was subsistence chief. Selection discussed openly; no feeling that appointment need be kept in family; "they picked the best man, someone not too old."

In "early" times, dancers circled around "tall pole in the middle [of the circle], just for fun"; Dellenbaugh (1926, 178) describes cedar tree, stripped of all branches, "but a small tuft at the top, and around this the whole band [?] formed a large circle, dancing and singing."

Fire built to one side of circle (only when performance at night?); dance chief stood there; joined singing but did not dance. Within circle was song leader, "a man who liked to sing"; sometimes a woman was song leader. Chief directed singer to start; he began singing alone, and others joined. Dellenbaugh (1926, 178) regards man within circle as "seeming to be the custodian of the songs and a poet himself. He would first recite the piece, and then all would sing it, circling round at the same time." Dance chief apparently selected song or songs; Sapir states that "in any one single dance only one song is sung."

Men and women alternated in circle, holding hands, fingers interdigitated. Faced inward. Movement clockwise. 2 steps described. Some dancers stepped to the left with left foot, then brought right foot up to it; then another step to the left. Others shuffled along, pivoting first on heels, then on toes. Sapir's description more specific:

All hold each other's hands. Left hand held down, palm facing body, interlocked finger for finger (thumb under, little finger on outside) in right hand of dancer on left. Right hand held palm away from body and interlocked (thumb inside, little finger on top) with left hand of dancer on right. Circled clockwise, facing in. Step to every beat in bar by lifting left foot slightly (toes at angle to left) and stepping to left; right foot (toes straight to front) dragged after it on end of beat.

Songs for circle dance evidently numerous. (Dr. Sapir writes [personal communication, June 20, 1932] that "there is also a good deal of material on Paiute music which perhaps we need not trouble with at the moment." He [Sapir, 1930, 300] mentions "a series of over two hundred songs, chiefly ceremonial.") G comments concerning them as follows: "There are many songs that go with a circle dance. [They] sing about the sun, clouds, stars, rabbits, mountain sheep, deer, birds, eagle.... In the fall they have a dance when they are hunting rabbits... this is a rabbit dance and [they] sing about rabbits. [They danced] two nights usually."

New songs acquired through dreams and then "tried out." This suggests Mohave focus on dreams might have percolated through the "Cry," but perhaps not, for Kaibab shamans acquired tutelary spirits in dreams and they provided "a song or songs to be used in curing" (Kelly, 1939, 152). Probably Dellenbaugh (1926, 178) is correct in assuming that "the poet seemed to originate some of the songs, but they had others that were handed down." He reports 1 theme concerned with the necessity of killing "your rabbit...before you eat him."

Circle dance provided opportunity for courtship and philandering; "used to marry at this dance."

Ghost dance.-- My data negative. G claimed to know nothing of ghost dance. M had heard of no dance to restore dead, nor of one "dreamed," nor of one that involved danger of being turned to stone. S heard first of such a dance when she moved to Moccasin reservation; thought "the Utes talked about it." Claimed never to have seen a performance. All information below from Sapir's informant:

Usually, but not invariably, dance corral prepared by stacking branches--preferably willow, sometimes cedar--to form circle 60 to 70 ft. dia. Branches piled to height of 4 or 5 ft.; 4 openings, each about 4 ft. wide. In center of corral, set up cedar pole 20 ft. tall. From its tip hung a string to which 2 feathers tied. One, a large feather from eagle's tail, painted red; other, from soft white feathers beneath tail. No restriction on touching pole.

Sometimes prophet (paaruguc, said to refer in later times to "anyone that composes a round dance"), whose dreamt songs were sung, set up serviceberry cane in place of central pole. Carved hook or knob at the top, from which the usual 2 feathers suspended. Only prophet might touch cane and feathers. At end of dance, he took cane home; stood it in doorway of dwelling or at head of bed, where nobody could touch it. Several prophets had such cane and feathers, and "some of them" were Kaibab. (The wording certainly implies non-Kaibab participants. In view of my informants' statements, it makes me wonder if Tony Tillohash may have been describing the ghost dance he witnessed among some neighboring group, not Kaibab.)

No activities by day. Dance usually started about 7 p.m and lasted until midnight. Continued night after night for many months, perhaps a year or two. Everyone supposed to attend; otherwise would turn into a crow, stone, or other animal or object.

Dancing clockwise, similar to ordinary round dance; no special costumes. During the dance, the prophets would fall suddenly into a trance; on awakening, would foretell various events, such as approach of a storm. They claimed dead relatives would return if people danced.

At conclusion of dance, "used to trill lips on high note"; this the signal for an extra-quick step. Song continued, but at much faster time. Some dancers fell owing to increased speed, which lasted about a minute.

Bear dance.--One Tom, already mentioned (p. 104) was prominent in introduction of bear dance. According to KC, he was a Koosharem resident among Kaibab; living in his house was another Koosharem named Moustache. Latter "sang every night"; taught bear dance songs to "men and women." Remained 2 years among Kaibab, then returned to Koosharem where, now blind, he still resided in 1932.

Sapir's informant described Tom as young man of Cedar City Paiute, "who has been much with the Utes." He credited him and a shaman named Mampuc* with launching of bear dance among Kaibab. Tom, who was at Moccasin during my stay, said he came originally from Yantarɨi, the "other side" of Henry Mountains, apparently between the Dirty Devil and Green rivers (pp.144-5). His

---

*There is uncertainty concerning the affiliation of Mampuc. In Sapir's notes on the bear dance he is described as one of the "Arizona Paiutes who had traveled much among Southern Utes." In a published account (Sapir, 1930, 473, 477, 534, fn. 102) he appears as "chief of the Cedar City Paiutes," and he and others of that group showed Tom and the Kaibab the bear songs and dance. There is not much possibility that Mampuc and Moustache are one and the same; at least, in Sapir's notes on the "Cry," both are mentioned--Mampuc arrived from Escalante (Kaiparowits country) to make arrangements for the ceremony, whereas Frank Moustache was said to be from St. George. The chances are excellent, however, that Tom of the bear dance is the Tom "Pickavits" of the "Cry," and apparently an innovator of both ceremonies. Lamentably, I did not undertake to disentangle these details in the field; at that time, it would have beem comparatively simple to have identified individuals and perhaps to have established dates more definitively.

mother was from Kaiviyɨgacɨ (mountain turn, presumably at the base of Circle Cliffs, in the Kaiparowits area (pp.143-4), and the family moved there when Tom was a "big boy." Prior to the move, he learned the bear dance and said that it reached the Yantari from the Uintah Ute. His statement follows:

I came here and married, about 47 years ago. I learned the bear dance before I went to Kaiviyɨgacɨ. The story is like this [Sapir, 1930, 351, has another version]:

Once in the fall a man came to where a bear lay asleep in her hole. The man took off his clothes; he was naked. He had two partners with him. He told his partners, "Come back in March (tamanɨ). He went in there and slept all winter with the bear.

His partners came back and talked to him. They asked, "Are you all right?" He said he was. He came out. He was all covered with hair. He could still talk. He told them not to be afraid; [that] he was still their partner. He said, "I'll give you a bear dance. I'll give you songs and the step. I will dance. My wife [the bear] and I will give them to you. Dance this in March. Now go and tell all the Indians." He told them, too, "Make a stick [rasp]; cut notches in it. When you come back next time, I'll go with you."

They told the people, "He will give us a dance and songs. He has a bear wife now. He is covered with hair; he has claws now."

Ten days went by. He told them to tie all the dogs or his wife might get angry. He said, "The two of us will come now." He went to camp. He sang for them. They did not understand the dance. "You will learn," he told them, "Dance and sing all day long." Near sundown he talked to them: "I give you song; I give you dance. All right. You learn. I never more here." Then he left with his wife. He told his partners, "For ten years, don't kill any bear; you might be killing me."

A long time ago the Uintah Utes did not have this dance. The Utes have it all the time in March. The Rabbit Valley people and the Kanosh people had it. The Yantari learned it from the Uintah when I was a big boy. Rabbit Valley people danced it in winter, until March. They think that if they sing the songs in summer a bear will kill them.

-ooo-

Tom said bear dance songs in Ute; confirmed by texts provided by Tony Tillohash (Sapir, 1930, 533, fn. 91). Tom claimed he learned songs from his grandfather, who had met 4 bears "who sang to him in Indian language." Graciously accepted responsibility of having taught bear dance to Kaibab; no mention of collaboration with Moustache or Mampuc. (Sapir's informant commented, puzzled, that when the bear dance was introduced, Tom ordered 6 holes to be dug in line, about 20 ft. apart, and had 10 ft. cedar posts set in them. He is said to have offered no explanation of this "fence" which, moreover, seems never to have been used.)

Information from my other informants summarized as follows:

Ute known to hold dance in spring, but Kaibab might have it "any time." Called "all the people, old and young," men and women. Dance held in afternoon and evening 2 to 4 hours.

Open plot, no enclosure. 4 or 5 men gathered to one side to sing. Placed tub over small pit and used it as rasp resonator (Pl. 7, d; Fig. 14). No recollection of basket resonator. Many songs, in "Ute language."

Male and female dancers formed separate lines, 1 either side of tub and singers. Women selected partners, using long wand to tap chosen man. If he did not want to accept, "some of the boys went after him." No dire consequences thought to follow refusal to dance, but if anyone should fall, performance halted.

Procedure not clear. One placed 1 hand on partner's shoulder and "sometimes the man's arm was around the girl's waist." Danced "in separate couples, back and forth."

Kaibab instrumental in carrying bear dance westward. One "Christmas we went to St. George and danced all night." A St. George informant concurred: "Tom, at Moccasin, used to live to the north. He brought it [bear dance] to Moccasin, and it came here from there."

Sapir's informant reported (cf. p. 174) bear dance sometimes performed by Arizona (San Juan) Paiute; those of St. George and of the Muddy (Moapa) had seen dance but did not perform it, for want of trained singers.

Sapir's notes include wealth of material on bear dance -- mostly on narrow strips of paper, apparently cut from pages with other topics. Below, I have organized his data somewhat; direct quotation if any doubt concerning meaning.

Bear dance (mama?koo?; Sapir, 1930, 564) generally held in March; sometimes in summer, whenever there was a general gathering or "good time." No visitors from other bands; danced by local people, with local attendance. Performance lasted 4 days--presumably each afternoon of 4 days, for informant declared dance ended about sundown. However, he also reported that well-versed singer could last the night without repeating his songs.

Interpretation of dance related to tale concerning its origin Sapir, 1930, 351). Women dancers represented bear women; the men, humans who danced with bears. Performance supposed to give power to escape from bear. Man who refused to dance when woman selected him as partner would have difficult time in actual encounter with a bear.

No formal dance leader; 2 or 3 "officers" either self-appointed, or agreed upon in advance by men; women had no voice in selection. Dance began when 6 to 8 men sat in circle on ground, surrounding dish pan (formerly, a round basket), inverted over shallow excavation. Rasps rested on pan (Pl. 7, d); they sang to accompaniment of rasping.

The singing "a sort of signal" for beginning the dance. Those who wished to participate joined; others observed. Women gathered on side "away from the singers"; men, near the singers. Female contingent advanced toward singers, on a flat, stamped-out dance ground. Did not approach in regular line nor keep time to music. Each woman selected a man as partner, touching him with willow wand or throwing pebbles at him. A man reluctant to dance prodded with a pole or branch carried by one of the "officers."

In time to music, each woman retreated backward, followed at a distance by the man to be her partner. Sometimes pair advanced and retreated several times before assuming stance of partners. Dancing pairs did not keep in line; each pair moved back and forth independently.

In time, if not immediately, partners faced one another. Each placed right hand on other's left shoulder. Left hand usually behind partner's waist; one statement to the effect that partners clasped their left hands.

Pair now moved together but apparently made no effort to keep time to singing and rasping; some pairs moved rapidly, some slowly. Direction of movement not clear. One passage describes dance as "the moving of the two lines toward each other, stopping, then moving back, and so on repeatedly." Step described as "sort of light springy walk or semi-hop."

If one member of the pair gave out, place taken immediately by a friend. The man and woman must not stop dancing at same time; apparently the pair, even with substitutions, must continue throughout. Probably this applies to a given song rather than to entire session, for it is said that, following interval between songs, other parties might dance, or same ones continue.

When a dancer stumbled or fell, it was said, "Alas, my friend, having a jack-rabbit stomach" (Sapir, 1930, 628), and one of the musicians ran quickly to the person, placed his rasp on the latter's back and rasped rapidly.

Rasp described as a long, "somewhat oblong stick," serrated along one side with angular notches (Fig. 14). Rested on dishpan resonator by an edge cut obliquely at one end, on side opposite notching (Pl. 7, d). Noise produced by rubbing cylindrical piece of wood along notches. Some rasps were large, some small.

Two styles of rasping. One used by Mampuc, the other by Tom (p. 107). Former rubbed in one direction only, toward himself, "two beats to each bar." In contrast, Tom rasped "four times to [the] bar, alternately toward and away from himself, [the] main beat coming on the rasp towards himself, with which he begins" [began].

Before start of singing, customary to have "one bar of rasping" --that is, with Mampuc, 2 beats toward himself; with Tom, 4 beats. Sometimes only half a bar was rasped. At end of a song, rasp played with strokes twice as rapid as those before, the last being outward and most accented. Musicians might follow either style; not necessary for all of group to rasp the same way.

On quiet evening, sound of rasping carried 2 or 3 mi.--much farther than singing. Each bear-dance singer sang as loudly as possible, which was not true of "Cry" singers. At conclusion of dance, resonator returned to its usual place; rasps and sticks left in the hole and abandoned.

Informant thought there must be several hundred bear-dance songs; old men who knew all of them would be able to sing the entire night without duplication. He said songs were in Paiute, but Sapir says texts he gave were Ute. Songs "seemed to follow in a certain order." Each song consisted of a statement or of a question and answer that referred to some incident of tale allegedly accounting for origin of dance (p.108; Sapir, 1930, 351).

When dance introduced to Kaibab, Mampuc sang first--his songs with Paiute words [sic]. Subsequently, Tom sang, but mostly songs without words; these considered the more difficult. One of Tom's songs with text, thought an original composition, ran thus: "Let us go back home, my friend.--No, we are traveling about just for fun."

Song usually lasted 5 to 10 min.; after short interval, another started and dancing resumed. Last song the longest; called "moving the longest distance," it lasted 20 to 30 min.

Games

The Kaibab had a fair number of games of chance and skill, most of them competitive. Gambling was associated primarily with the hand game, but wagers were made in shinny, and arrows were forfeited in target games. Women did not compete in the latter, nor were any games associated exclusively with them. However, they might play the hand game, presumably among themselves, and two female teams sometimes competed in shinny. The rabbit-skull variety of ring and pin was played by old and young, irrespective of sex. Most of the games and diversions reported for children seem to apply to boys.

Seasonal aspects were not pronounced, and there is specific mention that the hand game and shinny were played any time of year. However, ring and pin was a winter game; if played at any other season, there was risk of snake bite.

Hand game (naiaŋwɨpɨ; Sapir: naiyaŋwipi).--Said to have been learned "from people to the north" long ago, before informants' birth. A man's game (Steward, 1939, Pl. 10, a), although women sometimes played. No seasonal restrictions; could be played any time of year, inside house or outdoors. No way of insuring luck, although Sapir's informant thought a mirror placed secretly behind opponent aided guessing. Participants and spectators bet blankets, buckskin, arrows, even horses; wagers usually piled in front of opposing teams. Sapir: piled behind winners; horses need not be present to be wagered: "people remembered who bet horses."

Two teams, 6 to 8 persons each. At start, each team had 7 counters (naŋwitup), bunched and stuck in ground at an angle. Sapir: 8 to 10 counters preferred, in order to avoid short game and quick loss; more counters gave losing side chance for turn of luck.

Played with 4 small bone or wooden cylinders (Sapir: called naiyaŋ-wi numpii). 2 plain, 2 marked by being tied with a bit of string (Sapir: marked bone wrapped in center with sinew, glued with pinyon gum; Culin [1907, 311] wrapped with sinew or buckskin). Cylinders kept in small bag hung inside dwelling. 2 members of "hiding" team, each one with a plain and marked cylinder, "shuffled" beneath a blanket, sometimes tossing cylinders in air, eventually hiding them in closed fists. Sapir: playing side continued shifting bones (apparently until final guess). Several experimental guesses before final one. One of opposing team guessed; if successful, he continued perhaps several games; otherwise replaced by teammate.

Tried to guess location of plain cylinders. Sapir: bone to be guessed called pakau ? numpi; other bone not named. 4 arrangements of cylinders possible (X: marked bone):

	Name	Designated by
XOOX	sikavi, or wipi; Sapir: tiragwapi, between, center	Pointing between two hiders with forefinger or with hand in vertical plane
OXXO	wikavi; Sapir: wigaavi, summit	Extending hand horizontally, palm down, thumb and forefinger spread apart (Steward, 1939, Pl. 10, a)
OXOX	mɨwiviarɨkɨ; Sapir: tɨ, up	Waving arm in arc to left
XOXO	mɨwiviarɨkɨ; Sapir: tiva, down	Waving arm in arc to right

Sapir: guesser did not use above terms; exclaimed "A, i, " or "ei" when finally guessed. My informants said guess might be designated with either hand; a man clasped free hand on chest; woman did not. Sapir: guess designated with left hand, right fist on breast.

For incorrect guess, 2 counters forfeited to hiding team; for partially correct guess (e.g., OXOX for OXXO, etc.), 1 counter forfeited. Unlike Owens Valley and Surprise Valley Paiute (Steward, 1933, 286; Kelly, 1932, 173) who withdrew 2 cylinders from play at a "half correct" guess, hiding continued with 4 cylinders until a completely correct guess was made. Sapir: correct guess called "kill both." Thereupon cylinders relinquished to opposing team without transfer of counters. Game ended when 1 team won all counters.

Both sides sang at once; Sapir: guessing side did not sing; Culin (1907, 312, quoting Hillers): hiding team chanted first, then guessing team. Did not beat time; Sapir: sometimes playing side beat with sticks on small log in front of them.

Sapir: cheating by holding both cylinders in one hand; if opponents guessed hand without bones he lost ([?] apparently reference to version played with 2 instead of 4 cylinders). If they guessed hand with both bones, hider deftly jerked bone by pressure with index finger along inside of arm into other hand. Kaibab said once to have lost heavily to Moapa through this trick.

Stick dice (tačanaipi). -- Played by S's husband ("Chuarruumpeak," mentioned frequently by Powell), but "he played alone because no one else knew the game." S thought he might have learned from Cedar band. Played with 8 dice, one face red, the other unpainted. Thrown endwise on metate; scored according to number of upturned plain faces. S did not know method of recording but it was "by making marks on a board." Absence of game among Kaibab confirmed by M. But Culin (1907, 166-7) describes 2 sets from the "Paiute" of Southern Utah and speaks of "a large number of other sets of

Fig. 16. Stick dice, "white" and red. Scale not given. Sketch with Sapir's field notes; perhaps models made by Tony Tillohash, his Kaibab informant, 1910.

these cane dice." Sapir's account (Fig. 16) brief; differs from above in not specifying metate and in adding scoring details. Each upturned plain face counted 1 point; recorded by placing stick on ground at proper interval between series of sticks stood in a row. To complete game, traversed row of sticks and returned.

Four-stick game. -- Either unknown, or, through oversight, not recorded. Culin (1907, 334) describes a set in the U.S. National Museum attributed to the Paiute of southern Utah, accompanied by a statement from Hiller that the game was "played by Indians on the Muddy [Moapa] reservation." However, the Hillers plate reproduced by Culin apparently refers to the Vegas Paiute (cf. Steward, 1939, Pl. 4, a).

Basket dice.-- Apparently unknown.

Ring and pin (tasɨŋinipi; Sapir: tasin?nipi, rabbit-head game) -- Not a gambling game. Rabbit skull attached by sinew cord to sharpened stick of Chrysothamnus; nowadays hairpin or safety pin somethines substituted for stick. Culin (1907, 554) describes two ring and pin sets from southern Utah--1 "ring" is a rabbit skull; the other a small hollow tube with a notch cut through one side (Fig. 17). "Many people played" rabbit-skull game; seated in circle. 2 leaders chose members respective teams. Sapir; might be played by an even number of people, men, women, or children; divided into pairs (apparently within team) All on one team called nanarigiwuŋw, friends.

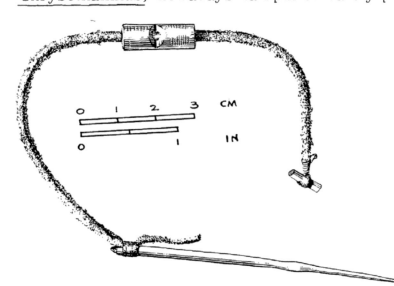

Fig. 17. Ring-and-pin game; bone bead, wooden pin. PM 9433. Palmer collection, southern Utah, 1875, band provenience unknown.

A person played until he failed to catch skull on pin, whereupon member of other team took turn.

Scoring: nose, ear, eye apertures, 2 points; tooth sockets, 5; small hole below ear opening, 10; tiny hole either side of nasal aperture won game. Sapir: tooth sockets, 3; one of 2 holes at end of row of teeth, 10, other parts of skull, 1.

Row of 10, sometimes 15 parallel lines drawn on ground, with long central line cutting across them at right angles; central line called creek, stream. Each team had stick marker (called togoni, mother's father). Marker placed on appropriate line according to points scored. Both teams started at same end, same side of "creek"; advanced to far end, crossed creek, returned on other side; reversed, and returned to starting point. In other words, traversed course 4 times, first and fourth laps on one side of "creek," second and third on other side. First team to complete course won game. No notion of "killing" opponent through coincidence of markers.

At conclusion of game, each side struggled for marker ("grandfather") of opposing team, trying to throw it in fire. Sapir says further that men of one team tried to protect their marker by tossing it in an obscure spot, meantime struggling for that of opponents. Sometimes marker passed from person to person, relay fashion. At start of game might agree not to burn each other's (tuguuhi) homonymous with "my snake." Danger of snake bite if game played any season but winter or if cord attaching pin broke during play.

Hoop and pole. --Denied by informants; absence confirmed by Sapir's notes, although Culin (1907, 498) figures a netted hoop and 2 feather darts from the Palmer collection in Peabody Museum, attributed to the Paiute of southern Utah.

Shinny (nanawapɨ; Sapir: nanauapɨ). --Played any time of year, men against men or women against women; usually 5 to 6 on a team. Field not measured (Sapir: might be 1/2 mi. to 1 mi. long). Stick set at either end as goal (Sapir: tree usually served as goal, kwa?a?nuŋwa). Shinny sticks (nanawapɨ; Sapir: kwipan?ɨmpi) curved at end. Ball of stuffed buckskin (Sapir: formerly filled with deer hair), sewn. Buried in center of field (Sapir: ca. 4 in. deep); knocked out by players of opposing team, who struck separately, not simultaneously. No goal guards; players scattered. Bets on outcome. Sapir: at conclusion of game teams changed goals for next game.

Single-goal ball (football). --Unknown.

Juggling. --Unknown.

Target games.--Numerous. One called nanawačapi, shooting (Sapir: naaŋwʔaičai). Root of narrow-leaved yucca tossed into juniper tree, several boys shooting as it fell. He whose arrow hit root first won; did not count if 2 arrows hit simultaneously. Winner took arrows of other lads and was entitled to pet squirrel. Others helped search for a squirrel. Sapir: root thrown into tree; if stuck, lads divided into teams to see who could hit it first. Root regarded as "deer"; he who hit it would be good hunter.

Another target game (maičtui; Sapir: maitʔuipi) same as preceding but root stationary. Sapir's account the reverse of mine: in former game, root stationary; in this spun in air. His description follows: several, perhaps 5, played. 1 player threw root any distance, others shooting immediately it touched ground. One who hit first had chance, as follows, to win arrows of others. He picked up root, spinning it in air and calling out, "maituʔi." Others, in line, shot at root. If 1 or more members of both teams hit root, tie declared and all retained arrows. Otherwise spinner had chance to win arrows that missed the goal. These he took, shooting them at root, which he himself spun in air, perhaps directly in front of his bow. Arrows with which he hit root then belonged to him; others returned to owners. Yucca root used because soft and did not blunt arrow point.

Sapir describes several more arrow games:

Narači kwuʔipi; could be played by 2, usually by 4, men or boys grouped as partners. 2 arrows placed slanting in ground about 100 yds. apart. Partners split, and paired opponents stood by each arrow. 1 pair shot first, individually, a first arrow, then a second. The one landing closest to fixed arrow scored 1 point; 2, if it touched. Then opposing pair shot. Game won with 12 points.

Paagauʔainapi; similar game, but arrow thrown as dart, without bow. Held with point in hand, nock up arm.

Načua kwiʔi; still another arrow game, played while walking, often on return from hunt. One player shot an arrow to serve as target; others, divided in 2 teams, tried to hit it. 6 to 8 counters held by 1 member of each team; counters delivered to custodian of side that won, 1 or 2 according to points scored. Scoring as above: 1 point for shot nearest fixed arrow; 2 for shot that touched it. Each player put up stake, such as an arrow, against that of player of opposing team. Group continued walking; when fixed arrow reached, it was shot forward again and game resumed.

Foot races; wrestling (nanaŋw?unai, throw one another) -- Considered modern by Sapir's informant; wrestling holds the same as those used by whites.

-ooo-

Children's games and diversions are mentioned below; much of the information concerning target games and sham fights comes from Sapir's notes.

Hidden object (na?apoguipi; Sapir: maavuguipi). -- A child's game; no betting. Player holding pebble trailed hand about ground in circle, dropping stone there after forming earth into 7 to 10 small piles, one of which contained pebble. Other players guessed in which pile pebble concealed. Correct guess won right to hide. Sapir adds: an incorrect guess eliminated that particular pile of earth; next player had one less from which to choose.

Tops. -- Not mentioned by my informants. From the Palmer collection, Culin (1907, 744) figures 2 " with clay whorls... cemented with gum, having wooden pins."

Cat's cradle (string figures). -- Not known to Kaibab; absence confirmed by Sapir's informant.

Tag (ininpiŋkiupi, ghost play; Sapir: inipintupi, ghost game, ghost making). -- One child pretends he is a ghost (inipic); chases others, tagging them anywhere on body, whereupon they become ghosts and help chase others. Sapir: when all are ghosts, start anew; game usually played on banks of a wash. A Hillers photo, attributed to the Kaibab by Dellenbaugh (1909, 134), shows boys playing "wolf and deer." Of this, I have no description.

Sling (siimu). -- Of untanned deerskin, with strings of yucca fiber. Boys threw stones, sometimes killing birds. Sapir: cords attached to rawhide sling through holes; one cord with ring at end for finger. Sling fights between 2 teams as sport.

Popgun. -- Described by Sapir's informant, who was not sure it was native. Pith tamped (pushed?) from length of [elder] by rosewood stick somewhat longer than resulting tube. The tube was wetted (?); 2 or 3 wetted rag balls inserted tightly at one end so that one partly protruded. Tube held slantingly upward; ball forced out "with a smack" by loose stick. New rag balls added as necessary. Boys had sham battles or deer hunts, in which one team pretended to be deer.

Fillip (waʔaampigu kukwʔinumpu, juniper-berry shooter).--Also described by Sapir's informant. Branch of juniper, 1/2 to 1 ft. long, whittled thin and flat at one end. Other end held in right fist. Cedar berry put on flexible end, which was held toward body; berry shot off slingwise. No sham battles or team games; in winter, piece of charcoal placed on snow to serve as target.

Mud fights (wianagukwi).--Also described by Sapir. Played by boys, sometimes by men. Soft clump of mud slapped on switch end of juniper branch. Latter swung, releasing mud. Sometimes shot at objects or animals (birds, rabbits). One young man said to have lost an eye in sham mud fight.

Stilts (paagainʔnumpu).--Sapir: while camping on Kaibab Plateau, boys played with stilts made of crotched branch of aspen. Crotch about 3 ft. from ground and just large enough to support foot. Not a regular game. My informants (M, S) thought stilts not native.

Dolls.--Little girls played with dolls (kiŋwaʔa), which they made of juniper bark (Pl. 6) or clay (Pl. 4, h-j). Latter rolled between palms, shaped; features gouged. Figures dried in sun, never fired. Dolls not dressed, but wrapped in rabbitskin. Today small girls ingeniously fashion rag dolls.

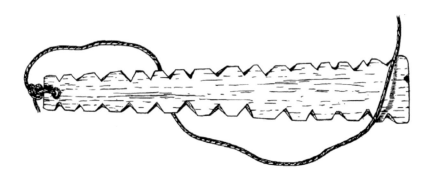

Fig. 18. Bull roarer. A toy, but may cause wind and attract evil spirits. Scale not given. Sketch with Sapir's field notes; probably model made by Tony Tillohash, his Kaibab informant, 1910.

Bull roarer.-- A man sometimes made bull roarer (nanimutanɨmpɨ) (Fig. 18) as toy for his grandchild. Dry piece of juniper, about 8 in. long; flat; both sides painted with "straight lines" in black and white; some "had dots." String about 1 yd. long, of milkweed or narrow-leaf yucca. Not a musical instrument. Mothers objected to bull roarer as a toy, because it "might make too much wind, and no way to stop the wind." According to Sapir, bull roarer might attract evil spirits as well as make the wind blow.

Slide.--Sapir reports that couples slid downhill on snow, seated on deerskin, hair side down.

Narration of Folk Tales

The circumstances surrounding the recitation of folk tales are poryed vividly in Sapir's notes; the following is taken directly from them:

Myths were never told in summer, for then snakes would bite the narrator; in winter, they were told, for there were no snakes at that time. Once a myth was started, it would be finished; otherwise, the winter would be lengthened, part of the summer becoming winter.

A favorite time for telling myths was in the evening when all had laid themselves away to go to sleep. Some man, generally an elderly person, would half-lie, half-sit, with his head propped up by a log or mass of blankets, and tell myths far into the night.... The auditors were expected to show their attention by comments (such as mgm or uuwai, "yes") or by laughing at the humorous passages. If the full point of any passage was not appreciated, it might be repeated, such repetitions often stringing out a story beyond its proper length.

Gradually the auditors dozed off; it rarely happened that most of them, particularly the children, were "lucky" enough to hear to the end.... If the narrator found that no one responded to his good points, he would suddenly stop and call out, "Are you listening?" If no one answered, he might wake the people and continue.

The older Indians still believe these myths to be true. An anecdote is related of a St. George Indian, who listened to the words of a white preacher at the mission church, as he told of the origins of things as related in the Bible. After he had concluded, the Indian arose and told his Indian friends, "Now this man has finished telling you stories. Now I am going to tell you Indian stories, and true ones." The anecdote was related from place to place and considered a good joke on the white man.

Sapir adds that myths, no matter how obscene, were told in the presence of women and children; "nothing was thought of this."

Kinship Terminology

The kinship terminology recorded is incomplete in designations for the great-grandparent and great-grandchild horizons and for relatives by marriage; additional detail on application of reciprocal terms also would be useful.

There is emphasis on age distinction in references to siblings and cousins, uncles and aunts, and nephews and nieces. Reciprocal terms are well developed in association with diminutives (Sapir, 1930, 171-2), and in this connection Gifford's (1917, 220) admirably clear statement is applicable: "the diminutive suffix... is often added to an identical reciprocal term to indicate the younger generation of the reciprocal relationship." Thus the terms for grandchildren are the diminutives of those for grandparents, and the terms for nephews and nieces, the diminutives of those for uncles and aunts.

Cousin marriage is barred. Cousins, both parallel and cross, call one another brother and sister--either older or younger, according to the age of the cousins,, not that of the parents. When informants speak English, they use "half brother" or "half sister" for a cousin. In spite of the fusion of siblings and cousins, the terms for parents are not extended to uncles and aunts, nor are the terms for one's own offspring applied to nephews and nieces.

Parallel and cross uncles and aunts are distinguished and are further segregated by age, except for the father's sister (no. 20, below); for the latter, the reciprocal term (no. 21) confirms the lack of age separation. There is, incidentally, a parallel absence among the Kawaiisu (Gifford, 1917, 235).

A whole series of terms clearly reflects the levirate and sororate. One (no. 18, below) groups the father's younger brother, the mother's younger sister's husband, and the stepfather; another (no. [24a]), the mother's younger sister, the father's (presumably younger) brother's wife, and the stepmother. Reciprocals for each (nos. 19 and [24b]) refer respectively to a man's older brother's child and to a stepchild; and to a woman's older sister's child and to a stepchild. There is, however, no age differentiation in a term said to mean "second husband" (no. 32) and applied to the husband's brother and to a woman's sister's husband, nor in one for "second wife" (no. 31), synonymous with wife's sister and a man's brother's wife.

As Steward (1938, 289) notes, the marriage of a brother and sister to a sister and brother is consonant with the use of one term for husband's sister and woman's brother's wife (no. 30), and to one for wife's brother and man's sister's husband (no. 29).

In grandparent-grandchild terms, the Kaibab share what Steward (1938, 286) calls a "universal feature of Shoshonean terminology," in that there is "segregation of the four grandparents and the use of a reciprocal term between each of them and the grandchild." When informants speak English, they refer to the mother's father as grandfather, but the father's father is "great grandfather."

One term (no. [32a]) is not defined. In a specific case, it was applied to a remote relative whose "grandmothers were some relation." It likewise was said to refer to "someone you feed"; hence certain obligation on the score of hospitality is involved.

In the listing below, numbers correspond to those used by Gifford (1917, 245-6) in his comparison of Kaibab and Kawaiisu terminology; later (pp. 126-9) that relationship will be examined anew, in the light of present data. Numbers in brackets refer to terms I have interpolated. All my Kaibab data come from KC, who gave three variants of most terms: the first refers to the speaker's relative; the second, to that of the person addressed; the third, to the relative of another individual, usually not present.

1. muani, mua?ami, muaŋi
    Father.
2. piani, pia?ami, piaŋi
    Mother.
3. tuani, tua?ami, tuaŋ
    Son.
4. pačɨni, pačɨ?ɨmi, pačɨaŋ
    Daughter.
5. pavicin, pavicimi, pavicaŋ
    Older brother, older male cousin.
6. čakaitinɨ čakaicimi, čakaiciaŋ
    Younger brother, younger male cousin.
7. pasicini, pacicimi, pacitɨŋ
    Older sister, older female cousin.
9. namecini, namecimi, nameɨcaŋ
    Younger sister, younger female cousin.

[5a]. tawaniwan
Brother [and presumably male cousin], older or younger; term of address, w. s.
8. yɨpiaŋwin
Sister [and presumably female cousin], older or younger; term of address, m. s.
14. kɨnuni, kɨnumi, kɨnuaŋ
Father's father; father's father's father; father's father's brother.
Reciprocal: kɨnucan (no. 15).
16. wicini, wicimi, wiciaŋ
Father's mother; father's mother's mother.
Reciprocal: wicicin (no. 17).
10. togoni, togomi, togoaŋ
Mother's father, father's sister's husband [latter evidently in error; probably should read mother's father's sister's husband].
Reciprocal: togocin (no. 11).
12. kaguni, kagumi, kaguaŋ
Mother's mother; mother's mother's mother.
Reciprocal: kagucin (no. 13).
[14a]. ɨwiʔɨni
Father's father's father; mother's mother's mother; not Kaibab; reported as Kaiparowits usage.
15. kɨnucan, kɨnucam, kɨnuciaŋ
Son's child, m. s.
Reciprocal: kɨnuni (no. 14).
17. wicicin, wicicim, wiciciŋ
Son's child, w. s.
Reciprocal: wicini (no. 16).
11. togocin, togocim, togociaŋ
Daughter's child, m. s.
Reciprocal: togoni (no. 10).
13. kagucin, kagucam, kaguciaŋ
Daughter's child, w. s.
Reciprocal: kaguni (no. 12).
[17a]. kuʔuni, kuʔumi, kuʔuaŋ
Father's older brother, mother's older sister's husband.
Reciprocal: kuʔucini (no. [19a]).
18. aini, aimi, aiyaŋ
Father's younger brother, mother's younger sister's husband, stepfather.
Reciprocal: aiʔicini (no. 19).

[21a]. kokweni, kokwaiemi, kokwaiyaŋ
            Mother's older brother.
            Reciprocal: kokwai?icin (no. [23a]).
 22.   cinani, cinancim, cinancaŋ [two latter terms presumably
            should refer to reciprocal].
            Mother's younger brother.
            Reciprocal: cinancin (no. 23).
 20.   pa?ani, pa?ami, pa?aŋ
            Father's sister, older or younger.
            Reciprocal: pa?acini (no. 21).
 24.   maŋwɨ?ɨn, maŋwɨ?ɨm, maŋwɨ?ɨaŋ
            Mother's older sister.
            Reciprocal: maŋwɨ?icin (no. 25).
[24a]. nimpian, nimpiami, nimpiaŋ
            Mother's younger sister, father's [younger?] brother's
            wife, stepmother.
            Reciprocal: nimpiacini (no. [24b]).
 19.   ai?icini, ai?icimi, ai?itin
            Older brother's child, m.s., stepchild [m.s.].
            Reciprocal: aini (no. 18).
[19a]. ku?ucini, ku?ucimi, ku?ucaŋ
            Younger brother's child, m.s.
            Reciprocal: ku?uni (no. [17a]).
 23.   cinancin, cinancim, cinanciŋ
            Older sister's child, m.s.
            Reciprocal: cinani (no. 22).
[23a]. kokwai?icin, kokwai?icim, kokwaicaŋ (also kokwaiaŋ)
            Younger sister's child, m.s.
            Reciprocal: kokweni (no. [21a]).
 21.   pa?acini, pa?aci?imi, pa?aciaŋ
            Brother's child, w.s.
            Reciprocal: pa?ani (no. 20).
[24b]. nimpiacini, nimpiacimi, nimpiacaŋ
            Older sister's child, w.s., stepchild w.s.
            Reciprocal: nimpian (no. [24a]).
 25.   maŋwɨɨcin, maŋwɨ?icimi, maŋwɨ?icaŋ
            Younger sister's child, w.s.
            Reciprocal: maŋwɨ?ɨn (no. 24).
 27.   kumani, kumami, kumaŋ
            Husband.
 32.   nain-kumani
            Husband's brother, sister's husband, w.s.; literal
            meaning said to be "second husband."

26. piŋwani, piŋwami, piŋwaŋ
   Wife.
[26a]. namu-piŋwani
   First wife.
[26b]. pina-piŋwani
   Co-wife.
31. nain-piŋwani
   Wife's sister, brother's wife, m.s.; literal meaning said to be "second wife."
30. antamuani, antamuami, antamuaŋ
   Husband's sister, brother's wife, w.s.
29. tantawavin, tantawavim, tantawaviaŋ
   Wife's brother, sister's husband, m.s.
[28b]. iyai?icin, iyai?icim, iyai?iciaŋ
   Child-in-law; parent-in-law.
28. munacin, munacim, munaciaŋ
   Daughter's husband.
[28a]. wicimpian, wicimpiam, wicimpiaŋ
   Son's wife.
[32a]. miotɨmpian [miotɨmpiam, miotɨmpiaŋ]
   Unidentified distant relative: "someone you feed."

Gifford's (1917, 245-8) comparison of Sapir's Kaibab kinship terms with those of the linguistically related Kawaiisu indicated that approximately one-third of the Kaibab words appeared similar in sound to certain ones of the Kawaiisu series but were "applied in quite a different manner," from which he concluded that "the position of Kaibab Paiute is anomalous." It now appears that Kaibab is much closer to Kawaiisu than Sapir's data suggested. Below (pp. 126-9) the Kaibab terms given by KC appear in the first column; in the second, Sapir's Kaibab terms; in the third, Gifford's Kawaiisu. To facilitate comparison, Gifford's numbering and sequence have been followed; numbers in brackets correspond to terms interpolated from KC's information.

In addition to resemblances evident from Gifford's comparison, numbers 10, 11, 12, 13, 14, 15, 16, 18, 19, 24, 25, and 29 likewise equate Kaibab with Kawaiisu. There are, moreover, a number of other similarities not demonstrated by the accompanying lists because the terms in question were not recorded by Sapir:

Nos. 17a and 19a, father's older brother and the reciprocal, younger brother's child, m.s.: Sapir has one term for brother and one for brother's child, m.s. (nos. 18, 19, second column).

	Kaibab (KC)	Kaibab (Sapir, in Gifford, 1917, 245-6)*	Kawaiisu (Gifford, 1917, 245-6)
1.	muani (father)	muani (father)	muwuni (father)
2.	piani (mother)	piyani (mother)	piyuni (mother)
3.	tuani (son)	tuwacini (son)	tuwuni (son)
4.	pačini (daughter)	paacini (daughter)	pedüni (daughter)
5.	pavicin (older brother)	paavi(ci)ni (older brother)	pavini (older brother)
			pavatcini (great-grandson)
[5a].	tawaniwan (brother [presumably also male cousin], older or younger; term of address, w.s.)		
6.	čakaitini (younger brother)	čakaičini (younger brother)	saka·ini (younger brother)
			saka·itcini (great-grandfather)
7.	pasicini (older sister) [pacicini]	paacicini (older sister)	patcini (older sister)
			patcitcini (great-granddaughter)
8.	yɨpiaŋwɨn (sister [presumably also female cousin] older or younger; term of address, m.s.)	yupiani (younger sister)	
9.	namecini (younger sister)	namincini (younger sister)	nama·ini (younger sister)
			nama·itcini (great-grandmother)
10.	togoni (mother's father, father's sister's husband [latter probably should read mother's father's sister's husband])	tuguni (grandfather)	togoni (mother's father)

*[Editor's note: Sapir's material has been phonemicized. Except for a few diacritics, Gifford's material is unchanged.]

-126-

11. togocin (daughter's child, m.s.) — togotcini (daughter's child, m.s.)

12. kaguni (mother's mother; mother's mother's mother) — kaguni (mother's mother)

13. kagucin (daughter's child, w.s.) — kagutcini (daughter's child, w.s.)

14. kɨnuni (father's father; father's father's father; father's father's brother) — kunoni (father's father)

[14a]. ɨwɨʔɨni (Kaiparowits, not Kaibab dialect: father's father's father; mother's mother's mother)

15. kɨnucan (son's child, m.s.) — kunotcini (son's child, m.s.)

16. wicini (father's mother, father's mother's mother) — hutcini (father's mother)

17. wicicin (son's child, w.s.) — hutcitcini (son's child, w.s.)

[17a]. kuʔuni (father's older brother, mother's older sister's husband)

18. aini (father's younger brother, mother's younger sister's husband, stepfather) — heeni (father's younger brother)

19. aiʔicini (older brother's child, m.s., stepchild [m.s.]) — heetcini (older brother's child, m.s.)

[20]. kuʔucini (younger brother's child, m.s.)

-127-

[20]. pa?ani (father's sister, older or younger)

paa?ani (father's sister, probably also mother's sister)

pahani (father's sister)

[21]. pa?acini (brother's child, w.s.)

paa?acini (brother's child, w.s.; probably also sister's child, w.s.)

pahatcini (brother's child, w.s.)

[21a]. kokweni (mother's older brother)

[22.] cinani (mother's younger brother)

šinani (male cousin older than speaker; mother's brother)

cinuni (mother's brother)

[23.] cinancin (older sister's child, m.s.)

šinacini (male cousin younger than speaker; nephew, probably also sister's child, m.s.)

cinutcini (sister's child, m.s.)

[23a] kokwai?icin (younger sister's child, m.s.)

[24.] maŋwɨ?ɨn (mother's older sister)

maaŋwɨ?ini (female cousin older than speaker; niece)

mawüüni (mother's older sister)

[24a] nimpian (mother's younger sister, father's brother's wife, stepmother)

[24b]. nimpiacɨnɨ (older sister's child, w.s., stepchild, w.s.)

[25]. maŋwɨ?ɨcin (younger sister's child, w.s.)

maaŋwɨ?icini (female cousin younger than speaker)

mawüütcini (younger sister's child, w.s.)

[26]. piŋwani (wife)

piŋwani (wife)

piwhani (wife)

[26a]. namu-piŋwani (first wife)

[26b]. pina-piŋwani (co-wife)

[27]. kumani (husband)

kumani (husband)

kupmani (husband)

[28]. munacin (daughter's husband)

munacini (daughter's husband)

mononi (daughter's husband)

-128-

[28a]. wicimpian (son's wife)

[28b]. iyai?icin (child-in-law, parent-in-law)

29. tantawavin (sister's husband, m.s.; wife's brother)

  tantaŋwaavini (sister's husband, m.s.)

  ci?entamuwaani (wife's brother)

30. antamuani (brother's wife, w.s.; husband's sister)

  atamwoni (sister's husband, m.s.)
  atamwoni (wife's brother)

31. nain-piŋwani (wife's sister; brother's wife, m.s.; said to mean "second wife")

  naimpiŋwani (wife's sister; brother's wife, m.s.)

  nebiwhoni (wife's sister; brother's wife, m.s.)

32. nain-kumani (husband's brother; sister's husband, w.s.; said to mean "second husband")

  naiŋkumani (husband's brother; sister's husband, w.s.)

  nekomwhoni (husband's brother; sister's husband, w.s.)

32a. miotimpɨan (unidentified distant relative: "someone you feed")

However, Kawaiisu recognizes the age differentiation, as does Uintah Ute (Gifford, 1917, 246-7, nos. 9-11). This is, accordingly, a Kaibab-Kawaiisu-Ute similarity.

Nos. 24a and 24b, mother's younger sister and the reciprocal, older sister's child, w. s.: Parallel usage now is recognizable for Kaibab, Kawaiisu and Ute (Gifford, 1917, 247, nos. 19, 20).

Attention may be called to a very few details:

Whereas KC distinguished mother's brothers by age, Sapir lumped them (nos. 21a, 22). The Kawaiisu have no such age differentiation (Gifford, 1917, 247) and, in this respect, my Kaibab data more closely approximate Ute (Gifford, 1917, 247, nos. 12, 14).

Sapir recorded two Kaibab terms for younger sister (nos. 8, 9, second column). KC considered his no. 8 a term of address, used by a man for his sister, irrespective of age, and gave a parallel term (no. 5a) used by a woman in addressing her brother, older or younger. There is no evident counterpart in Kawaiisu or Ute, and this datum should be checked in the field, probably among all three groups.

An identical reciprocal for child-in-law and parent-in-law (no. 28b) was given by KC, who also specified separate Kaibab terms for son's wife and daughter's husband (nos. 28a, 28). Sapir's Ute data (Gifford, 1917, 247, nos. 29, 30) show one term for spouse's parent and son's wife, with a separate designation for daughter's husband. Kawaiisu lumps the spouse's parents and uses separate designations for son's wife and daughter's husband (Gifford, 1917, 231). Among Kaibab, Kawaiisu and Ute, the terms for daughter's husband, at least, are very similar.

One could comment in detail and at great length about similarities and differences, but the foregoing seems sufficient to correct the impression that Kaibab and Kawaiisu kinship systems are comparatively remote from one another. The similarities are marked and far more numerous than appeared from the material available previously. If Kawaiisu relates to the Yuman systems (Spier, 1925, 81), so also does Kaibab and, by extension, Uintah Ute (Gifford, 1917, 246-8).

Miscellaneous Social Data

Under this heading is information concerning a number of social aspects not covered elsewhere.

Age Terms

KC provided a series of terms that correspond primarily to age; a few, to social and physiological condition:

pisoac, infant of either sex; naipac, boy (until 9 or 10 years); aip?apuc, young man, married or unmarried (no terms for newly married); ta?wac, man (30 to 35 years; no corresponding term for woman); na?puŋ, man (50 to 55 years); napɨc, old man.

na?ančic, girl (until 9 or 10 years; mama?uc, girl, woman, married or unmarried (called thus until middle age; no term for young woman); ma?puc, woman (50 or 55 years); masagwaic, old woman; suk?pianevi, menstruating girl, woman; nu?ogant, pregnant woman.

kač-pisoaroait (no child), sterile person, either sex; perhaps merely descriptive, in response to my query; tawanaverɨm, berdache (p. 100).

Names

Child not named immediately; name selected by "anybody"-- father, mother, grandparents. Some names declared meaningless; most evidently of nickname variety, based on physical or personal characteristics, or on what the person said or did (wide assortment mentioned, pp. 11-21). Sapir notes that the same name might be borne by man or woman. Occasionally a person known by two names. No disinclination to speak name of living. Used freely in conversation, but relatives usually addressed one another by appropriate kinship terms. Parents-in-law of one's offspring usually addressed by name; no parent-in-law tabu. Name of dead tabu for all time, but if by coincidence, a person happened to have same name as deceased, he would not change it.

Childhood

Small boys "played all the time". Swam in Johnson Canyon when possible and wherever else there was water; most could swim. Various games (pp. 118-20) as well as target competitions in which men and boys participated. Sometimes in winter, lad of 6 years or more, thrown naked into the snow; rubbed with snow; returned rapidly to house, before he could catch cold. This considered "training." Boys sometimes threw one another into snow. Half-grown lad expected to fetch water and wood in the morning, before eating (usually mush), and in evening. He ran, not because of compulsion, but "because he liked to and wanted to get back quickly." Lazy child whipped; no fear of this causing illness. Training in hunting techniques noted above (p. 47). No boys' adolescence rites; no vision quest. One lad had ears punched (p. 98) but this may not have been general.

Small girls played, mostly with dolls (Pls. 4, h-j, 6). When "a little older," learned to gather, grind seeds. Observances at adolescence described elsewhere (pp. 98-9).

Not disrespectful for child to converse at length with father. Orphans sometimes raised by mother's sister or, apparently more frequently, by father's sibling.

Division of Labor

S commented succinctly that "women dug roots and men ate them." Actually, women collected most vegetable products and prepared all foods. Men collaborated, however, in knocking cones from pinyon trees and, presumably as today, in roasting them. During the usual winter stay at Grand Canyon, women worked "every day," preparing mescal, while the "men hunted rabbits and sat around." Hunting the man's principal job. Some men tanned hides, but this primarily a woman's work. Women made most clothing, but men fringed the buckskin. Men made their weapons; women, their baskets. Both sexes apparently made Apocynum (si?ip) cordage. Both evidently shared the responsibility of training children, but details not recorded.

Greetings

Usual greeting is "maiku-tɨgivun" (hello, friend); return salutation the same. Sapir's informant gave maiki or maikuŋwašu. Nothing to correspond to our "good-bye"; one merely says, "I am going home."

Sapir's informant described arrival of a visitor from another tribe; "nearly everybody" gathered around. "After a while, he tells what he has to say. If he has nothing to say, he simply says he is going around just for fun." He thought it old custom to "grasp each other's hands, but not necessarily" to shake.

Natural and Supernatural

Under this heading are collected various data regarding the world, nature and the supernatural. Most of the available information on shamanism and curing has been covered in a previous paper (Kelly, 1939), but a few additional details will be found below, in connection with animal lore and spirits.

The World

The following information concerning the origin and nature of the world comes largely from Sapir's notes:

Wolf (Tɨvac, powerful one) was believed the most powerful being; his brother, Coyote (Sinaŋwavi, comic fellow), the next most powerful. Wolf was called "people's father" (niŋwumanc), because he made heaven and earth. Originally, all was water. Wolf told Coyote to make the earth, but he couldn't. So Wolf dived for clay at the bottom of the water and from it made land and animals.

He told Coyote that snow was to fall only on the mountains and was to be gathered by the people as if it were flour; but Coyote thought it better to have people leave tracks on real snow. Wolf wanted a person to return after death. Coyote said no, that he wanted people to mourn.

Although people refer to Wolf as "father," and are said to "worship" him, they do not address prayers to him (exception in Kelly, 1939, 152, fn. 6). Strangely enough, G claimed the term for prayer was sinawɨŋvi-ampagaga (coyote talk). He added that "these Paiute never prayed," but he had heard that those around Mount Trumbull (Uinkaret) used to do so. (In some context or other, G was asked how he "thought." He replied, with touching modesty, in the third person: "These Indians around here never think; they don't know anything but how to hunt rabbits.")

There is one report of an underworld, inhabited by porcupines in human form. Sapir's notes contain a long account, summarized below, of a visit to it by a Uinkaret shaman who once had cured Tony Tillohash, and to whom he gave an eye-witness description of his experiences:

Hunting one day, he followed porcupines into a hole and found himself in a great open country underground. No porcupines were in evidence, but he came to a camp. There people lived somewhat as in the upper world, except that at night they hunted and, by day, slept and copulated in full view. When they brought meat to camp, they prepared it, smelled it, then threw it away. When the visitor was about to eat the meat, they cried to him, "Don't; it is excrement." Nevertheless, he found the meat tasty; when he defecated, one of the porcupine men sampled his excrement, but it was not to his liking. Eventually, the shaman retraced his steps and returned to the upper world.

The earth is said to be round, flat and disclike. An earthquake is called "earth shake" (tɨwip-nɨnčɨkai) and is of unknown origin. The echo is "rock laughing" (tɨmpikiasoc); "they think it is birds calling back."

Cardinal directions.--There is confusion in the naming of cardinal directions. G gave the following terms: tɨwaʔ (south); tɨ (north); wagaičuk (east and west); tɨ (up); tɨwa (down). Apparently there is one name for north and "up," one for south and "down," and no distinction between east and west.

Sapir's series is equally brief; he reports no words for south or east, but gives tɨintugwantɨ as north and tɨivaiʔtugwantɨ as west. Separately, it is noted that panaŋkwa is north or "down"; tɨnaŋkwantɨ, "from west."

Time reckoning.--"The old men kept track of time," and there seems to have been some uncertainty about it; Sapir's informant recalled an anecdote in which two elderly men quarreled about the name of a month. Mnemonic devices were not used.

According to G, "the first month of the year began about September or October. They knew it because the wara seeds and the yucca fruit ripened and because of a [the] cold north wind.... They have known [knew] about this for a long time--learned it from Coyote." For S, the "year began when the leaves turned yellow" and the temperature dropped. Neither G nor S had heard of starting the year when a certain star or constellation appeared.

"The old Indians used to tell a story" about the solstice, but G had forgotten it; he thought Coyote responsible for the phenomenon. It had "nothing to do with" the months; he had "just heard that the sun comes back again."

There was a lunar calendar, but a partial one. A month (moatogoc, moon) began with the appearance of the new moon. Children watched for it but were not permitted to point (p. 137); the child who first saw the new moon told the others, and "the boys and girls ran a race."

Information from G and S appears in the first two columns of the accompanying resumé. Both named six months and agreed that "they didn't name the summer months"; S gave one term that applied to "all summer." G listed the months in numerical order, starting with the first month of the native year; S began with November and gave native equivalents to our months.

In the third column are data from Sair's informant. He remembered four month names but was uncertain how to equate them with our calendar; the sequence in which they are mentioned in the notes is indicated by the numbers in brackets. He reported the "greatest feast" (?) in connection with "some winter month" called kaaŋamu. Said to start when a star named kaŋa rises in the morning, children were sent out in the early twilight (morning?) to watch for its appearance in the east. One who could see the star would have good eyesight and be able to discern rabbits from afar.

For comparison, in the fourth column is a list of month names given by Dick--an informant whose data were relatively little used because of uncertainty as to whether they applied to Kaiparowits, Kaibab, or some Ute group. He remarked that "there are only 10 because the 'long moon' is half spring; summer is long, too." Nevertheless, he gave terms for "summer moon" and "middle summer moon." His names total nine rather than 10, because he could not remember the name of the month that preceded "fall." He started with the "long moon" and ended with the "sister month," as shown by the numbers in brackets.

On the whole, the same or similar names tend to run through the series and there seems to be agreement that summer months were not individually named. There are, however, discrepancies in sequence and in the equation of native months to those of our calendar.

For good measure, Dick named the seasons: tomorinr (winter); tamau (spring); tac (summer); wau (fall).

1. wanci-pisagaŋamɨ
   (wanci-antelope)

2. pisagaŋamɨ

3. gaŋamɨ (gan, cold; December)

4. nanavacimɨa (3-sisters)

5. paʔatogwamɨ (long month)

6. sovaramaruac (angry month, because wind blows all the time; March)

   tamarauac another name for same month (March)

7. tacamɨatogoc (all summer)

[1] iuanamac (fall; November)

[2] kaŋamɨ (December)

[3] navacimɨ (2-sisters ;January)

[4] paʔatɨkomɨ (long month; February) [sic]

[5] suvaramaruac (March)

[6] tamaruac (April)

[6] _____ [Name forgotten]

[7] ɨvanamatoic (fall)

[9] tɨwɨckamɨa (beginning of frost)

[10] navacimɨa (sister month)

[1] paʔatormoa (long moon; in middle of year; one half of this is spring month)

[8] sogawamatowoc (beginning of cold)

[2] tamaruac (second moon; beginning of spring)

[3] tamauc (tamau, spring)

[4] tacamuatos (summer moon)

[5] towɨtacmɨ-moatowoc (middle summer moon

[1] kaaŋamu (some. winter month; January or February)

[2] paʔatugumu (long month; some winter month)

[4] tamaruac (little spring, perhaps April)

[3] tamaʔucci (spring water-jar, probably March, when bear dance takes place)

-136-

More specific time reckoning appears in Sapir's notes as follows:

tava (sun, day); tavai (it's day); tašianti (early morning, before sun-up); ičuau (morning, at sunrise); ičuku tavai (forenoon); tguitavai (midday); tašipatavai (afternoon); tašipanti (time at sundown, dusk, early evening); šiapu (early night, after dark); tugwanu (night); tuguitugwanu (midnight); šiapuarugwanu (up to midnight); ta?šiatugwanu (after midnight, to morning twilight).

His informant added muatuguc (month); tuma (year; literally, winter); waa-tumania (two years).

S provided a somewhat similar list:

ičkus (early in the morning, before sunrise); suarugutavai (about 11 o'clock); tagutavai (noon; tav, sun); tava-pičuamik (afternoon); tavaiyakwa (sundown, to about 8 o'clock); siapi (after 8 o'clock); tasipak (evening); tukwon (night); tguitogon (midnight); tasiatogon (before sunrise).

Nature Lore

Heavens.--When the moon wanes, it was said "moon dies"; when it has a ring outside, it was said to "eat itself." To point at the new moon made one's finger sore. It might be even more hazardous: "They did not let the children point to it; they might put their hand in a rattlesnake mouth if they did that."

Stars used to be "the Indians' watch, just like an alarm clock; they turn around like a clock." One large (?) star (piav-puci, big star) (presumably Polaris) "does not move." Fields planted "about June first, when the morning star (tasiantu-pucipi; tašianti, early morning, above) appeared in the east." Milky way (tiwimpo; po, trail) said to be a road.

Orion's belt apparently called naagaŋw (mountain sheep); "there are three stars; you see them in the fall. They were not real mountain sheep. They are some Coyote made out of little stones he picked up. Then Mountain Lion had a son who killed the sheep. Coyote came along and said, 'My son killed them.' There is half a circle of stars around those sheep; they are Indians trying to get the sheep."

S apparently recognized Orion's belt as mountain sheep and thought the sword was Coyote's arrow; knew no associated tale. Had heard that one star, not identified, was "the arrow of Coyote's son."

Pleiades apparently Coyote's family (suniaŋw). "One is the mother; four are the daughters; and one is the boy. He is behind; that makes six stars." By Sapir's informant, said to be Coyote's daughters, who fled to the sky when he tried to have incestuous intercourse with them. Same informant likewise suggested identification with Dipper (Sapir, 1930, 463-5).

The Dipper "was caused by the Rat (kaac) brothers. The two brothers built a fire. The tail of the dipper is smoke; it is grass burning, not wood."

Cluster of stars (kam?winaračakac, stars close together) from description, should be Pleiades. Said to be hand stone or mano.

Water.--Waters of Lake Parowan (in Cedar territory) are "all right now; used to be bad." Called paaruugwantɨ (water fighter). Not a person or being, but water rose on approach of individual; dragged him into lake and he drowned if unable to escape.

"Water babies" (paan?apic, water baby) are "small, like babies, and live in water." Moreover, "they have wings; drag people into the water to drown them." One informant claimed "old people used to see women (paŋapic, water baby) in water. Like a person, with long hair." Had not heard they seduced humans. Best protection against them red paint, ashes (p. 141).

Weather.--Lightning (aŋkoguisarɨ, aŋkak?sɨt, red twitch) made by rain; said to be latter's walking stick. A twig of tonɨmpɨ (<u>Cercocarpus intricatus</u>) was smeared with red paint and put on the dwelling to protect it from lightning. Thunder (uunuuwarɨ) believed by one informant to cause rain; by another, the reverse. Thunder "is the rain talking." Sapir's informant thought thunder caused by rolling of a bear in his den.

Little weather control; Sapir's informant mentioned one shaman who claimed power to cause rain; apparently not common (Kelly, 1939, 153). Women used to shake their skirts and wave away rain (pauŋwarɨ), saying "marugwa, marugwa" (go away). Some "men and women might talk to rain and snow...saying 'Go away, no more snow;

I'm cold.'"

Rainbow (parukwanɨnɨt; uŋwarɨ-porogwa, rain cane) said to be rain's walking stick, as is the lightning. One who pointed at a rainbow would have a sore finger, or it would "come off."

Wind could be produced by bull roarer (p. 120). If day calm and breeze needed for winnowing, helpful to whistle; advisable not to do so unless wind desired. Whirlwind (turuniarɨ) thought to contain evil spirit (pp. 140-2).

Animals.--Today, women shriek on seeing lizard (sɨkupic); fear it may run up beneath dress, enter body, and lay eggs. When latter hatch, small animals consume woman's internal organs, causing death.

Only one kind of owl (mu?upuc). Feather occasionally used for arrows. Owl's cry the "voice of the dead"; presages death. Bird chased away; handful of ashes tossed toward it.

Deer on Kaibab Plateau once owned by Tukumumuc (big lion); "after that, a man called Kainsɨsapi got them away from him. That is what I think. Sometimes they see this man; sometimes he looks like a dog and then changes into a man."

Sapir's notes contain another version:

All the deer on Kaibab Plateau were owned by a supernatural being named Kai?našavi. During the hunting season his name must not be mentioned, or the luck of the entire season would be spoiled. A hunter may see him in one of 2 forms. On the hunt, a man may appear and, the next instant, disappear; he would know it was Kai?našavi and that his hunting luck had been ruined for that day. He might see 2 deer of more than ordinary size, into which the being had transformed himself. In attempting to follow the animals he would become lost, "all tangled up," losing sense of cardinal directions and estimate of distance. If a hunter offended Kai?našavi, the latter would confuse him by deer tracks that led to nothing. Sometimes, a man traveling in a canyon would hear or see rocks hurled at him; he would know it was Kai?našavi.

Data below are from Sapir's notes:

When wild horse (mustang) could not be caught, leaves of low plant (called kaagupuna?avu), growing near Colorado River, chewed; thereupon, pebbles moistened in mouth and thrown at animal to slow it. Remedy not advisable, because horse always slow and lazy thereafter. Leaves of another plant (kwaananumpu) fragrant; sometimes tied to armbands. Discarded on riding horseback because caused animal to sweat profusely.

Rattlesnake sensitive to plant called paaguntɨnavu; grows on slopes of wooded areas (Kaibab Plateau, for example); leaves, stalks carrot-like. Tied in small bundles, 1 to each ankle, to repel snakes. In case of bite, root chewed and applied to wound. Kaibab had special rattlesnake shaman (Kelly, 1939, 153).

To treat scorpion sting, fire built outside dwelling. Victim jumped over it, calling his own name. Confessed to any misdeed, such as rape, before all people present. Jumped as often as he desired; otherwise, wound would swell and perhaps cause death.

Omens

A sneeze (aŋwispi) means someone of opposite sex is thinking or speaking of one. If upper eyelid twitches, "someone has died somewhere"; lower lid, that "you will see something." Twitching leg muscle foretells arrival "of someone"; itching hand, ailment in hand or arm.

Dreams (nunušipi) apparently important. According to Sapir's informant, "If one dreams something will happen, it may or may not come true; it might easily happen." If a man dreams he won't kill a deer, "then probably he won't." Songs, shamanistic and others, come in dreams. Bad omen to dream of blood flowing, for "somebody probably will be killed"; if it is one's own blood, a relative will meet death. To dream of deceased persons is not evil portent; as S says, very sensibly, "it is because you think of them in the daytime, then dream of them at night."

Souls, Ghosts and Spirits

Most of the material to follow comes from Sapir's notes.

Every person has a soul (muguavi), which is his invisible double and which leaves the body at death; it becomes an inɨpic (ghost, evil spirit) and travels west, to the shores of a certain river.

Apparently, the shadow (avav) not related to the soul. G believed the latter resided in the breast, in "the heart" (piyɨni) and did not leave the body when seen in reflections or in dreams.

In contrast, Sapir's informant made good case for the latter, saying soul departed and experienced events that were dreamt. Dangerous to rouse a person suddenly if he is dreaming; "the soul might not get back in time." A wandering soul incapable of perceiving black objects, hence "older" Indians thought it inadvisable to have black cat near sleeping quarters; unwary soul might be caught by cat.

Visibility of wandering soul attested by Sapir's informant:

Once several Indians were sleeping in camp. During the night, 1 awoke and noticed a light (similar to a firefly) flitting about. Finally, it disappeared into a boot. The man stuffed something (such as a rag) in the boot and went back to sleep. In the morning, all awoke except 1 man; they could not rouse him. When 1 of the group tried to put on his boot, he found and removed the rag. Thereupon, the sleeping man awoke (for his soul had returned).

He also reported a practice that reflects concept of body if not of soul. When one has been traveling some time and then sits down to eat, it is necessary to wait--perhaps half an hour--to give the various parts of the body opportunity to come together and "set. Some part of the body might still be on the road."

Ghost and evil spirit (inɨpic, inɨpuič,) is one and the same. It may assume any form, but ordinarily "moves like the wind and looks like a shadow." Sometimes it is in the whirlwind. "They think inɨpic is everywhere. They put red paint on the face... inɨpic is afraid of that... afraid of ashes, too. Sometimes they burn pine gum." Apparently tobacco smoke also is useful in dispelling ghosts or spirits.

Sometimes a ghost is visible in the form of an elderly white man, with white hair; if addressed, he does not reply. Most frequently, a spirit is heard. Unusual noises on the trail and especially at night, near a travelers' camp, are attributed to spirits or ghosts. A whistle, a melancholy howl, giggling all are so interpreted, especially if the horses show signs of uneasiness. A spirit may make itself known by "whistling or yelling, like a real person," and is attracted by one who whistles in the forest at night. It also is attracted by the buzz of the bull roarer, and the latter is frowned upon as a toy for this reason, as well as because it may cause an uncontrollable wind. In camping, the spot should be selected carefully. One does not camp where those known to be dead have stayed, for ghosts might linger in the vicinity. Dellenbaugh (1926, 252) describes group singing at night to drive away the spirits.

Hair clippings and fingernail parings are thrown away, but toenail cuttings are buried for fear the inɨpic may "put them in one's throat." Illness also results when one shoots its "power" into a person; unless it is removed by a shaman, death follows. (Object intrusion thus may be caused by an evil spirit as well as by a malevolent shaman (Kelly, 1939, 152). Sapir's notes contain one reference to sorcery which may be put on record here. One (anyone? a shaman?) may bury an individual's excrement with macerated flint, following which the victim is unable to defecate and eventually dies.)

KAIPAROWITS

Identification and Neighbors

The large triangle of country northeast of the Paria River and northwest of the Colorado is barren and, even today, thinly populated. Concerning identification of this entire area, my information is confused. Below will be recorded what little material there is--including contradictory statements--in the hope that, some time in the future, following further study, the data may fall into place.

I have designated arbitrarily as Kaiparowits (Kelly, 1934) an area containing several population clusters in the desert zone immediately east of the Paria and in the nearby Potato-Escalante Valley. It adjoins the Kaibab on the northeast and the Panguitch on the southeast (map 1).

The few available informants tended to speak of themselves in terms of local place names, tacking on the suffix to designate "people." (The absence of a clear collective and the fuzziness concerning the location of some groups support Steward's [1938, 181] belief that some of the areas I have considered band territory contain "politically independent" groups.) The one name sometimes used in a collective sense would be hopelessly ambiguous, for it is virtually identical with that associated with the Kaibab of Kanab-Moccasin-Kaibab Plateau. It so happens that both the Kaibab and Kaiparowits plateaus are called Kaivavič (mountain lying down). Accordingly, anyone who camped habitually on the Kaiparowits Plateau--and, in fall, that included much of the population--might be referred to as Kaivaviči-niwincin or Kaivavičici.

Although by the latter term Kaibab informants sometimes designated those of the Kaiparowits area, they more frequently used local place names (p. 31), or lumped their neighbors to the northeast as "the people the other side of the Paria," or "the Escalante people."

Dialect difference between the latter and the Kaibab is indicated by remarks such as: "he talks like the Escalante people." The three major population clusters (p. 149) within the Kaiparowits areas were said to have had identical speech. There is mention of a "different voice" for a few families on the northeast limits, in the district called Kaiviyɨgacɨ (mountain turn). The name apparently was applied to the point where the scarp of the Aquarius Plateau swings south, at Circle Cliffs. Physically, this district necessarily is part of the Kaiparowits area.

Tribal affiliation of the Kaiparowits and some adjacent groups is uncertain. One informant called them "almost Ute"; most referred to them as "half Ute." The diagnostic of the latter seemed more sartorial (p. 33) than linguistic. L, chief informant for the Kaiparowits area,[*] wavered in

---

[*]See p. 3. L was born shortly before the arrival of Mormon settlers in the Escalante zone, perhaps about 1870. Her father lived in the vicinity of Kaiparowits Plateau; his father camped mostly at Saŋwawitɨmpaya (Escalante Valley) but wintered at the north end of Kaiparowits Plateau (p. 151). Her mother was from Kwaguiuavɨ (p.150) and there L spent most of her childhood. When she was very small, her father died. "The others" wanted to kill her, but "some relation" of her father married her widowed mother and accepted L.

When she was about 12, she moved to Panguitch. Later, she married a Koosharem and went to Koosharem to live. Following a second marriage, she lived at Avua (p. 149); still later, she moved to Moccasin, where she has been many years with the Kaibab.

L claimed she "used to speak" the dialect of the Kaiparowits area. Inspection of a brief vocabulary showed little difference between it and Kaibab, whereupon she claimed she had changed her speech in the course of long residence at Moccasin.

allegiance, practically from day to day, claiming first to be Paiute, then Ute. Some Kaibab declared flatly that she was Paiute and regarded her claim of Ute affiliation as affectation prompted by vanity (p. 33).

Those of the Kaiparowits area were "friendly" with the Kaibab; there was trade on modest scale (pp. 90, 165) and several specific cases of intermarriage. There also was a certain amount of contact with the San Juan Paiute; L reported that, upon occasion, her mother crossed the Colorado (p. 165) to visit the Paiute near Tuba City; a few instances of intermarriage were reported; and, presumably in comparatively recent times, "fancy basketry" was learned from the San Juan.

L and other informants mentioned groups with the complementary names of Impiŋwacɨn and Taviŋwac, whose translations are given below. It seems quite clear that the Panguitch people are to be identified with the Impiŋwacɨn; it was said that the Kaibab called them Pagɨv and that the lone survivor was named Rena (p. 3). On one occasion, L extended the term to include people of the Fish Lake area.

The Taviŋwac "talked like Paiute" and were "all dead." They lived on the "southern slopes," apparently on "the upper part of those rivers" that drained south to the Escalante. As far as I could tell-- and this is by no means certain--the name refers to the southern flank of the Aquarius Plateau, west of the "corner" district known as Kaivɨyɨgacɨ (mountain turn), at Circle Cliffs.

The translation of Impiŋwacɨn as near-side-of-mountain people and of Taviŋwac as far-side-of-mountain people complicates matters. Unless both terms originated among the Ute, perhaps at Koosharem, they describe locations precisely the opposite of those that apply from the Kaiparowits vantage point. Sapir (1930, 669) translates as "sun slope" a term very similar to Taviŋwac; it forms part of a group designation that he gives as cedar-bark sun-slope people and that he applies to the Uncompaghre Ute, "now at Ouray." The Taviŋwac mentioned by Kaiparowits informants almost certainly were closer to home. They may have been no more than another population cluster north of the Escalante River, yet they are not mentioned in association with the three main population centers (p. 149).

Yantarɨi (source of creek) is a name applied to an area and to its "almost Ute" residents. One man, whose father was of that group, located it "the other side of Henry Mountains, nearly to the Colorado River." Another identified the Yantarɨi as "by the Colorado and to the east." They talked like Utes; some used the Ute language." L had them " down by the Colorado River the other side of Aŋkawitimpaya" (red canyon). From the description, the latter is a Colorado tributary next upstream from the Escalante River, hence presumably the Fremont, or Dirty Devil. This would place the Yantarɨi along the Colorado, between the Dirty Devil and Green rivers -- an area that should have been Ute. L described their speech as different from hers and "a little like" Ute.

Unfortunately, I did not check with Kaiparowits informants the affiliations of the Koosharem. There is one statement that they spoke as did the Kaiparowits, but L claimed to have spoken both languages, which implies a difference. Kaibab informants were inclined to consider the Koosharem as Ute, but not "real" Ute (p. 33) and one statement in Sapir's notes has the Koosharem on East Fork, within what I have doubtfully considered Kaiparowits territory (pp. 34, 146). This would agree with L's claim, upon one occasion, that Bryce Canyon was the property of her father-in-law, a Koosharem.

According to L, "the Ute never came around in the old days, just recently." It is by no means clear what group or groups she considered genuine Ute. Before her time, the Kaiparowits had learned from the Koosharem to smoke skins (pp. 160-1) but, within her memory, several traits reached her people "from the north," presumably via Ute or near-Ute intermediaries:

> Fringing of buckskin; sewing with sinew; man's buckskin leggings sewn to "shoes"; woman's buckskin dress; moccasins. The dress and moccasins were adopted when L was 9 or 10 years old, hence 1880 or thereabouts. The travois and the 4-pole, canvas-covered tipi were introduced together, after L was married. The bear dance appeared when she was first married and before she had children; this seems considerably earlier than the date calculated for the same dance among the Kaibab (p. 104).

Of other neighbors, there was little mention. The Mukwic, to whom archeological sites are attributed, "left this country long ago; we never saw them." Nor had L seen an Apache. The Navajo used to cross the Colorado to trade (p. 165). They were called Pagaŋwic (cane, "because tall and slim") or Wekwec; the latter she said was the name used for them by the San Juan Paiute, and she thought it might be a Navajo term.

Habitat and Distribution of Population

The Kaiparowits area is rugged and traverse difficult. I did not attempt to establish a base there inasmuch as no Paiute remained in the vicinity.* Lack of first-hand knowledge of the country is a manifest handicap, and much of the confusion reported in the preceding section results from my unfamiliarity with the area. Place names have been identified largely on the basis of description and published maps; informants' efforts at drawing maps on the ground and on paper were conspicuously unsuccessful.

Nevertheless, it is possible to sketch the general aspects of the area, thanks to a recent monograph by Gregory and Moore (1931, 1-13), who characterize the region as one of "cliff-bound mesas, monoclinal ridges, and straight-sided canyons--all impressive alike for magnitude and ruggedness.... The region as a whole lies at an altitude of about 6,000 feet, and the downward departures from this level are approximately equal in amount to the upward departures." The same source gives the elevation of a number of major features as follows: Aquarius Plateau, 10,000-12,250 ft.; Table Cliff Plateau, 10,500; Canaan Peak, 9000; Kaiparowits Plateau, 7000; Waterpocket Fold, 6000; channels of the Paria and Escalante, roughly below 5000 ft.

In the heart of the Kaiparowits region there were three population clusters (p. 149); north, east, and south of them, imposing natural barriers forcibly determine boundaries. To the northwest, I am uncertain about the southeastern fringes of Paunsaugunt Plateau, together with Bryce Canyon and the headwaters of East Fork (p. 34; Kelly, 1934). Except for this ill defined stretch, the Kaiparowits country extended from the Aquarius Plateau on the north to the Colorado River on the south, and from the Paria River on the west, to Waterpocket Fold on the east.

The whole northern boundary is essentially a great arc, fringed by the High Plateaus (Paunsaugunt and Aquarius), by Circle Cliffs, and by

---

*L accompanied me on a hasty trip as far as Escalante, where we spent 1 night. She saw her homeland for the first time in 40 years, and her comment is a terse summary of the effects of white occupation: "This country is no good any more; everything is dry; the creeks are cut deep; the food plants are all gone."

Today, the sparse white population is concentrated in the little town of Escalante, on the river of that name, and in the hamlets of Tropic, Cannonville, and Henrieville, on the upper Paria. These settlements can be reached by car, but beyond there is no auto transport. [This was written in 1933-1934; a sketch of Escalante, from 1923 to 1950, has been published by Nelson (1952, 83-129).]

Waterpocket Fold. Within this arc, the province is crossed from northwest to southeast by the Kaiparowits Plateau, a narrow platform that extends from Table Cliff Plateau to the Colorado River. Its northeastern scarp, the Straight Cliffs, presents a vertical front, and its southwestern face, although less abrupt, is deeply dissected.

The Kaiparowits Plateau is a divide; the country to the west is drained by the Paria and the Colorado; that to the east, by the Escalante, which also enters the Colorado. The small streams that head in the High Plateaus and unite to form the Paria and Escalante rivers are perennial, but the flow in the lower course of the Paria itself is intermittent. The Escalante is said to be perennial throughout, but with its lower course so deeply entrenched that the waters are not accessible.

Some place names follow; others will be found in the text:

Paunsagantɨ (beaver place; so-named because of its profile), Paunsaugunt Plateau.

Paʔantakaipɨ (tall mountain), Piagaivɨ (big mountain), Avinkovagantɨ (white-faced peak[?]), alternate names for Table Cliff Plateau.

Sɨaripɨ (aspen), Escalante mountains.

Kwiumporočagantɨ (bear-dig[?]-roots place), Aquarius Plateau.

Aivɨ (sandstone), Aivavič (sandstone plateau), Circle Cliffs.

Tɨmpiavič (rock mountain, plateau), Waterpocket Fold.

Kaiparuwɨcɨ (mountain boy; said to be son of Table Cliff Plateau; named by Coyote), Canaan Peak, called also Kaiparowits Peak.

Kaivavič (mountain lying down), Kaiparowits Plateau.

Asikaivɨ (gray mountain, "all rocks, no trees"); not identified; south of Cannonville, east side of Paria River.

Mɨavɨ-pan (divide valley, "because it separates the mountains"), Escalante Valley, apparently downstream from point where river turns southeast.

Paga (big water), Colorado River.

Paria-pa (elk water; so-named because a lone elk once was seen to jump from a cliff into the stream), Paria River.

Soviuipɨ (cottonwood wash), Cottonwood Wash.

Parɨ, Paiyuin (water canyon), Paiyawiwe, Henrieville creeks.

-oOo-

No permanent camps on Kaiparowits Plateau, but several springs mentioned by name. One at north end, halfway up slope, called Spɨtapa (cold water)(p. 151). Others on plateau, from north to south: Orapac (dig water), Tɨnkanivac (cave water), Sovpac (cottonwood water), Siavac (squawbush water). Owned by sons of Asikɨvɨ (gray; a woman): Čičɨŋwɨgɨsui (smiles "funny"), Yɨŋɨvɨ (stinks), and Ogosɨc (pine-squawbush). Kaibab informant (G) remembered 3 springs along northeastern face of Kaiparowits Plateau. Northernmost had 2 names: Oitɨ (end of creek) and Oavac (salt water); could not recall names of others.

Vegetation is sparse and great stretches are devoid of plant life. Forests cover the highest plateaus, but the Kaiparowits Plateau has only juniper-pinyon growth on its summit, while Waterpocket Fold, according to L, is "white rocks with no trees, no cactus, and no seed plants." The three plant zones that Gregory and Moore (1931, 25-6) recognize may be summarized thus:

(1) Cottonwood, cactus and yucca, in the Colorado and tributary valleys, to about 5000 ft. (2) Pinyon, juniper and sage, 5-8000 ft., on top and flanks of Kaiparowits Plateau, both sides of Waterpocket Fold, and on slopes of Paunsaugunt, Table Cliff, and Aquarius plateaus. (3) Yellow pine, spruce, and fir, 8-11,000 ft., with yellow pine dominant on upper slopes and top of Aquarius, Table Cliff, and Paunsaugunt plateaus and on Canaan Peak, to 9000 ft., followed upward by spruce and fir.

Understandably, the aboriginal population was sparse. The Paria Valley south of Cottonwood Wash and the entire lower course of the Escalante were uninhabitable. In the mid-1870's, Mormon settlers met only four or five families in Potato Valley (Gregory and Moore, 1931, 27), and a "communal drive" with five or six participants suggests very limited numbers.

Regarding both population and organization, L's information is not very helpful, because her memory dates from some years after the Mormon entry, when camp life had disintegrated. She had heard that in earlier times springs were privately owned, but when she was young, "we went all around, camping anywhere, and nobody owning springs." Nevertheless, she identified the owners of several springs. She knew little of chieftainship or property (pp. 155, 166).

Economic Clusters

In pre-white days, there seem to have been three population clusters (map 1):

XI. Avua (pocket-between-hills; Sapir, 1930, 551, semicircular valley).--This is the upper Paria Valley, extending south along the east bank, to Cottonwood Wash.

XII. Kwaguiuavɨ ([var.] -seed valley).--Described as lying between Kaiparowits Plateau and the Paria River, "below" Cottonwood Wash. It must refer to the comparatively open area between the wash and the plateau. Both resources and population notably scant.

XIII. Saŋwawitɨmpaya (sagebrush-canyon mouth).--Potato Valley and a strip along the Escalante Valley, apparently to the bend of the river at Circle Cliffs. In conversation, informants referred to Escalante Valley as "Tɨnɨ valley," declaring this to be its "white" name.

Within these three areas, campsites were governed by the availability of water and fuel. On the whole, land utilization followed pretty much the same pattern as among the Kaibab: the valleys supplied seeds, cacti, and small game; and the plateaus, visited chiefly in fall, provided berries, pine-nuts and larger game.

Further information follows on the three clusters just mentioned:

XI. Avua.--Water obtained from 1 spring (Sagova, green water) and the following streams: Henrieville creeks; Paria River; a small stream called Oavac (salt water), called also Sagankwiči ("from a kind of willow"); another stream, Sagankwicič (also from willow); and Aŋkaŋkwintɨ (red stream). Dry sage the chief fuel. In winter, obtained juniper from cliffs west of valley, either camping on top of bluffs or tossing wood over cliff for use in camps at base.

Spring and summer campsites: (1) foot of cliffs at north end of Paria Valley; (2) above Cannonville, on east bank of Paria; (3) west bank of Paria, at intersection with Henrieville Creek; (4) low red hill (Aŋkapokorɨ, red knoll), southwest of Henrieville.

Fall: hunted deer on Table Cliff and Kaiparowits plateaus. Sometimes joined Panguitch band in latter's territory on Paunsaugunt Plateau, camping and hunting with hosts. Winter and spring occasionally passed in Escalante Valley, but usually in Avua. No caves for shelter. Winter camps located at base of red cliffs bounding valley to the west, or on top of cliffs, because of fuel supply.

L could not remember number of Avua camps nor names of occupants, but said the spring and streams "belonged" to 1 person, who was the br of L's second h and the f of a man called Aŋkaŋkwintɨ (red stream). Kaibab informant (G), who had visited Avua, recalled 3 br, of whom the youngest, named Nagagtuks (mountain-sheep ass [?]) was chief.

XII. <u>Kwaguiuavɨ.</u>--Water obtained from potholes and from the one large wash in the area; called Oauipi (salt wash [?], apparently Wahweap Creek. Latter owned by Uinpucɨ (pine tree), who was L's br; she thought he received it from his f or his f's y br. L's m and her 3 ss camped here. The mother of Kaibab informant A from here originally; she was an older half-ss of L.

Chief fuel was iyɨmpɨ (<u>Fraxinus anomala</u>). Apparently juniper found only on Kankarɨ (boulder knoll), a small hill near the Paria; accordingly, this site favored for winter camps. Rest of country described as treeless; said to be "open desert," with rabbitbrush and greasewood.

Spring usually spent in Kwaguiuavɨ, although Kaiparowits Plateau sometimes visited for roots, eating, while there, seeds stored from preceding fall harvest. In summer gathered seeds in Kwaguiuavɨ. Summer and fall hunting trips to Aŋkaigavɨ (red rough), between Canaan Peak and Kaiparowits Plateau. Same place popular in fall, for seeds, berries, roots, pinenuts; part of harvest left there, stored in caves. In winter returned to Kwaguiuavɨ, camping at Kankarɨ hill.

XIII. <u>Saŋwawitɨmpaya.</u>--Water from upper Escalante River and tributaries; sometimes reliance on melted snow. Winter camps well up valley slopes to insure adequate supply of juniper fuel.

Spring and summer along fringes of Potato Valley and downstream, west of Escalante village and south of river. Sometimes moved below

Escalante, to hill called Siapiŋwavɨ, above town cemetery, and on hill behind the latter. Lower Escalante drainage completely uninhabited. In summer, considerable scattering of camps within Potato Valley-Escalante area, for seed harvest.

In fall, camps united for trip to plateaus, sometimes Kaiparowits, sometimes Aquarius. Usually returned to lower elevation in winter, often camping along small northern tributaries of the upper Escalante; "all those hills have names." Occasionally remained on Kaiparowits Plateau, living on cacti and stores of seeds and pinenuts.

L remembered 3 camps in Saŋwawitɨmpaya area, but thought there used to be more: (1) Muavigaipɨ, or Muaviŋapun (mosquito man), his w, and 2 d, together with another couple and latter's s. Usually camped toward eastern limits of Saŋwawitɨmpaya, at foot of Circle Cliffs, presumably about where the Escalante swings southeastward. (2) Nakavaiptinkaipi (no ears), his w, 2 d; one of latter married a Kaibab; other, a San Juan Paiute. (3) Tumunsokont (black moustache) and his w; he was L's pat grf. He owned a spring called Spɨtapa (cold water) halfway up slope, at north end of Kaiparowits Plateau, and sometimes wintered there.

-ooo-

There may have been two more population clusters concerning which I have virtually no information. One, called Kaivɨyɨgacɨ (p. 143) apparently was at the base of Circle Cliffs, where the cliffs join the Aquarius Plateau. From description, this should be the same general area where Muavinapun (see preceding paragraph) habitually camped, but he was reckoned a resident of Saŋwawitɨmpaya.

Another cluster may have been that of Taviŋwac. Presumably this name refers to the same district, but farther west, along the southern face of the Aquarius Plateau, on the small streams that head there and drain south to the Escalante.

Subsistence

For a nonagricultural population--even a small and dispersed one-- subsistence problems in the Kaiparowits area must have been acute. Anything but plenty is indicated by the casual comment that the Kaiparowits, when starving, ate their own children. Only pride and group loyalty can account for L's contention upon another occasion that "in the old days there was plenty to eat--all kinds of seeds; it was the Kaibab and Ankatɨ people who were always starving."

As among most of the Southern Paiute, seeds were regarded as the chief vegetable staple; roots and berries were more important than among the Kaibab. Probably the seasonal data given below for individual plants are inaccurate, as L's statements were frequently contradictory. However, it is evident that seeds and roots were available from summer through fall, with the addition in the fall of pinenuts and berries. Winter and, particularly, spring, were times of stint, when stored products and cacti were the chief sustenance.

As for game, resources, although diversified, appear to have been pretty strictly limited in quantity, certainly much more so than in Kaibab habitat. Hunting was a year-round pursuit but reached a peak in late summer and fall with trips to the neighboring plateaus. Large game animals included: deer and bear on the plateaus; mountain sheep in the upper Paria and the rough country to the east; and antelope "this side," presumably southwest, of Table Cliff Plateau. Elk was not common enough to be hunted despite the native name for Paria River (Paria-pa, elk water), which tradition derives from the fact that a lone elk once was seen to jump from the cliff into the stream. Smaller game animals are enumerated below, in connection with hunting.

Food stores were deposited in a bark-lined pit and covered with bark and stones. When possible these caches were located in caves or rock shelters.

Wild Plant Products

Seeds.--Gathered with seed beater in flat parching tray and poured into conical container. Latter a skin-covered frame, not a basket. Seeds prepared as among Kaibab. Metate (maracɨ), mano (muacɨ) similar to Kaibab; one side of metate used. When possible obtained from prehistoric site. No mealing brush.

A number of seed plants, mostly grasses, unidentified; partly because brief visit to Kaiparowits country did not permit extensive collection, but chiefly because of displacement of native plants.

Unidentified seeds: kwaguivɨ (from which Kwaguiuavɨ takes its name); pagankwak; soniantɨkwoi; nanancikwuiki; aŋcɨ; wanci; kovi (in fall); yɨsakɨ (similar to akɨ, but larger); kwakwe; ko (plateaus, in fall); tɨmarɨ (seeds? leaves? possibly Stanleya ?).

Valley seeds (i.e., Avua, Kwaguiuavɨ, Saŋwawitɨmpaya) ripe in summer, unless specified otherwise. Sawavɨ (Artemisia filifolia [?] ; a taller sage growing along streams called kakapɨ, but its seeds not eaten), ripe in fall; wa?a (wai?i; sand bunch grass, Oryzopsis hymenoides); aka (Helianthus petiolaris); tu-puipi (Amaranthus blitoides); ku?u (Mentzelia); wara (Chenopodium atrovirens Rydl.); pago (Chenopodium salinum Standl.), found in bed of Paria River, ripe in fall; nɨavi (probably Muhlenbergia; Gregory and Moore, 1931, 26, note occurrence of M. trifida); okɨntakwa (okontɨkwogwe,"fat kwakwe, because of large seeds; Epicampes rigens); kuiyokɨmpɨ (Sphaeralcea marginata); mua-puipi (fleabane, Erigeron canadensis); akɨ (Descurainia).

Plateau seeds ripe in fall. Pasɨ the most important; 4 kinds, of which 2 collected: sɨ?ɨkura-pasɨ (squawbush-neck-pasɨ, "because the seeds are long," Artemisia gnaphalodes Nutt.) and uiša-pasɨ (dark pasɨ, A. dracunculoides). Wa?a or wai?i (sand bunch grass, Oryzopsis hymenoides); aka (Helianthus petiolaris); cičagantɨ (Balsamorrhiza sagitata); siŋwa (gravel; stickseed, Lappula occidentalis Greene), found on Flake Mountain and on knoll called Aŋkapokorɨ, near Henrieville.

Berries and fruits.--On plateaus: tɨvicɨ (strawberry), beneath aspen trees. Eaten fresh; dried and stored in buckskin bag. Nagauwɨnatɨmpipi (raspberry) found only on Table Cliff Plateau. Not dried. Gathered early fall in finely wrapped carrying frame. Kunukɨ (elderberry) and tɨwampɨ (serviceberry) ripe in fall; dried, boiled, and drunk. Tonopɨ (chokecherry) ripe in fall. Eaten fresh, uncooked; not dried. Kaiŋ-apipi (a currant, Ribes cereum) eaten occasionally; not dried.

Lower elevations: I?isi (squawberry) found sparingly in canyons, as along Paria River. Not eaten fresh. "Cleaned" with hot ashes to improve flavor; care taken to prevent mixing pebbles with ashes; otherwise ground in with berries. Fruit rubbed between hands; winnowed, rubbed with "rag." Dried; stored in sack. Ground and made into a drink "like canned tomatoes."

Wiampɨ (Mahonia haematocarpa); on flat about Avua. Ripe in fall; eaten raw; not dried. Pa-upi (buffaloberry, Shepherdia argentea) found along streams, especially Paria. Eaten fresh; dried and ground on metate. U-upi (different from Kaibab berry of same name), a blue berry "kind of sour." Grew only in Paria Canyon; ripe in late summer. Eaten fresh, or dried and ground.

Roots.--Found mostly on higher elevations; in fall, according to L, but many of following specified as summer foods. Digging stick (poroc) of any kind of wood, often serviceberry. Butt placed beneath ashes to soften it; bent into crook, and tied with buckskin. Point not fire hardened; sharpened with stone knife.

Nagastarɨnɨmpɨ (Astralagus [?] ; name said to refer to mountain sheep eating leaves); lower elevations; spring; cooked in ashes. Cičagantɨ (Balsamorrhiza sagitata); mountain slopes; young roots eaten fresh. Ciŋ (Cirsium arizonicum); mountain slopes; summer. Pigi, unidentified root; Kaiparowits Plateau; summer. Sigo?o (sego root), called also musɨgwi and mu?unapac; common on plateaus; summer. Cooked in special kind of earth oven called pasuyaikɨ: fire built in pot-shaped pit; opening smaller than diameter below. Roots poured in; sprinkled with water; covered "quickly and tightly" with damp earth. Kaŋɨ, unidentified root; Table Cliff Plateau; summer. White daisylike blossom. Cooked same way as preceding. Na?ani, root resembling sego but double "like twins." Gathered Kaiparowits Plateau; summer, fall. Kwiyu?u, a long root, blackish, evil-smelling (two latter characteristics suggest Valeriana, whose occurrence is noted by Gregory and Moore, 1931, 26); Aquarius Plateau, fall. 4 women supervised cooking; roots assembled in large pile; hole in ground lined with stones; fire kindled; ashes raked out; roots deposited in oven, with individually owned lots separated by bunches of grass. Covered with grass, stones, hot ashes; no vent; breaks in covering filled to prevent escape of steam. Cooked overnight; not dried. Tasiu (said to be same as Kaibab tasiu, Peteria); along mountain slopes; all year; roasted overnight in earth oven (urapɨ).

Miscellaneous.-- Pinenuts (tɨwai) harvested on Kaiparowits Plateau in fall. Cacti (tasɨ, nɨaras, munč, wisi, yawɨmpɨ) on Kaiparowits Plateau; important winter and spring. Mescal found in small quantities along Paria River. Yucca (wide-leaved) fruit eaten; also "cabbages" (base of stalk, čuarɨ) of narrow-leaved yucca. Sawa-u?u (Orobanche ludoviciana, Nutt.) grew beneath the plant called nagamavɨ, which is similar to rabbitbrush but smaller; ripe in fall; boiled. Kučuavi (Cercocarpus flabellifolnis Ryd.) leaves made into tea. Aspen sap not utilized; no sugar substitute.

Tobacco.--Called sagogoapɨ (Nicotiana attenuata). Whole plant pulled in fall; stacked; left to dry. Brush not burned to encourage growth of tobacco. Tobacco mixed with ararɨmpipɨ (manzanita), dried separately. Mixing regarded as old custom; not attributed to recent Ute borrowing.

Men smoked, also women shamans. Pipe tubular, a length of elder with pith removed. Not lined; "when it burned you made another."

Hunting

Kaiparowits hunting methods are attributed to Coyote; in recent times a boy received instructions from his father.

First-game observances.--Boy could not eat first game but gave it to old people. If woman ate it, lad would be lazy. When 15 or 16 years old, killed first deer. Mother thereupon bathed boy, painted his body red. Gave him taste of meat, which he might not swallow but must spit into fire; otherwise, would be lazy and kill no more deer. Parents then ate meat. Boy still too young to smoke; "not until a man."

The Kaiparowits had one hunting chief (niavi) for deer and mountain sheep and another for antelope; both addressed the people early in the morning. No esoteric elements appear to have been involved in the selection of such an individual, for dreaming and singing were not a customary preliminary to the chase (although L remarked that "the Navajo always sang before hunting or trading"). Practical considerations probably governed selection, for the antelope "chief" was the man who built and owned the one antelope pound in Avua. It is possible, but unlikely, that the construction was the consequence of his office rather than the reason for it. This, incidentally, was the only mention of private ownership in connection with hunting.

Large game.--Deer, antelope, mountain sheep, and bear; latter rarely hunted because "hard to kill with arrows." No elk.

Deer hunted chiefly summer and fall; on "mountains," often Aŋkaigavɨ, near Canaan Peak. Stalked; no disguise. Individual hunter encountering fresh tracks or several deer in cul de sac summoned assistance. Party of 5 or 6, with chief, might hunt. No surround; sometimes ran deer into cleft in rocks; onto promontory, cutting off retreat by fires; or over bluff. Kill divided; head, hide, 1 hind leg to successful marksman; ribs, sometimes a leg, to chief. Latter shared equally with others. Meat dried; head baked in ashes.

Antelope hunted in fall "when meat tastes strong"; found "this side," presumably southwest, of Table Cliff Plateau. Stalked; no disguise besides tuft of brush held in hand for concealment.

Drive, a small-scale affair with few participants: 5 or 6 men, headed by antelope chief. Latter announced hunt early in morning. No singing; no rasp; no "charming." Corral (waŋcinkwiɨpi, wanc-ičunɨpi; wanc, antelope): stones piled in circle perhaps 200 ft. dia.; walls about 2.5 ft. high (animals often jumped over). Opening flanked by stone wings; latter not straight but curved back, almost following line of corral wall. Owned by antelope chief; built by him with aid of other men. Only 1 corral in Avua country. Chief posted 2 men at pound, 1 either side of entrance, between wall and wing. Sometimes chief remained at corral but usually accompanied driving party. Man who shot antelope got head, hide, 1 hind leg. Head cooked in ashes; meat boiled; dried. Women shared cooked meat with neighboring camps.

Mountain sheep hunted in upper Paria district and in Kwaguiuavɨ, at Asikaivɨ (gray mountain; said to be "nothing but rocks"), south of Cottonwood Wash. Stalked by lone hunter crying "paga, paga," in imitation of call. Sheep difficult to hunt and heavy to transport. Lone hunter butchered and hung part from limb of tree for subsequent transport. Parties, headed by chief, ran sheep into cleft; or on promontory, cutting off escape by fires; occasionally ran them off bluff. Meat boiled; head roasted. Hide utilized same as buckskin.

Several kinds of bear recognized: tocakwiacɨ (white bear), found north end Table Cliff Plateau; gasikwiacɨ (gray bear, said to be gray mixed with black; evidently grizzly); ontonkwiacɨ (brown bear), on Aquarius Plateau; and aŋkakwiacɨ (red bear) very scarce. Bear called kwiacɨ (said to be Moapa term for rattlesnake) or kwiagant; all bears likewise called kagun (maternal grandmother)(cf. p. 48). If one cried kwiacɨ to bear, it pursued him; if called kagun, it fled. Seldom hunted bear, but if man saw tracks, he summoned aid and killed animal. When about to shoot hunter said, "Old woman, I am going to kill you. I want to eat your meat. Do not be angry; do not kill me." Head roasted; flesh boiled or cooked in pit oven; no parts taboo to either sex. Hide used for blanket.

Small game.--Rabbits tracked in soft snow; hit with straight stick of oak. L saw curved rabbit stick first when she visited Kaibab reservation. Rabbits taken any time year in drive; although actually communal, scarcely sufficient participants (5 to 6) to be designated as such; "not enough Indians." No rabbit chief. Net (p.164) about 3 ft. wide. Set in straight line across trail. Man stood at one end; at other placed stick tied at top with sagebrush to simulate a man. Other men (never women) drove rabbits into net; no fires. Hunter killed entangled ones, apparently by swinging to break neck. Women roasted kill. In summer, roasted in skins; in winter, skinned (pelts saved), cleaned, and laid in ashes, heads all 1 way, for about an hour. When cooked, distributed to various camps.

Beaver (paunsɨ) found on mountains "where there is plenty of water." Shot; skinned (sacklike or with ventral cut); boiled. Meat sometimes dried; hung on bushes or horizontal bar. Hide used extensively for moccasins and leggings.

Marmot (yaŋampuc) found on plateaus in summer; shot; roasted in skin or boiled. Squirrels shot among rocks at cliff base; not trapped; sometimes hit with stone. Baked whole in ashes. Prairie dog (aiyavuc) abundant on Paunsaugunt Plateau, but originally none in Avua. Introduced in post-white times from Sevier Valley by Maggie Johnny, a young Kaibab (cf. p. 52). Became plentiful. Water poured into burrow; animal hit with stick as it emerged. Tossed into fire, removed, scraped, gutted. Belly pinned together with twigs; placed in ashes to bake; sometimes boiled. Chipmunk baked whole in ashes. Gopher (miɨmpuc) eaten to induce pregnancy (p. 166).

Rats of two kinds: tɨnakac, living "halfway up the rocks"; kacɨ, living in open desert. Shot; sometimes hauled from nest by long serviceberry stick, not hooked. End dampened and twisted in skin. Roasted whole in ashes; pelts not used.

Porcupine (yɨŋɨmpɨc) clubbed in tree. Singed and plucked; scraped with stick; roasted. Badger (ɨnampucɨ) hunted all year in valleys. Smoked from hole and clubbed. Roasted. Hide, with fur outside, used for moccasin uppers. Wildcat (tukupic) clubbed in tree or shot; roasted, hide for blankets and quiver. Young coyotes (sinaʔavɨ, šɨnavɨ) lured from nest by hunter, who called and offered rabbit guts as bait. Cooked in ashes; hide (skinned sacklike) for quiver.

Sagehen (cičaiya) the "best" of the birds. Shot in spring on sage flats on Paunsaugunt Plateau. Feathers not used. Wild turkey (kaɨmpuc) "stayed on big mountains like Paʔantakaipɨ" (Table Cliff). Shot in spring; plucked and baked in ashes; not dried. Other birds: mourning dove (aiyɨvɨ); flicker (aŋkakwanawavi); quail (shot in snow in Kwaguiuavɨ); owl (muʔupɨc); eagle (kwananc). Two latter considered "meat, just like rabbit." No bird blind; no bird of any kind taken in net or trap; some shot, but usually young ones caught when learning to fly.

Yellow "caterpillars" (piɨgɨ) found "everywhere." Collected; pulled, head down, between thumb and first finger to clean; "braided" into "rope" 2 to 3 ft. long and roasted between 2 heated stone slabs.

Game not eaten.--Skunk ("never saw one in that country"); fox (yuguvɨc; hide for quiver and blankets); full-grown coyote (hide for blankets); wolf (scarce and dangerous; would attack camp if its young were stolen); lion (difficult to hunt; skin used for blanket); mice; lizard (sikɨmɨc; regarded with great aversion; L shivered at mention of name (cf. p. 139); snake (addressed thus, "Grandfather [togoni, mother's father, p. 123, no. 10], where are you? don't bite me!"); grasshoppers, ants, ant larvae.

Salt

Reddish colored salt (uʔagampɨ) was obtained in Escalante Valley and caves along Paria canyon. Mixed with water, it was used to season mush.

Shelter

The shelters described are similar to those reported for the Kaibab; L attributed the sweathouse to late Navajo influence.

In winter lived in cave when possible; fire built in mouth. Either side of entrance flanked with green juniper boughs; none across entrance. When no cave at hand, constructed house (kani) similar to Kaibab, leaning juniper posts against horizontal limb of tree. No smoke hole; juniper-bark thatch. Juniper bark for mattress.

Remainder of year used a dome-shaped (?) shade or a rectangular shade (flat roof on posts), both called avagan; or a circular brush enclosure (nuvipi).

Learned use of sweathouse from Navajo when L was "grown" (1885-1890?). Lodge (nasaʔa, nasa-kan) dome-shaped frame covered with blankets; entrance faced any direction. Water poured on hot stones, which were to left of entrance (as one entered). Two, sometimes 3, sweated together; sexes separately. Came out of lodge to roll in sand ("got pneumonia when they came out like that") and returned to continue sweating. Curative and "just for bath." No singing, praying; "Navajo sing and yell but we didn't know how."

Dress

As among the Kaibab, the traditional clothing evidently was of bark, although L remembered this type of garment only for women. The latter adopted a Plains-type skin dress within her memory (about 1880?), presumably through Ute or "nearly Ute" influence. Prior to this, however, there was some sort of woman's garment of mountain sheep hide. Moccasins came about the time the woman's buckskin dress was adopted.

The woman's "skirt" (kasumpi) of cliffrose bark or soft inner bark of cottonwood; either double apron or "wrap-around" similar to Kaibab. Leggings of same material; sandals, of narrow-leaved yucca. In winter, feet wrapped with cliffrose bark.

Buckskin dress (paramun) and moccasins "recent"; adopted when L was 9 or 10 years old (ca. 1880?). Previously, woman had garment of mountain sheep hide; L uncertain if apron or some sort of dress. Buckskin dress took 2 hides; 3 for large woman (gores inserted). Sewn across shoulders and under arms; hides hung head downward. Sleeves short, unfringed; probably not separate pieces. Seams fringed; separate strip of hide sewn straight across bottom of garment and fringed. Buckskin belt. No porcupine quill decoration; manufacture of bead trim learned "recently" from Ute.

Women bareheaded. Hair hung loose; mescal fiber hairbrush obtained in trade from Kaibab. No basket cap.

For men, L remembered only buckskin "pants" and shirt (perapɨ); moccasins. Latter same pattern as Kaibab; sometimes of beaverskin; sometimes soles buckskin and uppers, badger hide (fur left on, outside).

Men wore hair with central part, 2 braids; string tied at top and bottom of braid.

Both sexes painted faces daily; red ordinarily; for dances, several colors applied in designs. Red paint, a clay(?), found at Impit-impaya (paint-canyon mouth; Birch Creek Valley [?]) near Table Cliff Plateau. Found on surface, but could be dug out if desired; boiled; spread on buckskin to dry; not ground or pounded. Traded to Kaibab. Site of paint "owned" by Muavinapuŋ (mosquito man), who sometimes camped there (p.151) but he did not own paint: "anyone could gather it."

No tattooing. Some of both sexes had ears punched by mother when about 10 years old. Not associated with puberty rites. Twig of rabbitbrush worn as ornament.

Blankets of bear, wildcat, lion skins; several fox or coyote pelts sewn together. Woolen blankets, worn as wraps, obtained in trade from Navajo.

Rabbitskin blankets woven only by women. Cottontail or jack skins either alone or interspersed; cottontail said to be "warmer when the blanket is old." Skinned with ventral cut, not sacklike. Pelt cut into continuous strip, starting with hind leg and cutting back and forth, not quite severing edges of skin. 7 to 10 such strips joined to form long string; looped. Looped end tied to stationary object; Apocynum string attached to other end and twirled between palms (downward movement of right palm on left), twisting looped fur. Resulted in "rabbitskin rope"; hung to dry.

Two kinds of frames: (1) 2 parallel rows stakes over which "rope" warped; (2) 2 horizontal bars, each supported either end by stake. Warping started lower right (as one sits before frame), proceeding back and forth about bars. L regarded latter frame as "easier." In both cases twining (Apocynum cord) continuous, starting lower right corner. Blankets used as bedding and robes; worn across shoulders, tied on chest with Apocynum cord.

Crafts and Manufactures

The handicraft tradition was conspicuously weak and focused on basketry; no pottery was manufactured. A two-holed flute was mentioned, although the Kaibab reported no such instrument.

Tanning

Tanning a woman's job. Skin hung on post resting against tree; scraped on fleshy side with stone or deer cannon bone (foreleg). In recent times, dried after initial scraping; soaked overnight; de-haired. For tan, used "any kind" of brain ("even rabbit, but not coyote") or marrow, pushed from spinal column with small stick. Marrow boiled, sprinkled on hide; preferable to brain tan, because skin turned out softer. Six applications of tan; skin rubbed and pulled after each one. Smoked on hair side; a smoked skin remained soft, even if it became wet. Smoking process learned from Koosharem who, in turn, learned from Ute father north; this was before L was born.

Some hides tanned with hair on. Fleshy side scraped with stone; skin spread on ground, pegged down. Sometimes, with hand, brains and water sprinkled on skin; allowed to dry; rubbed with stone; pulled and worked in hands. Hide buried in damp ground to make it pliable; worked again; hung in sun. L thought when hair left on burial in ground was sufficient; brain application not essential.

Weapons

Bow (ačɨ); self-bow (ta?auɨ-ačɨ); sinew-backed bow (taŋačɨ); horn bow (nag-ačɨ, mountain sheep bow). Self-bow of juniper; sinew-backed, of oak. Sinew (tamupi) from leg of deer or mountain sheep applied in lengthwise strips. Single application; attached with glue made from boiling neck and horns of fawn; less frequently, glued with pinyon gum (sanapi). Grip slightly constricted, wrapped with buckskin. Inside of bow coated with pitch and red paint. Ends notched for sinew string (pagawi). L thought horn bow not manufactured locally but received in trade from Kaibab. Latter mentioned horn bow as trade item obtained from Kaiparowits

Arrows (kwiyu) of serviceberry, currant, cane; not of rose. Cane arrows tipped with serviceberry points; others had stone heads found archeologically. After whites arrived, nails used as points. Arrows 3-feathered; tail feathers of eagle or any kind of hawk were split, attached with pitch and sinew. No arrow poison.

Five to 10 arrows carried in quiver (ugunain). Latter made by man; sewn with sinew. Wildcat, fawn, or other skin used; stick sewn into seam. Coyote pup skinned sacklike and hide used for quiver. Packline of Apocynum cord.

Fire Making Equipment

Percussion technique known; sometimes struck "red and white stones" from archeological sites over shredded bark. Drilling more usual. Juniper hearth, with stem of narrow-leaved yucca for drill; L does not remember if latter simple or composite. Slow match (kosɨvɨ) of bark, tied with strands of narrow-leaved yucca.

Juniper the best firewood. When new camp pitched, burned down 4 or 5 trees to obtain fuel; this practice called kov?kopɨ.

Horn Spoon

Each household had horn spoon (agoc) or ladle for stirring mush; presumably similar to Fig. 1, a, b. Made by the man but "belonged to the woman." A man stirred mush with a stick. Mountain sheep horn warmed in ashes and cut off below tip. Latter formed into handle; lower part of tip scraped and flattened to make bowl. Warmed again and sprung while soft. Not carved.

Spoon not used in eating. Mush scooped to mouth with stick (rarely), usually with first and second fingers.

Basketry

Baskets the chief receptacles. Pottery not manufactured and no use made of vessels occasionally found archeologically.

L learned to make baskets from her mother; "fancy basketry" apparently introduced later, from San Juan Paiute. Kaiparowits preferred willow to squawbush; latter too brittle.

No conical burden basket, either twined or coiled. Seeds gathered in subconical, skin-covered receptacle.

Carrying frame (kaŋavi) in wrapped stitch (model, Pl. 3, a) used for yucca fruit, pine cones, etc. Model made as follows:

Two serviceberry sticks crossed at right angles; juncture tied with yucca strand. Another serviceberry wand bent to form a hoop. Ribs made by bending crossed sticks upward, forcing them inside hoop, and tying them with buckskin; near-conical frame thus produced. Wrapping of yucca strands; broad-leaved yucca preferred because stronger; specimen figured is of narrow-leaved yucca, since no other available. Leaves torn in strips and knotted together to form long strand.

Frame held on lap with opening to worker's left; 1 end of strand tied to rib, near encircling hoop; carried forward (away from worker), passing over rib, coming out beneath it and to right of superior strand; this wrapping continued from rib to rib, spirally from rim of frame to apex. If specimen viewed from above mouth, progression counterclockwise.

Frame now held with apex in worker's lap. New strand attached at apex, just to left of rib. Wrapping carried forward and away from worker, engaging with each already-wrapped strand. When rim reached, frame reversed and wrapping continued from rim to apex, always away from worker. Active strand manipulated with right hand; left holds previous "stitch" in place. Each of the 4 "faces" of frame worked as described, except the last. With this, for no apparent reason, strand carried up center of face instead of following rib. When horizontal and vertical wrapping completed, extra courses added wherever spacing unduly wide. Tump of 4 to 5 buckskin thongs, not braided, fastened to 2 ribs. Model of an essentially similar carrying frame, but with apex more pointed, collected from Shivwits Paiute.

Parching and winnowing trays both twined and coiled. Latter said to have been made on 2-rod foundation. Specimen (Pl. 3, e) made by L, of 3 rods arranged vertically; progress right to left, convex side the work surface. Coated with old yucca root pounded with water.

Cooking and food baskets called kwicičuac; coiled. Former about 1.5 ft. tall; latter, smaller. Inside made watertight by application of yucca root.

Seed beaters of twined and of wickerwork (Pl. 4, c, a, respectively). Twined specimen more elongated than Kaibab; bowl not circular, but angular at base; outer warps do not cross over top of bowl (as among Kaibab), but all warps bunched to form handle. Twine downward. Both kinds of beater had wooden blade.

Water jar (uci) coiled. Start single-rod, changing to 2-rod. Flat bottom. Handles of horsehair; L does not know what was used in pre-horse days, "maybe squawbush." Stopper of sagebrush bark; juniper bark discolored water.

No basket cap.

Cradle made by L shown in Pl. 5, c. Body of diagonal (upward) twine; no separate frame, but body encircled by rods (in old days, of avagunimpi, *Symphoricarpos*) attached in coiled stitch; encircling rods extended to form handle at top. Awning of simple twine; sides nearly parallel. Attachment differs from that of Kaibab; Kaiparowits awning in same plane with body of cradle; Kaibab awning attached at sharp angle (cf. Pls. 5, c, d).

Nets of wi?ivɨ (<u>Apocynum cannibinum</u>) fiber. Gathered in fall by men, who made cord and nets (wanai, called also wani). First row of netting made over a stick; no measuring apparatus; "they know without measuring." Rabbit net about 3 ft. wide.

Musical Instruments

No rattle; no drum (but known to be used by Ute); no musical bow. The only instrument a flute (uiyuinɨmpɨ) of willow (?) or elder; pith pushed easily from latter. Flute about 1 ft. long; 2 holes, bored with stone drill found archeologically. End blown. Played by men in daytime; no singing accompaniment; no association with courtship or dances.

Communications and Trade

The Kaiparowits region was pretty well traversed by trails. Because of the rugged relief, some routes were circuitous, and because of the scarcity of springs and pot holes in certain areas, water was carried in basket jars. Trade seems to have been slight, probably owing to poverty as well as to difficult traverse.

Routes

Potato Valley (that is, Escalante Valley, upstream from the town of that name) to Kaiparowits Plateau. Route extraordinarily roundabout, going the full distance to the Colorado River, presumably along the base of the Straight Cliffs, thence climbing to the summit. A traveler spent 2 nights on the way and carried water.

Potato Valley eastward to Henry Mountains. Apparently the only trail was via Kaivɨyɨgacɨ, where Circle Cliffs and Aquarius Plateau come together; route crossed north of Circle Cliffs. No established trails over Waterpocket Fold; forbidding and seldom traveled; if necessary, "crossed anywhere."

Potato Valley to Aquarius and Table Cliff plateaus; same route as present road, up Birch and Sweetwater canyons.

Potato Valley to Avua. Apparently via upper Potato Valley.

Avua to Ankatɨ, in Kaibab country (map 1, springs 40-45). Trail down Paria Canyon to fork, where 1 branch turned west, up canyon, passing north of Kaivaku?-uwaiyac (standing-up mountain, probably Mollie's nipple), and on to nearby Ankatɨ.

Avua to Kwaguiuavɨ. At start, same route as preceding, to fork, from which point, eastward to Kwaguiuavɨ.

Kwaguiuavɨ to hunting grounds (Aŋkaigavɨ, p. 150) between Canaan Peak and Kaiparowits Plateau. Route followed southwest flank of Kaiparowits Plateau.

Kwaguiuavɨ to Kaiparowits Plateau; upstream along Colorado Canyon (not in sight of river), apparently across heads of tributary canyons, to southern tip of plateau, thence to summit. Travelers carried water from Oauipi (presumably Wahweap Creek).

Kaiparowits trail crossed Colorado River. Ford said to be at southern tip of Straight Cliffs (of Kaiparowits Plateau) and, on far shore, at point just northeast of Navajo Mountain. Called nɨnwɨnparo (people crossing, i.e., Paiute crossing). Location sounds upstream from Crossing of the Fathers. L claimed her mother passed river here on visits to San Juan Paiute and that Navajo traders used same ford.

Commerce

Kaibab gave Kaiparowits mescal fiber brush in exchange for red paint. Also gave buckskin for bows, arrows; apparently 2-way traffic in bows (pp. 90, 161).

Utes visited but did not trade; buffalo (moguikuč) hides not obtained from them. Navajo came on foot, blankets on back. Somewhat larger than saddle plankets, undecorated; 1 to 3 buckskins for a blanket.

Dogs (šɨnavɨ, coyote) introduced by whites; called thus: "ya papi" (here, puppy). Horses (pukuma, pet; also kava, from Spanish) introduced by whites. 5 buckskins, never children, given for horse.

Miscellany

Below are a few oddments that may be placed on record.

Eagle nests: apparently not considered private property by L. She knew of one to which a man was let over cliff, by means of net tied about the waist. Young birds taken to camp; nest built for them; fed rabbits, squirrels, snakes thrice daily. In former times, grown birds plucked, killed, eaten; when L was young, they were freed after feathers had been pulled.

Menstrual customs: seclusion 4 to 5 days in hut. No meat, salt, cold water (caused cramps). Scratching stick used; likewise by parturient. Goldenrod (oatɨnapɨ, Solidago missouriensis Nutt.) made into tea to relieve menstrual pain. On return from hut, barren woman ate gopher in belief that conception of male child would follow.

Love charm: plant called nasasi (Ximenesia exauriculata [Verbesina]) said to attract one of opposite sex; Kaibab interpreter KC thought L indicated wrong plant.

Mourning: women mourners cut hair; men did not.

Constellations: Milky way called togoravɨ (sky cane, pole). Pleiades(?) said to be a mother and daughters, with Coyote's son just outside the group; L uncertain how many stars in cluster. Evidently refers to familiar tale of incest (Kaibab version, Sapir, 1930, 463-5). Orion's belt: mountain sheep. Two lone stars nearby, one "at top" and one "at bottom" are hunters; former driving sheep toward latter, in ambush behind rocks.

Ghosts: a ghost (inɨmpɨc), male or female, in whirlwind. Wings of flicker sewn into baglike affair; in early morning person set out, opening and collapsing feather "bag," trying thereby to kill ghosts. Context not clear.

Therapy: Shamans sang; did not use feathers; L "afraid to say" if they sucked. Her ff or fff (kɨnuni) was rattlesnake shaman (togoa-vuagant). Root called togwogwasi (loco weed, Oxytropis lamberti) applied to snakebite. In old days, bull snake eaten as remedy for "sore legs," perhaps rheumatism. Leaves of oicɨkwasipi (squirrel tail, Achillea millefolium var. lanulosa) pounded and applied to pustules. Sore eyes "bathed" in steam from sagebrush tea; latter used also as an emetic.

SAN JUAN

These few and uncertain notes on the San Juan Paiute were obtained in the course of three or four days, without opportunity for subsequent checking. They are being put on record because there is no published material on the group, except for casual mention in the Reports of the Commissioner of Indian Affairs.

The accompanying material comes from two informants (p. 3), Jodie (J), at Marble Canyon, and Joe Francis (JF), at Tuba City. Work with the former would have been more profitable had an interpreter been available; we were obliged to communicate in pidgin English, supplemented by my limited Kaibab vocabulary. JF worked through a Navajo-English interpreter. Potentially an excellent informant, he disappeared at the end of the first day and could not be located, either then or a year later, when I was again in Tuba City.

If one could take time to go to Piute Canyon, where most of the remaining San Juan seem to be concentrated, it is almost certain that good material could be obtained. To be on the safe side, it might be well to take along an interpreter, perhaps Kaibab. The San Juan have had less white contact than other Southern Paiute, but Navajo, Ute, and probably Pueblo influences must have been strong.

Territory and Neighbors

The distribution of the San Juan Paiute has been indicated previously (Kelly, 1934). Roughly, the area extended from Monument Valley to the Little Colorado and from the San Juan River to Black Mesa and Moencopi Plateau, without including either of the latter (map 1). It comprised the northwest corner of the region Gregory designates as Navajo country.

In spite of this territorial extent, the San Juan seem to have kept pretty much to the western half of the zone, because of Navajo aggression. Travelers seldom ventured east of Moonlight Creek; Monument Valley was little visited "because there was no water." In my informants' youth, the San Juan rarely camped in Piute Canyon or eastward; they "would go there, then come right back"; they were "afraid of the Navajo."

When J and JF were young, Moencopi Plateau was uninhabited. The Navajo were mostly on "Calabaza Mesa," said to be a "mountain east of

Kayenta." Although it is south rather than east, reference seems to be to Black Mesa. There were a "few" Navajo in the vicinity of Tuba City and one Hopi lived where Moencopi village now is situated. Several sources (Bartlett, 1932, 31; W.W. Hill, 1936, 4; Spier, 1928 95, 362-5) indicate a Navajo thrust westward in the 1860's.

No mention was made of the Paiute on the far side of the Colorado Canyon, although Kaibab and Kaiparowits informants spoke of occasional visits to the San Juan group and of a few cases of intermarriage. There is one Kaibab report of San Juan traders who came to offer rugs, presumably Navajo, in exchange for buckskin (p. 90).

The area north of the San Juan River was unoccupied, but "probably Ute." Bluff City was said specifically to be Ute, as was the region of Henry Mountains (Antari; cf. Yantarii, (pp. 144-5).

West of the Little Colorado were the friendly Havasupai, with whom the San Juan Paiute hunted deer on Coconino Plateau and with whom, it was said, they intermarried.

J thought there might have been Apache in the area north of Flagstaff; he had heard that there they once fought the Havasupai and Paiute.

Habitat and Settlement

The area of the San Juan Paiute is a great stretch of mesas, buttes, and canyons, whose middle elevations are arid, with little perennial water and scant vegetation. An extract from Gregory's (1917, 14) description follows:

> At altitudes below 5,000 feet vegetation of all kinds is sparse and over large areas nearly lacking. Between 5,000 and 6,000 feet sagebrush (Artemisia) and greasewood (Sarcobatus), with scattered groves of juniper (Juniperus monosperma) and piñon (Pinus edulis) are conspicuous. At elevations between 6,000 and 7,000 feet juniper and piñon enclosing parks of sagebrush and grass make up the larger part of the flora.... Within the zone of yellow pine, between altitudes of 7,000 and 8,500 feet [Navaho Mountain] forests of merchantable timber are found.... Above 8,500 feet the flora resembles that of humid regions. Engelmann spruce is the chief timber tree, but groves of aspen, willow, and oak are found.

The few data on settlement refer to a time when the Paiute already had scuttled westward. Although informants remembered several semi-permanent camps, with gardens, at Kayenta, occupation seems to have been chiefly in the areas of Navajo Creek and Moencopi Wash. In 1776, on the return to Pueblo country, and some 8 leagues beyond the Crossing of the Fathers, Escalante's party came upon an encampment of "yutas payuchis" (Documentos 1, 1854, 539), evidently in the Navajo Creek area.

Even before the devastating effects of recent erosion, campsites were restricted by available water. When JF was young his father planted at Willow Spring in Navajo Canyon, or at Tuba City, at a spring called Aŋkankwinɨ (red stream; "where the street ends in Tuba City"). Moencopi Wash (Pankwinti, water stream) had no plantings.

Nevertheless, JF's family spent considerable time about Shinumo Altar (Tukwarɨri black hill), in the desert flat west of Echo Cliffs (Skiwakavɨ). Lacking springs, this district could be occupied only during summer rains and winter snows. As the snow melted, camp was broken and the people scattered--"some toward Cameron, some toward Navajo Mountain, some to Tuba; they went anywhere."

JF remembered 14 individuals with camps at Shinumo Altar: (1) Tɨnɨsta (ram) and his several children. (2) Manesagarɨ. (3) Pasɨc (sunflower). (4) Napacɨ. (5) Paguicɨ. (6) Tɨnwɨtɨgaivɨ. (7) Čaiyagai (8) Wɨšɨyavɨ (big nose). (9) Šanapɨ (pine gum). (10) Siapasɨ. (11) Powɨskis (no tooth; "a Paiute with a Navajo name). (12) Panakarɨ, who later moved to Piute Canyon. (13) Kunagai. (14) Kavapikuananc (horse rides sideways).

If the population centered anywhere, probably it was along Navajo Creek, where J's father lived. From the bend(?) downstream the canyon is known as Pagamtɨpaiya (cane canyon); and, upstream, Tonotɨmpaiya (probably Sarcobatus-canyon). According to description, the canyon was well watered, with willow, cane, and many cottonwoods. Plots near the various springs were cultivated. Summer was spent in the canyon; winter, nearby, on top of the mesa to the west, where there "was lots of snow but plenty of juniper" for fuel.

Subsistence

The present data are too fragmentary to give a very clear idea of the economy of the San Juan Paiute. At best, the country is one of little water and limited resources. Supposedly the subsistence pattern was similar to

that of the Kaibab but more restricted. For example, deer and pinenuts--
of which the Kaibab had an ample and dependable supply--were less plentiful. Maize was grown, but so casually that it was probably no more than
a supplementary item in the diet.

Agriculture

Paiute learned to plant from Hopi; JF does not know how long ago,
but his grandfather raised corn. When he himself was young, maize
the only cultigen; when he was adult, beans and squash also grown.
J gave following names for plants: maize, kumi (cf. Kaibab name for
modern corn, p. 39); beans, muruis; squash (or pumpkin), na?gɨtis(?);
watermelon, piarkanɨmp; cantaloupe, muruna; sunflower, mukwivi.

At Willow Spring, in Navajo Canyon, JF's father selected an open
site (hence no need of clearing), near spring. Worked soil "with
any kind of stick"; with hands, dug ditch from spring in order to
water plot. Planting not in rows. Apparently little cultivation; occasional weeding by hand. Planted in spring; thereafter left site to
gather wild foods ripe in summer; returned to harvest agricultural
products.

Wild Plant Products

A superficial check on basis of wild plant foods known in Kaibab
area indicates similar range, but presumably somewhat different
emphasis, according to local circumstances. Herbarium specimens
not collected--chiefly, for want of time, but also because recent
changes in vegetation make many plants mentioned by informants
now difficult to find. A good many of the names listed below probably can be equated roughly with similarly named plants among the
Kaibab.

Seeds: wa?a; kwakwe; wara; tupui (a prostrate plant); akɨ; ku?u
(formerly plentiful at base of Echo Cliffs); kumutɨ; pasɨ; wiakɨ; pana
("like wheat); 2 latter not mentioned for Kaibab.

Berries: wapampɨ (juniper berry); ogompɨ (current?; plentiful
near Tuba City in former times); tonapɨ; ciampɨ; ɨpɨ (gathered between Willow Spring and the Colorado Canyon); is; kainapɨ. No
wiyɨmpipi (Mahonia); several other berries reported by Kaibab not
mentioned locally.

Pinenuts eaten; likewise yucca fruit and base of stalk, both roasted in ground. Yucca root avoided; caused vomiting. Mescal: baked 2 nights in earth oven, then dried. Cacti: iuavɨ (prickly pear), tasɨ, nɨaras eaten. Roots included: kwičas (wild onion); kusau?urɨ (gathered on sand hills); tun, tagɨ (disappeared); kwiu root found only in canyon west of Kayenta and not "good." Aphis "sugar" from cane eaten; likewise tu?u (probably broomrape; grew in sand).

Tobacco: plot burned to encourage growth. Tobacco considered scarce; unobtainable for several years, then plentiful; "maybe the rain plants it". Tobacco mixed with manzanita, smoked in green stone pipe with cane stem. Stone collected "this side," presumably southwest, of Bluff City, on San Juan River.

Hunting

First-game observances.--Boy would be lazy if he or his mother ate first kill. Lad painted red and told to run south before sunrise. (Volunteered that Hopi boys run according to direction of Milky Way). Running perhaps a general observance for adolescent boy, not connected specifically with first game.

Large game.--Deer hunted upstream from Cameron and outside Paiute territory: on Coconino Plateau (Havasupai) and north of the San Juan River (Ute). Antelope found upstream from Cameron and on Kaibito Plateau. Informants claim Paiute killed 1 or 2 at a time, but "the Navajo, on horseback, killed all." Antelope impounded in corral, 1 hunter either side of entrance, others driving. 1 headman for both deer and antelope; "talked but did not sing." Mountain sheep found on Navajo Mountain; bear, upstream from Cameron, but probably not hunted.

Small game.--Rabbits tracked in snow, shot; also trapped. Sometimes pulled from hole with straight stick, whose end was moistened in the mouth, so as to catch in the fur. Rabbit drive known to J by hearsay only. Directed by a chief (tavuc-nɨavɨ). Drive lasted all day; hunters returned to camp at night. Rabbit net of wipi, presumably *Apocynum*.

Rats eaten, mice not. Porcupine edible after quills scraped off (no quill embroidery). Wildcat also eaten. Snakes and coyote not used as food, although Hopi said to eat coyote as emetic.

No fishing in former times, although some fish in Navajo Creek; nowadays eaten.

Dogs.--None, although both Hopi and Navajo said to have had them.

Salt

Collected in a "cave where the water dripped all the time"; situated on Little Colorado, some "30 miles above Cameron."

Shelter

The winter house was conical, with a forked-post frame. Informants claimed there was no ax in former times and branches were broken from a tree. They described a frame of two interlocking, forked posts that supported auxiliary poles. Women stripped juniper bark from the trees and heaped it loosely over the frame, leaving no smoke hole, and covering the floor with it.

FJ thought that no shade or arbor was used; "in summer, we lived under the trees," and took refuge in rock shelters from the rains.

According to J, use of the sweathouse was inspired by the Navajo; he could give no date, but his father practiced sweating. The lodge was earth-covered, with a blanket over the doorway. Water was poured on hot stones, placed to one side of the entrance. Anyone who entered called, "Paa" (presumably, water); otherwise a ghost or spirit (inɨpɨc) might close the entrance and death result. "Lots of Navajo die while sweating."

Dress

Men used skin clothing. There was no mention of leggings, but the shirt was sleeveless; it was a one-skin garment, of deer, antelope, or mountain sheep hide. They wore a cap of wildcat or antelope skin. Moccasins had a badger skin sole and buckskin upper; in winter, bark was stuffed into them to protect the feet. A man invariably made the moccasins, but a woman might make the shirt.

The woman's garment was a double apron of skin, probably of cliffrose bark when hides were scarce. "Some women wore bark shoes." No basket cap was used.

The rabbitskin blanket, with Apocynum-fiber weft, was made by the women; J declared that no frame was used, and "that is the way" he saw his maternal grandmother make blankets.

Crafts and Manufactures

As among all Paiute, handicrafts are not well developed, except for basketry. Basketry is of special interest among the San Juan, for this group appears to be the source of the so-called Navajo wedding baskets.

In spite of comparative proximity to the Pueblos, no pottery was manufactured.

Tanning: men tanned. Formerly hides not smoked. Dyed with a concoction of tonɨmpɨ; (unidentified plant; reference may be to the alder-mountain mahogany dye used by the Navajo [Amsden, 1934, 81-2], particularly since J said his people and the Navajo used the same dye for skins); boiled, and liquid allowed to cool before hide immersed.

Weapons: horn bow known, but scarce. Sinew backing applied to oak bow, using glue made from boiling a horse hide "about 5 nights." J thought perhaps mountain sheep hide used in pre-horse times.

Arrows of serviceberry or cane, latter tipped with tonovɨ (Kaibab: Sarcobatus). Three feathers, of eagle, chicken hawk (kavɨ), owl (mu?upic), or unidentified bird described as "small eagle," with rear parts yellow. Quiver of wildcat or antelope hide.

Fire drill: of yucca; hearth of cottonwood.

Pottery: none. Stoneboiling in baskets usual; sometimes cooked in pots found archeologically.

Basketry: both coiled and twined, as well as wrapped stitch for carrying frame. Techniques not determined for each kind of vessel. Squawbush, willow used for coiled and twined wares; yucca for wrapped stitch. Water jar rubbed with sheep dung, red paint, prior to application of pine gum.

Decorated coiled baskets made for Navajo trade (p. 174; Franciscan Fathers, 1910, 291). For the so-called wedding basket, material was dyed red with tonɨmpɨ (above); black, with burned pine gum mixed in water. No Martynia. Several such decorated baskets, supposedly San Juan Paiute, in the Michael Harrison Collection, Laboratory of Anthropology, Santa Fe. Some have continuous design; of those with discrete, geometric motifs, three repeats (occasionally five) as frequent as four. All have "herringbone" rim finish.

In addition to woven burden baskets (apparently twined) and wrapped-stitch carrying frame, used (presumably for seeds) a conical frame covered with antelope hide or buckskin (p. 162).

Trade

Commerce with the Paiute north of the Colorado was not mentioned and probably was infrequent (p. 90). From the Ute, buckskins and buffalo hides were obtained in exchange for arrows. The buffalo skins were made into blankets and passed along in trade to the Navajo and Hopi.

A small buckskin or an antelope hide was given the Navajo for a blanket; a child was the standard price for a horse. The Navajo are said to have stolen Paiute children, trading them later to the Hopi. Coiled ware "wedding baskets" were made for the Navajo, apparently on a cash basis; each brought $5.00. J thought the San Juan Paiute the exclusive source of such baskets (p. 173).

The Hopi (Mukwic, Oraivɨ) gave maize and wafer bread for firewood and rabbit-fur "rope."

Red paint, from a deposit east of Red Lake, and eagle-feathered arrows were exchanged for mescal, apparently with the Havasupai.

Miscellany

A few oddments may be added:

Disposal of the dead: "long ago they burned a man, now they bury him" (J).

Bear dance: not known to San Juan Paiute (J) (cf. p. 109).

Datura: used externally as medicine. J knew of "just one boy who chewed the roots; talk, talk, talk, just like drunk."

PANGUITCH

Identification and Neighbors

North of the Kaibab and northwest of the Kaiparowits were the Panquitch. The last survivor of this group is Rena (R), who now lives at Cedar City. She was born some years after the white occupation and, in her youth, the native population had dwindled to six camps.

She declared that the Panguitch were Paiute, not Ute, and gave the group name as Pagɨvgai, from pagɨv (fish), very similar to the term applied to her people by the Kaibab (p. 31).

Holdings coincided roughly with the basin of the upper Sevier, centering in Panquitch Valley and on west, south, and east, extending at least to the watersheds (map 1; Kelly, 1934). The western boundary was quite definitive--beyond it, to the northwest, west, and southwest, at lower elevation, are Parowan, Cedar City, and Kanarraville, all in Cedar territory. R called these neighbors Kamparɨ-niwɨ (hard-rock people), from the name of a hill "across Cedar Valley," where they sometimes wintered.

To the south, the divide between the Sevier and the Kanab-Virgin drainages separated the Panguitch and the Kaibab, which latter group R designated as Kaivavič. To the east, the line is fuzzy. R magnanimously ceded to the Avua people (p. 149), Bryce Canyon and the eastern flank of Paunsaugunt Plateau, but the chief Kaiparowits informant thought the former, at least, was Koosharem. Bryce must not have attracted a hunting and gathering people and probably was unoccupied. R said that East Fork was not Panguitch; with respect to this strip on the Kaiparowits-Panguitch border, Sapir's information and mine are similarly contradictory (pp. 34, 145-6).

To the north, Panguitch limits terminated with Circle Valley, just upstream from the junction of East Fork with the Sevier. Inclusion of Circleville fits with a statement made by Kaibab informant G (p. 33) to the effect that "many Circleville people moved to Koosharem [Ute reservation] and now think they are Ute."

Despite the charge that the Panguitch stole children for the slave trade, relationships with Paiute neighbors seem to have been amiable. Those from Avua (Kaiparowits) went to the Paunsaugunt Plateau for deer, camping and hunting with the Panguitch (p. 150). Occasionally the Kaibab fished in Panguitch waters, and the Panguitch visited the Kaibab Plateau for deer (p. 32).

Likewise attracted by the fish, the Cedar people visited the upper Sevier basin, and the Panguitch went to Cedar territory to obtain Apocynum fiber for nets. Sometimes they went as far as Toquerville; this area was attractive to visitors in spring because of a green called kwivavɨ (Rumex); in summer, for "sugar," presumably aphid; in fall, for Opuntia fruit.

R made little mention of relationships with the Ute; unfortunately, I seem not to have asked, for she should have been able to clarify the impact of the Koosharem on the Paiute. She did not attribute great cultural innovations to the Ute, but from them the Panguitch had learned to mix "manzanita" with tobacco and to substitute egg for brains in tanning. In R's youth, "the young people" adopted the drum from the Ute, and the bear dance almost certainly came from the same source.

Habitat and Distribution of Population

Panguitch Valley is a longitudinal depression between the Paunsaugunt and Markagunt plateaus and lies at approximately 7000 ft., with the bounding tablelands 1000 to 2000 ft. higher. Through it the south fork of the Sevier flows in a general northerly direction and eventually, far to the north, swings westward, then southwestward, to empty into Sevier Lake, in the Great Basin. Accordingly, although Panguitch Valley is in the heart of the High Plateaus, drainage allies it ultimately with the Basin.

In contrast to the Paiute areas treated previously, the Panguitch zone is comparatively well watered. The flow in the Sevier itself is considerable, and the eastern slopes of the Markagunt abound in springs and small creeks. Low on the same slopes is a depression occupied by Panguitch Lake, a small body of water fed by a number of little streams and drained by Panguitch Creek, a tributary of the Sevier.

Upon one occasion, R said that small streams and springs were private property but were used by "anyone," regardless of tenure. Later she denied individual ownership. Such ownership may have been weakly developed because of the abundance of water; and it may have lapsed completely soon after the white advent, from which time R's memory dates.

A number of streams were named as follows: Sevier River: Avapa (much water); Panguitch Creek: Paguitua (end of lake); Sanford Creek: Nawiŋvinkwit (skirt water); unnamed creek next south: Usɨnuavɨ (from "nettles"); unidentified: Pakwanui (frog jumping in water), Aŋkankwint (red stream), Tɨavɨnkwint (serviceberry water).

Sage is the dominant vegetation in Panguitch Valley, but it is possible that, in pregrazing times, parts may have been grassland. Along the valley fringes, the sage is dotted with juniper and, at higher elevation, both give way to pine forest. The latter covers the western slopes of Paunsaugunt Plateau and parts of its summit, although a considerable area of the summit is open sage desert. Markagunt Plateau has forests of pine, spruce and aspen, which descend to the shores of Panguitch Lake, there supplanted by juniper and sage. As far as vegetation is concerned, Panguitch habitat parallels that of Paiute groups already described in that it consists of three main zones: sage, juniper and conifer forest.

It is not possible to estimate the numbers of the Panguitch people nor to locate their campsites. R had heard that in prewhite days houses were clustered along the lower slopes of Markagunt Plateau, within easy reach of water and fuel, and in Circle Valley, to the north.

When she was young, only six camps remained:

(1) Taŋavɨ (crooked knee), the o br of R's m. Lived with his br, Tɨratap (no beard). Both unmarried. On death of R's m, Taŋavɨ raised R and her ss. (2) Kwitɨkwai (left-handed), a widower, and his 3 s: Aakačɨkwi (horns), Kucankaq (pine bark), and Si?inoragwac (always urinating). (3) Sagwogaivɨ (green mountain) and his w were R's grp. (4) "Squash"-napuŋ (squash-man; native name forgotten) and his w, Wara (from wara, the seed). (5) Nagaukusac (mountain sheep leggings), his w, d, and s. (6) Minarɨ (legs stretch over; referring to his walk), his w, and 2 s.

Another man, called Pasɨpit (running eye) belonged to the group, but R did not remember his camp affiliations. She did not identify her father by name, and he seems to have been pretty much of a free agent on the score of residence. He seldom stayed with the other Panguitch, but sometimes camped at Orderville and Glendale, on the upper Virgin, within Kaibab territory, and "on the other side of Cedar Mountain."

Except in early summer, when the households scattered widely, the Panguitch of R's youth seem to have moved as a body, shifting seasonally within their territory. R remembered the cycle as follows:

Winter: camped along the northwest shore of Panguitch Lake, near the mouths of small streams. Situation favorable because within the range of timber, yet free from heavy snows of higher elevation. Lived on stores of seeds, berries, roots, pinenuts; on fresh roots; and on game: deer, rabbits, porcupine, beaver, sagehen. Also fish, fresh and dried.

Spring: all camps traveled together to Markagunt or Paunsaugunt plateaus to hunt, fish, and gather roots and cacti.

Summer: camps scattered in early summer over plateau, moving frequently. Hunted deer, groundhog; gathered roots. In late summer, all united in valley, near present settlement of Panguitch, to harvest seeds, buffaloberries and to hold rabbit drives.

Fall: returned in a body to higher elevation. Hunted; collected plateau seeds, yucca fruit, (Calochortus) root. Late fall, returned to Panguitch Lake for winter. Held rabbit drives.

In spite of the somewhat greater altitude of Panguitch terrain, the already familiar Paiute land-utilization pattern held without much fundamental change. There were, to be sure, substitutions, such as aspen instead of juniper for house posts, and a few distinctively local food staples, such as fish and sagehen. Nevertheless, as elsewhere, the valley supplied seeds and small game, while the higher lands provided roots, berries, and larger game.

Chieftainship

The Panguitch had not one chief (niạvi), but two: Minarɨ and Sagwogaivɨ (the latter, R's grf), who alternated days of service. The first-mentioned was a leader for the deer hunt and, as such, he received the "best meat"(p.181). The latter—perhaps because of the informant's desire for reflected glory--was a "big chief" (pia-niavi), for both deer and fish. The apparent duplication may result from the fact that originally there were at least two clusters of camps in Panguitch country(p.177). It is likely that, with the dwindling of the band and the concentration of the survivors about the lake, leaders from two originally distinct districts came to live in a single settlement.

R knew nothing of inheritance of chiefly office and had heard of no chief prior to those mentioned above. In the morning, Sagwogaivɨ stood by the door of his house and called to the people, "Get up. The sun is up. Do something: fish or hunt." In the evening, all the men--but none of the women--gathered at his camp to smoke and talk.

As a "deer chief," Sagwogaivɨ led hunting trips, but his duties as "fish chief" were not parallel. When guests arrived, he sallied forth alone, trapped several fish and, as "fish chief," presented them to the visitors.

There was no chief for hunting bear; the leader in the rabbit hunt was one of the men who owned a net. R said that there was no dance chief.

Subsistence

The Panguitch were nonagricultural and, as noted above, their wild-product resources varied somewhat from those of other groups.

R considered seeds, both valley and plateau, to be the chief vegetable staple but, because of the accessibility of the higher plateaus, considerable reliance was placed on roots and berries. Cacti were eaten sparingly in spring. Pinenuts, which grew only in the small stretch between Panguitch Lake and the modern settlement of Panguitch, were limited in quantity and not of great importance. "There was enough," but the local supply was supplemented through trade (p. 188). Of animal foods, fish and sagehen were distinctive local staples. R had heard that long ago there was elk in the region, but there was neither mountain sheep nor antelope. The principal game was deer and rabbit; rabbit drives were held all year, but particularly in summer and fall.

Food for winter consumption was stored in rock shelters or caves near Panguitch Lake. It was placed in a pot-shaped hole, lined with bark and covered with earth and stones. Meals were twice daily, morning and evening.

Wild Plant Products

Seeds.-- Valley seeds ripened at different times of year. Spring: niavi (Muhlenbergia?). Summer: akɨ, tamakɨ (said to be "like a sunflower"), wai?i (the most important seed food), ku?u, monɨ. Fall: aka (Helianthus petiolaris?), pia-akɨ (big akɨ), kwakwe, kumutɨ, kuiyokɨ (mallow seed; kuiyokɨmpɨ, the plant), ko, saŋwavɨ (Artemisia tridentata).

Most plateau seeds ripened later. Summer: čičagantɨ. Fall: kučapasɨ (white pasɨ, Artemisia frigida), wɨpɨvas or wɨpɨ-pasɨ (dark pasɨ, from stalk color, Artemisia dracunculoides), tu-puipɨ (Armaranthus californicus?), wara (Chenopodium humile Hook.), ugwivuipɨ, mutakɨ (Gymnolomia), wiyɨkɨ (larger than preceding, with yellow blossom), tavuic or tovuicɨ (Phacelia heterophylla var.), papuipɨ.

Fruits and berries. - Berries of one kind or another available from summer into fall. Strawberries (tɨwi?is) and raspberries (nagawɨa-tampopɨ, mountain sheep penis) eaten fresh in summer. Other berries usually dried. Squawbush (i?is) and buffaloberry (paupɨ) ripe in summer. (A distinction was made between paupɨ (water upɨ) and aŋka-upɨ (red upɨ). Specimens of both have been determined as Shepherdia argentea.) Ripening later were buffaloberry (aŋka-upɨ), serviceberry (tɨwampi), elder (kunuki), and chokecherry (tonopɨ). Latter dried and boiled; pits removed after cooking. Currant (pogompɨ) and gooseberry (wɨsɨvɨgompɨ, thorn currant) dried.

Roots. - Dug with a stick having the handle "hooked like a cane." Boiled or roasted in earth oven. Some roots gathered on plateaus all year: kwiu, kusau?urɨ (Trifolium), kani (possibly Oenothera, although specimen may be incorrectly identified by informant). Other roots seasonal. Kwičasɨ (said to resemble sigo?o dug in spring wič una (Oreogenia linearifolia Wats.) available spring, summer; sigo?o (Calochortus), summer and fall.

Miscellaneous. - In spring, ate fleshy "leaves" of several cacti: minčɨ, nɨaras, navumpɨ, tasɨ (cf. p. 45), and blossoms of sarɨmpɨ (Opuntia whipplei Englem and Bigel.). Fruit of local cacti not eaten, but prickly pears sometimes gathered in Toquerville area in fall. Yucca fruit collected in fall, along slopes of plateaus.

Saŋwaru?u (sage tu?u, probably Orobanche multiflora) found beneath sagebrush, from spring to fall, and a similar plant beneath rabbitbrush. Boiled, not dried. In spring, roots of tule (sainpipɨ) and, in winter, roots of cattail (touivɨ) eaten; cattail seeds a summer food.

Leafy part of kwičasɨ (listed with roots) eaten; another green, "like rhubarb," called kwivavɨ (Rumex), sometimes gathered on spring trip to Toquerville. Occasionally visited Toquerville in summer, eating "sugar," supposedly aphid; none found locally.

Tobacco. - Plot burned to encourage growth of tobacco (sagwogoapɨ) (Nicotiana attenuata). No subsequent care. "Manzanita" (bearberry?) mixed with tobacco in post-white times; learned from Ute. Women did not smoke unless they were shamans. Pipe of clay with cane stem or of soft stone with elderberry mouthpiece. Shape apparently similar to Kaibab.

Hunting and Fishing

First game.--Small boy did not eat his first kill, although his mother might. When "old enough," his mother bathed him and painted him red; trimmed his hair. He ran, pursued to camp by others (boys?). Carried nothing in hand. Afterward could eat game he killed.

Large game.--Deer and bear the 2 large-game animals. Deer hunted mostly south and west of Panguitch Lake. No stalking disguise. Lone hunter chancing upon deer in cul de sac kindled fires across entrance. Sometimes hunted in pairs, 1 man hiding along trail and other circling about, chasing game past concealed marksman.

Usually several hunted together. Might run deer on promontory and build fires behind them, but never surrounded with fire. No chute and pound, although R knew this technique from Parowan (Cedar) area. When group accompanied by hunt leader, leader headed procession from camp, stationing men at strategic points. Chief entitled to any part of kill and took the best meat. Hide and head went to successful marksman; meat divided among others of party. If a man hunted alone and was successful, wife took some of the game to neighboring camps.

Bear plentiful; probably seldom hunted. No bear chief. 1 man located bear and thereupon summoned assistance. Prey surrounded, but fire not used. In winter, pounded on den and animal emerged; 10 arrows needed to kill a bear. No address complex, but bear was called kagun (mat grm). Flesh eaten; skin used as blanket.

Small game.--Rabbits most important. Stray jacks shot; cottontails pulled from holes with straight stick twisted in fur. Rabbits caught singly in small baglike net hung on trail; held in place by 2 posts and propped open by a third, which fell as prey entered. "White rabbits" (probably Rocky Mountain snowshoe rabbit) taken on plateaus in nets.

Rabbit drives in area south of modern town of Panguitch; all year, but especially summer and fall. Throwing stick not known. Nets (wanai) of Apocynum, obtained through trade (p. 188). In R's youth only one Panguitch man knew how to make nets. About 3 nets set up in half circle, with hunter at each intersection. Rabbit chief, who was owner of a net, stood at 1 end of arc. Others chased game toward nets; only in summer was brush fired.

Rabbits killed by pressing with hand on breast. Long wand run through necks and carried on hunter's shoulder. No division of spoils; each man kept own kill. Rabbits baked in ashes or boiled; surplus meat dried 1 or 2 days; kept well. Backbone cooked, pounded on mealing stone, eaten at once.

Beaver shot in winter along Sevier River and mountain streams; meat boiled; skin for quiver. Marmot plentiful about lake in summer; shot or clubbed; skin not used. Rock squirrel trapped. Prairie dog abundant throughout year in lake region; not trapped; water poured in hole and animal clubbed as it came out. Gopher shot as it emerged from hole. 2 kinds of wood rat; one, in open valley, other, among rocks. Usually trapped; not pulled from nest with stick. Nest sometimes fired.

Porcupine clubbed, often in tree; roasted; quills for belt ornament. Badger cooked in ashes; hide for cap and moccasin soles. Fox, young or adult, shot; roasted in ashes; "tasted like rabbit." Wildcat shot; sometimes smoked to death in rocks, then extracted with stick. Mountain lion (piarukɨ and tukumumɨci) shot; cooked in ashes; skin for blanket.

Birds apparently important, particularly duck, sagehen, and unidentified bird called parɨnwɨnt. Flicker (aŋkakwanawanc), mourning dove, and others eaten. Ducks shot from blind or edge of lake; blown ashore by wind; no dogs to retrieve; no balsa or other craft. Sagehen shot in early morning from blind near watering place. Not dried. No use made of feathers.

Lizard, particularly "bull lizard," eaten in summer, roasted in ashes.

Game not eaten.--Bat (too small); skunk (contradictory statements); coyote ("never killed them long ago, not even little ones"); wolf (hide for blankets); mouse; ant larvae; snake (contradictory statements).

Fishing.--Local fish described as reddish along sides, with flesh of same color. Eaten boiled; fish and eggs dried.

According to R, fished chiefly in spring. Man stood in stream and speared catch with long willow stick, with chokecherry point. In winter, chopped hole in ice, presumably of Panguitch Lake, using a "long, hard, white stone." Fisherman stuffed grass in his moccasins and stood on ice, spearing fish through hole. R also reported use of open-twine basket trap, of willow, at outlet of lake and in Sevier River. Stream dammed with willows either side of trap. Kaibab (and Cedar Paiute, p. 176) sometimes visited Panguitch in spring or summer to fish; S had accompanied such a party. She described fishing at point where stream entered lake. Borrowed open-twined willow trap from hosts; trap called wan, as is net. Held in place by 2 men, one either side. Catch dumped on shore; fish hit with a stick to kill them. S added that to dry catch, fish cut open and hung over long pole supported by 2 uprights, probably forked. Never smoked nor pounded; dried fish boiled.

A "big chief" (p.178-9) went out alone to fish and presented catch to visitors.

Shelter

In keeping with local resources, the Panguitch house often had aspen posts and a covering of rye grass and pine bark. There is mention of a type of shade not reported for the Paiute described heretofore. In ground plan this was rectangular; in profile, arched. Walls and roof were continuous and there was no ridgepole (see below). In addition to the Panguitch occurrence, a similar structure was described for the Cedar, Gunlock and Paranigat bands. The Gunlock informant thought his people "borrowed it from the Moapa, who got it from the Mohave," and the Paranigat informant considered it of late introduction. A somewhat similar structure--but evidently triangular in section, and with a ridgepole--was reported for the Chemehuevi; a Las Vegas informant mentioned a gable-type shade but could not remember whether it had a ridgepole.

Winter Dwelling

Ground leveled and, if on side hill, excavated slightly, but not normally semisubterranean. Holes dug for 4 posts, unforked, of aspen; their upper extremities leaned together and tied, forming conical frame. Upper part of posts exposed above covering. Latter of juniper bark or of wild ryegrass (wavi, Elymus triticoides), held in place with transverse willow withes. Bark slabs from old pine trees applied over grass and similarly held by transverse willows. On one occasion, I understood grass covering in form of mats; on another, grass was "just heaped on." Doorway and floor covered with ryegrass mats; used also as mattress. Because of fire hazard, parching done out of doors, although food could be boiled inside house.

Less Substantial Structures

The usual circular enclosure (siaŋkagan, juniper-leaf house) was reported.

Shade had a frame of 2 parallel rows of aspen posts, 4 in each row. These bent, tied together at top (no ridgepole), and covered with fresh aspen boughs. Sometimes built entirely of juniper.

Sweathouse

Sweathouse not considered of recent introduction. None when R was young; she heard of sweating from her grf. When many Indians still living near present site of Panguitch town, had 2 sweathouses, one for each sex. Excavated about 2 ft., built bark-thatched house, and covered it entirely with earth. Doorway closed by juniper-bark mat. Large stone (presumably heated) in center. Sweated only occasionally; curative. Jumped in water at conclusion. Grf did not mention singing or "talking" in connection with sweating.

Dress

Body Clothing

Men wore buckskin shirt, leggings, breechclout. Women used buckskin dress or double apron of wildcat hide or buckskin. R's grf spoke of ryegrass "skirt" of former times, but she never saw one; evidently the equivalent of Kaibab cliffrose bark apron. No cliffrose in Panguitch territory. Men made all the skin clothing, including woman's dress and moccasins for both sexes. Also made buckskin belt, with sewn ornament of porcupine quills in natural color; worn by men and women.

Footgear, Headgear and Ornament

Moccasins of buckskin, with badger soles. Pattern similar to Kaibab (Fig. 6, a), but tongue V-instead of U-shaped. No mention of wide cuff for women. Most women, in fact, wore yucca "shoes," said to be "turned up at the toe and kind of pointed." Men wore badger-skin cap; women invariably used close-twined basket hat; once finished, designs rubbed on with crushed buffaloberries. Both sexes tattooed chin, cheeks, forehead--at any age. Red paint also used; obtained locally.

Blankets

Of bear, wolf, mountain lion skins.

Rectangular (not trapezoidal) rabbitskin blankets woven by both sexes. Sometimes strips of wildcat hide incorporated. Rabbits skinned in sacklike fashion by cutting around fore and hind legs and slitting latter to crotch. Skin then peeled off. Beginning with hind leg, tubular hide cut spirally, resulting in long, continuous strip. About 10 such lengths joined by tying legs together. This composite strip doubled on itself; looped end secured to a tree; 2 loose ends tied to short stick. Stick twirled between palms, twisting the doubled strand of fur. Hung from tree to dry. Fur "rope" warped over 2 rows of pegs and twined with buckskin thongs. Belly fur and skin of white rabbit sometimes kept separate and used to make stripes.

Crafts and Manufactures

A few details concerning handicrafts are of interest in the light of comparative material from other Paiute groups. Although the Panguitch learned from the Koosharem the use of eggs in tanning, R considered smoking of hides an old trait among her people and did not attribute it to recent Ute influence as, apparently, did both Kaibab and Kaiparowits. I do not recall from other groups the use of the inner bark of old pine trees in tanning.

The Panguitch did not have the horn bow and apparently did not acquire it in trade.

The similarity of the Kaibab-Panguitch-Beaver ceramic tradition already has been remarked (p. 70). Pottery must have been more firmly established among the Panguitch than among the Kaibab, for R reported no stone-boiling in baskets.

Tanning

Both sexes worked hides, scraping them with cannon bone from deer foreleg. Brain and spinal cord marrow used as tan; in post-white times, learned from Koosharem Ute to substitute eggs, raw or boiled, for brain. Hides stretched by skewers; smoked. R considered both these traits old. Had never seen hide tanned with hair on but "knew" it was sprinkled with dust from inside bark of old pine trees, then scraped with a stone. Not buried.

Weapons

No horn bow. Used juniper, serviceberry, oak, mountain birch (kaisɨwimpɨ). Sinew backing. Paint applied over latter and on inside of bow. String of sinew.

Arrows of serviceberry, wild rose, currant; stone points; three eagle feathers. Cane arrows had chokecherry points; butts not plugged.

Quiver of fawn, buckskin, beaver, fox, or wildcat hide. Bottom a hide disc to which sides sewn; not a common Paiute pattern.

Fire Making Equipment

No percussion technique; R knew it from Cedar neighbors.

Drill composite, with shaft of mountain mahogany (tunɨmpɨ) and point of greasewood (tonovɨ). Pine hearth, with 2 holes. Juniper-bark tinder. Fire making apparatus (kwitunuinɨ) of narrow-leaved yucca obtained in trade, but source forgotten. Slow match of juniper bark, wrapped with same material.

Pottery

Clay pots (wiavɨnpuni) flat bottomed and sun baked; not fired. R insistent on these points. Had not witnessed manufacture and did not know if observers barred. Pottery made by women from red clay found at 1 site; latter not privately owned.

Nothing but water added to clay; not mixed on metate. Lump flattened for bottom and rolls added (apparently concentrically) to form straight sides. Method of smoothing unknown. Punched below rim by way of decoration. Set in sun to dry, then used for cooking. R's uncle had such a pot. No basket for stoneboiling.

Basketry

Coiled and twined techniques, plus wrapped stitch for carrying frame. No cooking basket, clay pots used; no description of food bowl.

Coiled ware: "plates, turned up a little along the edges," presumably parching trays. Said to have had 2-rod foundation.

Water jars both coiled and twined. Former preferable; vessel stronger and did not crack if dropped. Started with 1 rod then changed to 2-rod foundation. Handles of sinew from along backbone of deer. Exterior smeared first with juniper leaves, ground on metate; then coated with red paint; finally, sealed with pinyon gum. Inside pitched by inserting gum together with hot pebbles.

Twined ware: conical burden baskets, both open twine and closed twine. Former a general utility container; latter, rubbed with cactus to seal interstices, for collecting seeds.

Fan-shaped trays both open and closed twine; former for winnowing berries, pinenuts; latter, for seeds. Seed parcher smeared both sides with pine gum. Seed beater evidently similar to Kaibab (Pl. 4, b); had oak blade.

Twined water jar not pointed on base; sufficiently flat to stand alone. Woman's basket cap of close twine; design rubbed on finished specimen with crushed buffaloberries; no woven designs.

Cradles of squawbush, presumably with twined body; no details. Some had buckskin covering. Chid had 3 cradles, successively larger. First cradle thrown away.

Wrapped-stitch carrying frame. From description, similar to Kaiparowits (Pl. 3, a). Frame of serviceberry; wrapping of yucca leaf or of buckskin thongs.

Communications and Trade

The Panguitch had no dog for transport and no balsa or other craft.

Routes

Several trails mentioned, but obviously many more. Panguitch to Beaver: "straight over the mountain." To Cedar: likewise "straight over the mountain"; forked, one branch coming down Coal Creek Canyon, the other down spur immediately north. To Toquerville: along watershed of Markagunt and Kolob plateaus, entering

Cedar Valley just north of Kanarraville, thence downstream to Toquerville.

Commerce

Within Panguitch territory, those of lake area traded pottery to Circleville. Some of latter made own ceramics; others obtained pots in exchange for rabbitskin blankets.

With Kaibab: Panguitch went to Kanab to exchange rabbitskin blankets, buckskin, and serviceberry canes for Apocynum nets. Kaibab informants commented that Panguitch sometimes stole children and traded dogs, horses, knives and firearms.

With Paiute west and southwest: Panguitch offered buckskin or rabbitskin blankets to Cedar people, receiving in exchange moccasins with badger soles (p. 184). With Paiute of Indian Peak area (Beaver), Panguitch exchanged pasɨ seed (Artemisia) for pinenuts.

Miscellaneous Social Data

Below are odd bits of information concerning various aspects of Panguitch society.

Property: contradictory statements concerning ownership of springs and small streams (p. 176). Certain hunting spots--as, for example, a cul de sac--said to have been privately owned, but anyone could hunt there merely by asking permission. Ownership rights terminated at death. Eagle nests individually owned and passed, at death, to a man's son.

Marriage: "some men had more than one wife." No polyandry although, when grown, R saw " a woman at Hiko (Paranigat band, far to the west of Panguitch country) who had two husbands."

Death: corpse and best personal possessions of deceased hidden in rocks; " a sort of graveyard" among lava boulders just south of Panguitch Lake. Dwelling demolished and burned, together with personal property not deposited with corpse. Mourners cut hair.

Dances: no dance chief. No drum; "young people" learned of it from Ute. Presumably from same source the bear dance was introduced when R was young (early post-white times).

BIBLIOGRAPHY

Amsden, Charles A.
    1934   Navaho Weaving, its Technic and History. Fine Arts Press, Santa Ana.

Bartlett, Katharine
    1932   Why the Navajos Came to Arizona. Museum Notes, Museum of Northern Arizona, Vol. 5, No. 6, pp. 29-32.

Bolton, Herbert E.
    1928   Escalante in Dixie and the Arizona Strip. New Mexico Historical Review, Vol. 3, No. 1, pp. 41-72.

Bowman, Isaiah
    1911   Forest Physiography. John Wiley and Sons, New York.

Culin, Stewart
    1907   Games of the North American Indians. Bureau of American Ethnology, Annual Report, No. 24, 1902-1903.

Dellenbaugh, Frederick S.
    1909   The Romance of the Colorado River. G. P. Putnam's Sons, New York.

    1926   A Canyon Voyage. (2d ed.) Yale University Press, New Haven.

    MS   Kaibab Paiute.

Documentos para la Historia de Mexico
    1854   Diario y Derrotero de los RR. PP. Fr. Francisco Atanasio Dominguez y Fr. Silvestre Velez de Escalante [1776]. Segunda serie, Vol. 1, pp. 375-558. [Ciudad de] Mexico.

Dutton, Clarence E.
    1882   The Physical Geology of the Grand Cañon District. United States Geological Survey, 2nd Annual Report, pp. 47-166.

Fenneman, Nevin M.
    1931   Physiography of Western United States, McGraw-Hill, New York.

Franciscan Fathers
    1910   An Ethnologic Dictionary of the Navaho Language. St. Michaels, Arizona.

Gifford, Edward W.
    1917   Tübatulabal and Kawaiisu Kinship Terms. University of California Publications in American Archaeology and Ethnology, Vol. 12, No. 6, pp. 219-48.

Gregory, Herbert E.
    1917   Geology of the Navajo Country. United States Geological Survey, Professional Papers, No. 93.

Gregory, Herbert E., and Raymond C. Moore
    1931   The Kaiparowits Region. United States Geological Survey Professional Papers, No. 164.

Guernsey, Samuel J., and Alfred V. Kidder
    1921   Basket-Maker Caves of Northeastern Arizona. Peabody Museum Papers, Vol. 8, No. 2.

Hill, Joseph J.
    1930   Spanish and Mexican Exploration and Trade Northwest from New Mexico into the Great Basin, 1765-1851. Utah Historical Quarterly, Vol. 3, No. 1, pp. 1-23.

Hill, W. W.
    1936   Navajo Warfare. Yale University Publications in Anthropology, No. 5.

Hodge, Frederick W. (Ed.)
    1907,   Handbook of the American Indians North of Mexico.
    1910   Bureau of American Ethnology, Bulletin, No. 30, Pts. 1, 2.

Kelly, Isabel
    1932   Ethnography of the Surprise Valley Paiute. University of California Publications in American Archaeology and Ethnology, Vol. 31, No. 3, pp. 67-210.

  1934 Southern Paiute Bands. *American Anthropologist*, Vol. 36, No. 4, pp. 547-60.

  1939 Southern Paiute Shamanism. *University of California Anthropological Records*, Vol. 2, pp. 151-67.

Little, James A.
  1881 Jacob Hamblin, a Narrative of his Personal Experience as a Frontiersman, Missionary to the Indians, and Explorer. *Faith-promoting Series, Juvenile Instructor*. L. D. S. Church, Salt Lake City.

Lowie, Robert H.
  1924 Notes on Shoshonean Ethnography. *American Museum of Natural History, Anthropological Papers*, Vol. 20, Pt. 3.

Mason, Otis T.
  1904 Aboriginal American Basketry. *United States National Museum, Report,* 1902.

Nelson, Lowry
  1952 *The Mormon Village.* University of Utah Press, Salt Lake City.

Powell, John W.
  1875 *Exploration of the Colorado River of the West and its Tributaries.* Smithsonian Institution, Washington.

  1961 *The Exploration of the Colorado River and its Canyons.* Dover Publications, New York.

Sapir, Edward
  1930 The Southern Paiute Language. *Proceedings of the American Academy of Arts and Sciences,* Vol. 65. (Cited: Sapir, followed by page reference.)

  MS *Kaibab Paiute.* (Cited: Sapir, without page reference.)

Spier, Leslie
  1925 The Distribution of Kinship Systems in North America. *University of Washington Publications in Anthropology,* Vol. 1, pp. 69-88.

1928   Havasupai Ethnography. <u>American Museum of Natural History, Anthropological Papers,</u> Vol. 29, Pt. 3.

Steward, Julian H.
- 1933   Ethnography of the Owens Valley Paiute. <u>University of California Publications in American Archaeology and Ethnology,</u> Vol. 33, pp. 233-350.

- 1937   Linguistic Distributions and Political Groups of the Great Basin Shoshoneans. <u>American Anthropologist,</u> Vol. 39, No. 4, Pt. 1, pp. 625-34.

- 1938   Basin- Plateau Aboriginal Sociopolitical Groups. <u>Bureau of American Ethnology, Bulletin,</u> No. 120.

- 1939   Notes on Hillers' Photographs of the Paiute and Ute Indians Taken on the Powell Expedition of 1873. <u>Smithsonian Miscellaneous Collections,</u> Vol. 98. No. 18.

Wissler, Clark
- 1910   Material Culture of the Blackfoot Indians. <u>American Museum of Natural History, Anthropological Papers,</u> Vol. 5, Pt. 1.

Explanation of Plates

Abbreviations have been explained elsewhere (p. 3).

Pl. 1. Landscape and vegetation, Kaibab habitat. a, Houserock Valley; b, view west, from near mouth of Johnson Canyon; c, view east, from Moccasin; d, White Cliffs, above Three Lakes Canyon.

Pl. 2. Kaibab seed collection and preparation. a, wielding the seed beater; b, winnowing, with basket tray; c, parching, in commercial container; d-f, grinding on mealing stone.

Pl. 3. Basketry. a, subconical carrying frame, wrapped stitch; dia. ca. 20 in.; AMNH 50.2/3477. b, conical burden basket, open twine; dia. 20.5 in.; AMNH 50.2/3446. c, fan-shaped winnowing tray, open twine, used chiefly for pinenuts; max. width, 18.75 in.; AMNH 50.2/3449. d, fan-shaped tray, closed twine, for winnowing and parching; max. width, 23 in.; AMNH 50.2/3461. e, circular tray, coiled, with 3-rod foundation; for parching seeds; dia. 17.5 in.; AMNH 50.2/3474. f, water jar, coiled, pine-gum coating; hgt. 13 in.; MNM 9975/12.

a, b, f, models. a, e, made by Lucy (L) (called also Rosie), Kaiparowits; others, by Sarah Frank, Kaibab.

Pl. 4. Basketry, yucca footgear, clay dolls. a-c, seed beaters; d, e, modern basketry, made for sale; f, g, models of yucca footgear; h-j, model clay dolls, unfired (h, female; i, male; j, child).

a, wickerwork; same scale as b; AMNH 50.2/3476. b, twine; max. width, 10.5 in.; AMNH 50.2/3448. c, twine; same scale as b; AMNH 50.2/3475. d, coiled; dia. 7.5 in.; AMNH 50.2/3462. e, coiled; same scale as d; MNM 9985/12. f, checker work; same scale as g; AMNH 50.2/3470. g, checker and twine; length 11 in.; AMNH 50.2/3441. h, length 4.75 in.; MNM 895/12(f). i, same scale as h; AMNH 50.2/3458. j, same scale as h; MNM 895/12(j).

a, c, made by Lucy (L), Kaiparowits; b, by Minnie Tom, born in Cedar territory, but sharing Kaibab culture; d, h-j, by Sarah Frank, Kaibab; e, by Minnie Frank, affiliations complex, but learned basket making among Kaibab. f, a type of footgear said to have been common in Ankati area, Kaibab zone; made by Maggie Johnny, according to description furnished by Mose (M), Kaibab. g, likewise by Maggie Johnny, Kaibab.

Pl. 5. Cradles. _a_, oval hoop supporting body of longitudinal rods; twined awning; hgt. 30.5 in.; PM 50663. _b_, model cradle for newborn infant; twined body, awning; miniature; hgt. 20 in.; AMNH 50.2/3442. _c,d_, cradles for older child; twined body, awning; cover of mattress ticking instead of buckskin; _c_, same scale as _d_, MNM 9940/12; _d_, hgt. 38 in.; AMNH 50.2/3443.

_a_, Powell collection, southern Utah, 1873; band provenience unknown. _b, d_, made by Sarah Frank, Kaibab; _c_, by Lucy (L), Kaiparowits.

Pl. 6. Juniper-bark dolls. Models, painted on inner bark of tree (_a_, female; _b_, male; others, not specified). Length of _a_, 6.75 in.; others to same scale. _a, b_, MNM 894/12 (_b, a_); _c-e_, AMNH 50.2/3454-3456. All made by Sarah Frank, Kaibab.

Pl. 7. Postures associated with bow and arrow, rabbit stick, rasp, rattle, and hand game. Tony Tillohash, Sapir's Kaibab informant, Carlisle Indian School, 1910. Photographs provided by Dr. Sapir.

_a, b_, use of bow and arrow; informant apparently shoots left-handed. Bow, a Ute specimen, collected by Sapir in Ouray, Utah, 1909. _c_, throwing rabbit stick; _d_, using rasp for bear dance; _e_, rattle, in Bird song of "Cry"; _f_, rattle in Roan song of "Cry." _g, h_, playing hand game; bones and counters, Ute specimens from Ouray, 1909.

Plate 1

Plate 2

Plate 3

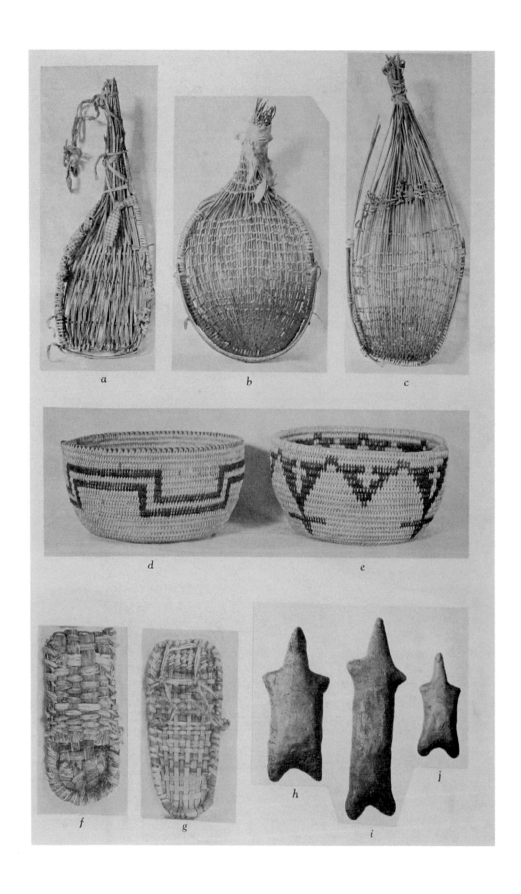

Plate 4

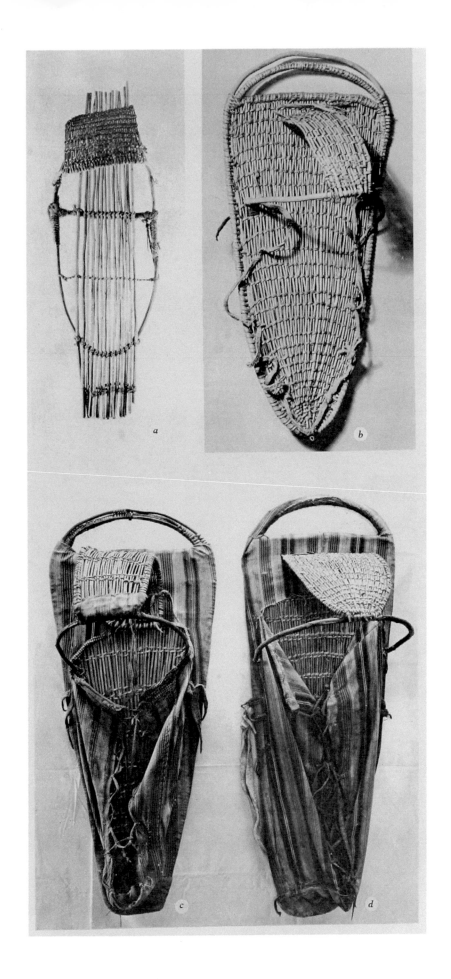

Plate 5

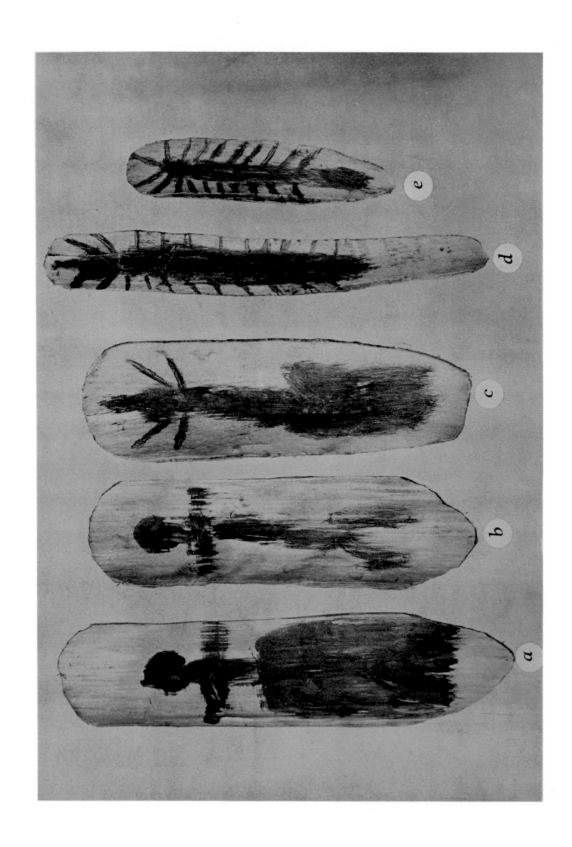

Plate 6

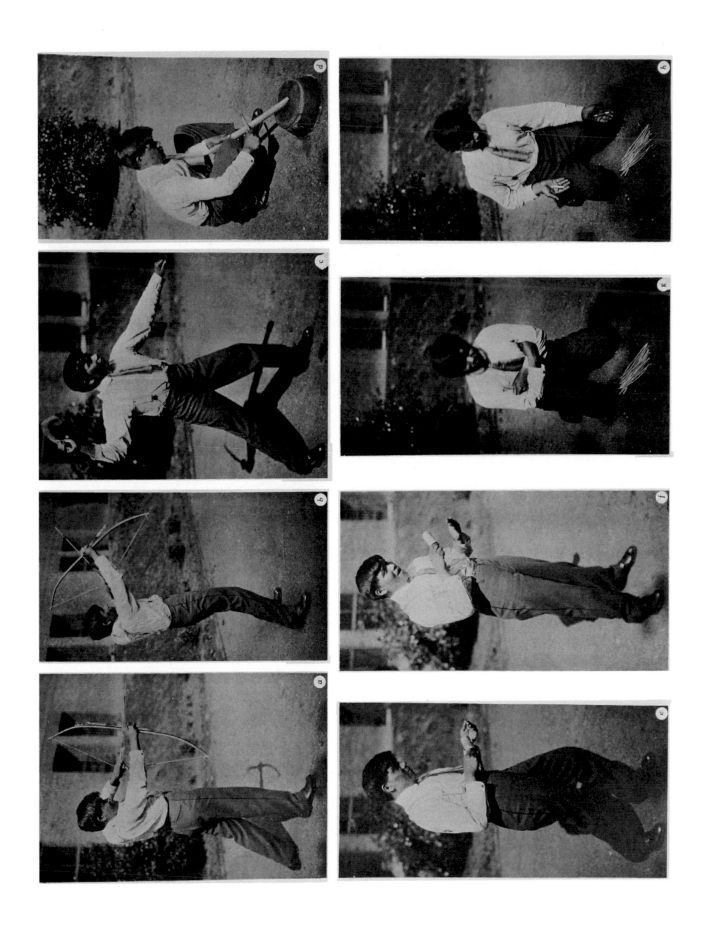

Plate 7